THE WORLD COURT
WHAT IT IS AND HOW IT WORKS

The Peace Palace at the Hague

THE WORLD COURT

WHAT IT IS AND HOW IT WORKS

by

SHABTAI ROSENNE

Ambassador of Israel

THIRD REVISED EDITION

A. W. SIJTHOFF – LEIDEN
OCEANA PUBLICATIONS INC., DOBBS FERRY, N.Y.
1973

Library of Congress Catalog Card Number: 62-9743

© 1973 by A. W. Sijthoff International Publishing Company B.V., Leiden

ISBN 90 286 0213 5 (Sijthoff)
ISBN 379-00206-X (Oceana)

First edition 1962
Second edition (revised) 1963

Chinese edition, Taipeh 1966
Spanish edition, Madrid 1967

Illustrations I-II: United Nations
Photographs as credited

Printed in the Netherlands

FOREWORD

In the foreword to the first edition of this book, in 1961, we wrote:

"The present book is intended to serve the politician, the diplomat, the member of parliament, and the enquiring members of the public at large, all who are interested in international affairs and the organs through which they are conducted, as a guide and introduction to the main factors which make the Court what it is and cause it to work as it does."

That remains the aim of this book.

In the eleven years that have elapsed, much has happened in connexion with the Court, which has found itself the subject of polemical discussion to an extent probably unparalleled in the history of international adjudication. Decisions rendered in difficult political circumstances have given rise to much controversy.

As part of the reaction, political circles, including the General Assembly of the United Nations as well as important academic bodies on the one hand, and the Court itself on the other, have embarked upon a series of thorough-going reviews of the Court's role, its activities, and its manner of work. Some of the results have been made public in the revised Rules of Court adopted on 10 May 1972.

These new Rules, together with the not inconsiderable judicial activity of the Court since 1961, have required a revision of this book, to bring it into line with these developments.

If the Court has not yet been able to meet all the expectations which we expressed in 1961, it nevertheless, in its capacity of the principal judicial organ of the United Nations, remains an important instrument through which international relations can be conducted. We have continued treating the subject on the basis that the proper presentation of the material must place in due perspective the interplay of the political and legal factors bearing upon the Court and its role. It is our hope that this book will contribute to a better understanding of what the Court is and how it works.

Beth ha Kerem, Jerusalem   *Shabtai Rosenne*
September 1973

NOTE

All references in this book to the Rules of Court are to the 1972 Rules, unless otherwise indicated.

TABLE OF CONTENTS

WHAT THE COURT IS

HOW THE COURT WORKS

WHAT THE COURT IS

In the last resort, recourse to international justice depends on the will of governments and on their readiness to submit for legal decision all which can and should be preserved from the arbitrament of violence. As for the Court, it means to accomplish to the full the duties incumbent upon it; and it will not weaken in that resolve—
Judge J. Gustavo Guerrero, President of the Permanent Court of International Justice (1936-45) and of the International Court of Justice (1946-49), on 4 December 1939.

CHAPTER I

THE FORERUNNERS

The idea of resolving international disputes through disinterested third parties deciding the dispute on the basis of law and justice, as an alternative to direct settlement of the dispute by means of violence after diplomacy has failed, is a deep-rooted human aspiration. Its origins can be found in religious sentiment which tended to recoil from the horrors of war and seek other ways of eradicating conflicts of international interests. At times the idea was expressed in Messianic terms, as by the Prophets Isaiah and Micah: "And it shall come to pass in the end of days ... And He shall judge between the nations, and shall decide for many peoples; and they shall beat their swords into plowshares and their spears into pruninghooks; Nation shall not lift up sword against nation, neither shall they learn war any more."[1] At others, it is cast in the language of political programme, as by Hugo Grotius, the father of modern international law: "Christian kings and states are bound to employ this method [arbitration] of avoiding war ... And for this and many other purposes, it would be helpful—as a matter of fact, necessary—for the Christian powers to hold conferences, where those whose interests were not involved might settle the disputes of the rest, and even take measures to compel the parties to accept peace on fair terms."[2]

EARLY BEGINNINGS

As an ideal, this concept seems to have been widespread: in practice, however, its application was far from general. It was found, for instance, in the early periods of Middle Eastern history and in sacred codes of the Far East,[3] and it is encountered in the experience of Islam.[4] But it was in Europe that the concept most took root. Its attraction for the European mind was that it sought to transfer the absolute values of the discipline of the law, on which the well-being of the national society in Western Europe was thought to depend, to the problems of the international community. The Greek city-states, for instance, possessed a well-developed system of third-party settlement of their disputes, within the framework of their own Hellenic culture, especially through the instrumentality of the Delphic Amphictyonies.[5] Here, indeed, there is something approaching true disinterested third-party judgment between nominally equal political units—the city-states—on the basis of a rudimentary system of law or custom by which the correct behaviour of those political units might be judged. With the growth of the big empires—Macedonia, Rome, Byzantium—this form of third-party settlement fell into disuse, partly, no doubt, because of the impossibility of finding any true disinterested third party, and partly because the general imperialist and expansionist tendencies of those super-Powers, and their centralized system of government, would not easily be reconciled to the idea of the settlement of *their* disputes by application of "law" (however rudimentary international law might have been at that time). On the other hand, the classical historical writings contain many circumstantial accounts of those Powers "deciding" disputes between their various clients and vassals through a procedure which resembles partly a system of arbitration, and partly a system of mediation and conciliation—and partly a mere concealment for force.

In medieval Europe, too, both types of "arbitration" are found.

For instance, in Switzerland, where peculiar geographical conditions impressed their stamp on the political organization in a manner reminiscent of that of ancient Hellas, several cases are known in which disputes between two or more cities were arbitrated by disinterested ecclesiastical and secular authorities, who tried to reach a settlement by a combination of methods of persuasion and of decision.[6] Something similar seems once to have existed for the city-states of Italy. On the other hand, the tradition of the Roman Empire was largely continued by the Popes and Emperors, whose system of government contained built-in machinery for resolving disputes between their vassals and subordinates. Here it has been said that the major premise was that the church knows what is right and wrong, and that the peace-maker, if he is the delegate of the church, must begin by judging, not by conciliating, the parties.[7] It was in this period too that the theologian-jurists began developing the theory, that the existence of central institutions in the Papacy for the settlement of disputes implied that the princes were not entitled to take the law into their own hands—an idea closely connected with the theory of the just war and the unjust war or (as we would say today) the war of aggression.

THE NINETEENTH CENTURY

The origins of modern arbitration are usually traced to the so-called Jay Treaty of 19 November 1794, between the United States and Great Britain, putting an end to the American War of Independence. This provided for the setting up of three different commissions for the settlement of outstanding questions. Two of these commissions succesfully completed their task, but the third ran into difficulties which were only resolved later by direct diplomatic means. The commissions were composed of American and British nationals exclusively—a fact which negatives any idea of third-party settlement. However, the proceedings before the commissions were conducted on the model of court actions, and the commissioners tried to reach their decisions by applying rules of law.[8] This type of proceeding was in substance diplomatic rather than judicial in character, since there was no impartial arbitrament between the two parties represented on the commissions. But the Jay Treaty and these processes led to a renewal of general interest in the possibilities of using legal and judicial techniques as a method of resolving certain types of international conflict, especially, though by no means exclusively, when there is involved in the international dispute a large number of private and individual claims. Occasionally instances are found, in the early part of the nineteenth century, in which true third-party settlement of a dispute is invoked—the third party being nominally either the Head of a State or one of its organs, acceptable to the two litigants. When this happened, the process begins to lose its purely diplomatic character, and to assume that of true judicial arbitration.

A major development in the history of international adjudication occurred in the well-known *Alabama* case, arising out of the American Civil War. This, commonly regarded as the watershed of modern international litigation, was a spectacular affair, which, because it involved fundamental questions of the law of neutrality and of warfare at sea, touched upon serious political interests of Great Britain, the defendant. The dispute, which originated in the departure of the *Alabama* from the Merseyside shipyards on 29 July 1862 to join the Confederate Forces and prey upon U.S. shipping in the Atlantic, caused great political bitterness on both sides. It was not until the Washington Treaty of 8 May 1871 that the two countries agreed to submit it to arbitration. The significance of this act lies in the nature of the tribunal, which was composed of one national of each of the two parties, together with three neutral members—nationals of Italy, Switzerland and Brazil. The Treaty also contained another innovation: it specified some (though not all) of the basic legal rules concerning the duties of neutral states, which the Tribunal was to apply. After complicated proceedings held in the Hôtel de Ville at Geneva the Tribunal handed down its award (reached by a majority of four to one) on 14 September 1872.[9] Despite the dissent of the British arbitrator, the British Government paid the damages to the tune of over $ 15,000,000 within the time stipulated. The spectacle of two important countries submitting a dispute of this character to impartial third-party settlement on the basis of law, and then complying with the terms of the award, naturally gave a great fillip to the development of the concept of international arbitration as an alternative to allowing political tension to smoulder indefinitely. On the other hand, the fact that the two countries were both English speaking, and shared the same basic legal culture of the common law, undoubtedly made it easier to carry out the political decision to settle the dispute in this way.

THE HAGUE CONFERENCES OF 1899 AND 1907

The experience of the Geneva Tribunal, and other important instances of arbitration proceedings in its wake, provided the point of departure for a new development which came to a head, on the initiative of the Tsar Nicholas II of Russia, in the First Hague Peace Conference of 1899, and which was consummated in the Second Hague Peace Conference of 1907. [10]

Among other things, these conferences attempted to find a way of repairing a number of obvious cracks in the system and practice of international arbitration, as it had been developing during the nineteenth century. The agreements to have resource to arbitration had all been reached *ad hoc*. All the instances of international arbitration up to this time, even when succesful in settling the political dispute, had been marked by acute political difficulties in reaching agreement on the composition and procedure of the arbitral tribunal and on fixing precisely the point or points on which it was to be asked to decide. This was because no standing arbitral machinery existed, and no clearly accepted concepts of international arbitral procedure, and it is rarely easy to reach agreement on these highly complicated and at times extremely technical aspects in the heat of a political controversy which may leave little room for manoeuvre. This added to the difficulties of invoking disinterested third-party judgment and increased the psychological obstacles which, in the nature of things, always make it difficult for a government to empower outsiders to reach binding decisions on delicate matters of direct concern to it. This had the consequence that if political passions became too inflamed, the governments concerned might find it politically impossible to agree to settle the matter by arbitration even if they wanted to, or, what was worse, they could make illusory agreements, or frustrate their declared intentions by other means. For reasons such as these, enlightened persons, and governments, began looking for a method by which permanent arbitration machinery could always be at the disposal of States: some went even further, and began thinking of the possibility of making it *compulsory* for States to have recourse to arbitration, if not for all then at least for certain types of international disputes.

At this point two almost insuperable problems made an appearance. They are mentioned here because they have dogged the whole history of international adjudication and their influence is felt in the International Court. The first was the composition of the Tribunal. The second was how to define *in advance* its jurisdiction. Neither of these problems were fully solved by the Peace Conferences of 1899 and 1907.

On the question of composition, the experience of the diplomatic arbitrations of the nineteenth century showed that even if the balance in an arbitral commission should be held by neutral arbitrators or a neutral umpire, States, for reasons which are essentially psychological, could not normally be expected to agree to submit their disputes to a tribunal in which there was not a single national of their own. This aspect was the easier to resolve, basically on the principle that the balance in an arbitral tribunal, in which the parties too should be represented, should be held "neutral" members. More significant, however—and it was this which really made it impossible then to establish a permanent arbitration court—was the attitude of the Great Powers of the time. Loosely organized in the Concert of Europe, these felt that their international interests and responsibilities (including their general responsibilities to preserve the peace between the Small Powers and to maintain the balance of power between themselves) were sufficiently heavy and universal to justify a demand that if any permanent international court were created, they should be represented on it. Experience showed—and this was no more than a matter of political reality—that it was one thing for Powers, even Great Powers, to agree to settle their existing disputes through arbitrators of their own choice: it was quite another thing to expect them to agree *in advance* to submit their future disputes, with parties and on matters unknown, to a permanent tribunal whose composition was already fixed and on which they might not be represented.

The difficulty of setting down in advance and in general terms the jurisdiction of a tribunal had its roots no less in experience and political realism. It derives from the view which is firmly held and valid as a matter of political doctrine (however repugnant it may be to legal theory) that not every international dispute, especially when it is one involving a serious clash of interests, or of aspirations, can be said generally and in advance to be suitable for settlement through disinterested judges applying legal techniques and criteria exclusively. Many of the most intractable and dangerous international disputes are born out of a desire to alter the law, for instance when the law is embodied in an unpopular, but legally binding, treaty. This difficulty, which is a real one, has led to a long series of attempts to define the types of disputes which can be inherently regarded, in advance, as suitable for settlement by arbitrators or judges, to set down the tests for the "justiciability" and "non-justiciability" of disputes, to employ a common term (borrowed from the experience of the United States Supreme Court in dealing with certain constitutional matters). These attempts may be regarded as satisfactory technical advances: it would be an illusion to think, however, that they have solved the problem, as can indeed be seen by the frequency with which respondent States challenge the jurisdiction of the Court (see p. 76 below).

In 1907, no workable solution was found to either of these problems (partly because German militarism thought that an effective system of arbitration would give their enemies a useful instrument for delaying political events, and thus enable them to overtake the German superiority in armaments). As a result, a compromise was adopted. The idea of compulsory arbitration, even for limited categories of disputes, was for the time being dropped. It was replaced by a system of voluntary arbitration which required, for each instance, the consent of the States concerned, both to the composition of the Tribunal and to its terms of reference. On the other hand, it was recognized that certain types of disputes were probably more suitable for arbitration than others. The value of the institution of arbitration had proved itself, and there was a widespread desire to transform it from an exclusively *ad hoc* diplomatic process into one having elements of permanency. The attempt was made to formulate the main lines of arbitration procedure (which, nevertheless, States were free to modify at will). This technical aspect was important as a step towards simplifying the drawing up of arbitration agreements and thus reducing the opportunities of frustrating a political decision to resort to arbitration.

THE PERMANENT COURT OF ARBITRATION

The element of permanency was created by the establishment of the Permanent Court of Arbitration. In fact this institution is misnamed, for it is neither a court nor permanent. It consists of a panel of arbitrators nominated by the contracting parties (they may each nominate not more than four persons, of known competency in questions of international law, of the highest moral reputation and disposed to accept the duties of arbitrator). From this panel the States may choose a Tribunal to decide their particular case, the balance in the Tribunal being, of course, confided to neutral arbitrators. The Permanent Court of Arbitration has an Administrative Council, consisting of the diplomatic representatives at The Hague of the contracting parties, and a small permanent Secretariat. Its headquarters were established at The Hague (where they still are).

The First Hague Convention of 1907 for the Pacific Settlement of International Disputes (replacing the First Convention of 1899), therefore contains an elaborate code covering a number of processes for the settlement of international disputes, in the event of failure of diplomatic negotiations to produce satisfactory results, and arbitration is included among them. Others are the procedures of good offices, conciliation and mediation, and arrangements for international commissions of enquiry, essentially for the elucidation of disputed facts. [11] The Convention defined the object of international arbitration as "the settlement of disputes between States by judges of their own choice". It imposed no obligation on the Parties to have recourse to arbitration, but Article 38 stated that: "In questions of a legal nature, and especially in the interpretation or application of international conventions, arbitration is recognized by the contracting Powers as the most effective and at the same time the most equitable means of settling disputes which diplomacy has failed to settle". Consequently it was desirable to have recourse to it in that type of case. But it was never obligatory, even after arbitration had been decided upon, to have recourse to a panel of the Permanent Court of Arbitration: that was maintained primarily as machinery to facilitate recourse to arbitration.

These difficulties, above all, made it impossible, at The Hague, to establish any general obligation to have resort to arbitration. All that could be done was to create machinery, and to lay down a series of general rules, for the conduct of arbitration proceedings, [12] leaving their actual application in a concrete case to the unfettered will of the States concerned. Therefore, in order to set arbitration proceedings in motion, there must be a special agreement for that purpose (sometimes called technically, even in English, a *compromis*)—whether an agreement, bilateral or multilateral, providing for the submission of certain types of disputes to arbitration, or one providing for the submission of a specific dispute to arbitration.

Even before the 1899 Conference, two other developments in the practice of States started to make an appearance. The first was the inclusion in general treaties of a "compromissory clause"—a stipulation to refer disputes arising out of the particular treaty to arbitration. The second was the conclusion of general treaties of arbitration, as distinct from special agreements, sometimes coupled with other machineries for the settlement of disputes, between pairs of States. In these treaties too the problem of defining in advance the type of dispute which they were intended to cover was found to be extremely difficult. Usually they excluded from their scope disputes involving the vital interests, national sovereignty, independence or honour of the contracting parties, and in so far as this formula granted the State concerned a right of unilateral determination that a given dispute came within that category, the treaty was to that extent illusory.

Despite these weaknesses, the Hague Conferences gave a great impetus both to the process of including bilateral arbitration treaties, and to the invocation of arbitration proceedings. It has been estimated that between 1900 and 1914 more than 120 general arbitration treaties were concluded between pairs of States. Between 1902 and 1920, fourteen disputes were handled by panels of arbitrators chosen from the Permanent Court of Arbitration and more than fifty other disputes were arbitrated in some other manner. [13] Since the end of the First World War to 1970, over seventy cases of international arbitration are known. [14] Of these, twenty-five are claimed to have taken place before panels of the Permanent Court of Arbitration or with the co-operation of its Bureau, and the balance before *ad hoc* arbitration tribunals. In addition to these, both under the Peace Treaties of 1919, and under the 1947 Treaty of Peace with Italy and the long series of corresponding arrangements with the Federal Republic of Germany, a number of Mixed Arbitral Tribunals, Conciliation Tribunals and the like were established, and these dealt with an extremely large number of cases. Since one of the parties was an individual, these cannot be regarded as international arbitrations proper: that term is rightly limited to litigation in which only States, or at the most international organizations composed of States (inter-governmental organizations), are parties.

By the outbreak of the First World War, the main lines of international arbitral procedure were firmly drawn. From the starting point of the voluntary character of the whole process, the following are the principal features that may be noted:

Firstly, it had become accepted that if in the course of the proceedings a dispute should arise concerning the Tribunal's jurisdiction, *that* dispute should normally be settled by the Tribunal itself, and should not be referred back to the diplomatic channels, unless the arbitration agreement provided otherwise. Thus one way of frustrating the work of the arbitration tribunals was blocked.

Secondly, it was accepted that the arbitrators should all be persons of recognized competence and of the highest standards of integrity. Where the Head of a State was appointed arbitrator, as was frequently done, he was entitled to delegate the actual work to his own officials, but the award was promulgated personally and under his own authority. The mixed diplomatic and judicial quality of international arbitration was generally preserved by the appointment of national arbitrators (who in the Tribunal tended to cancel each other out), leaving the real power of decision in the hands of a group of neutral arbitrators or even a single Umpire. [15]

Thirdly, accepted elements of the normal judicial techniques, including features such as the equality of the parties, the right of both parties to an equal hearing, and, of course, the independence of the arbitrators, were fully incorporated into international practice. International political thought began to appreciate the implications of the maxim, that justice must not only be done but that it must be seen to be done.

Fourthly, the outlines of fairly regular patterns of procedure began to establish themselves. These included both written and oral pleadings, closed deliberations of the Tribunal, the promulgation of its award (unless for any reason the parties desired to keep the whole arbitration secret, which they were entitled to do), the duty of the Tribunal to give reasons for its award, and the right of any member of the Tribunal to express his dissent (this latter was not invariable: the custom of dissenting opinions is essentially of a "common law" origin, and is not familiar to continental jurists).

Finally, it became established as a rule of law, not requiring to be specifically written into arbitration agreements, that the agreement to have recourse to arbitration automatically contained the obligation to abide by the Tribunal's award, and to carry it out in good faith. The award was "final" and "binding" as a settlement of the dispute. It is this which distinguished arbitration from other diplomatic processes such as conciliation and mediation, in which the binding quality was not always present or was even deliberately excluded.

These essential features of international arbitration have been preserved to this day, and have exercised a potent influence on the development of international adjudication proper, through the International Court. [16]

THE LEAGUE OF NATIONS

One of the reasons for the difficulties which attended all the earlier attempts to establish permanent international tribunals of general jurisdiction was the absence of any central political administration for the international community. Before the First World War, no regular international machinery existed, neither on the political-diplomatic level nor on the administrative level. The so-called Concert of Europe of the time was an informal system of consultation between the Great European Powers of the epoch; it lacked all the attributes of system and constitution, and its machinery was that of the traditional techniques of diplomacy.

The establishment of the League of Nations by the Peace Treaties of 1919 changed this. Especially significant was the differentiation between the Council and the Assembly. The Council was conceived as a small executive body in which the political responsibility and power were concentrated. It was composed of a number of permanent members, who were the surviving Great Powers which were members of the League, and elected members. On the other hand, the Assembly, which met once a year in regular session, was the general deliberative body of the total membership. The League was equipped with an administrative organ, the Secretariat, and a regular budget. Obviously, the existence of such a pattern of international organization opened new perspectives for a permanent international judicial organ.

The relative success of the 1907 Conference—which only served to highlight the obstinate political difficulties in the way of true international adjudication—inspired a significant movement which was not satisfied with the partial solution and looked forward to the day when a permanent tribunal with compulsory jurisdiction would exist. The Hague Conference itself had adopted a resolution admitting the principle of obligatory arbitration as well as a project for the creation of a court of arbitral justice, but nothing had come of it. Important bodies, however, kept hammering away at the theme, including the Institute of International Law (resolution of 1911) and others. During the War, the Scandinavian neutral States prepared a joint plan for the organization of an international judicial organ, and this was followed by other plans prepared under the aegis of the Swiss (1918) and Netherlands (1919) Governments. The movement also had powerful backing in the United

States, and among the Western Allies in general. It was a movement which, therefore, could not be ignored by the peacemakers of 1919.

By the time the early drafts of the constitution of the League of Nations were circulating at the beginning of 1919, the notion that permanent machinery for international adjudication must be included seems to have been accepted. It was perceived that the establishment of the League, in which the Principal Allied and Associated Powers would have a predominant position (they would be permanent members of the Council), opened the way to a solution of the problem of the composition of such a tribunal. It was also felt that the existence of a regularly established international organization might facilitate a solution for the question of the extent to which the principle of compulsory arbitration could become feasible. Obviously, however, a great deal of work was required before these ideas could be translated into the language of reality. Article 12 of the Covenant contained a general obligation to submit to arbitration or settlement by the League Council any dispute likely to lead to a rupture, as well as provisions for the execution of decisions, and Article 13 contained a general declaration about the types of dispute which were regarded as generally suitable for submission to arbitration. [17] These included disputes as to: *(a)* the interpretation of a treaty; *(b)* any question of international law; *(c)* the existence of any fact which if established would constitute a breach of any international obligation; or *(d)* the extent and nature of the reparation to be made for any such breach. The first of these categories had appeared in Article 38 of the Hague Convention of 1907. The others, however, were new, and indicate the extent of the intellectual advance achieved since 1907. If the matter could be disposed of merely by means of definitions and classifications, the four categories together are broad enough to cover every international *dispute*, though not necessarily every type or instance of international tension which might occur. This formula has come to exercise a significant and on the whole fruitful influence on the work of the International Court.

Articles 12 and 13 contained general obligations binding on the Members of the League, obligations which were vague and of indefinite scope it is true, but nonetheless obligations. That was as far as the Peace Conference could go in the time at its disposal. It could not establish the permanent judicial organ, and it therefore decided to leave future developments to the organs of the League. Article 14 of the Covenant consequently imposed on the Council the duty of formulating plans for the establishment of what was termed the Permanent Court of International Justice, which would be competent to hear and determine any dispute of an international character which the parties thereto submit to it. This Article also introduced a completely novel idea into international practice, by providing that the Court might give an advisory opinion upon any dispute or question referred to it by the Council of the Assembly. This is discussed on pp. 80 ff. below.

The Council lost little time in getting down to work and already at its second session in February, 1920, appointed a committee of ten eminent jurists (several of whom had participated at The Hague in 1907), from allied or neutral countries, to submit a report to the Council. The Committee's attention was called to the plans which had been drawn up in the meantime, and to certain assurances that had been given to the German and Austrian Governments in the course of the Peace Conferences. By July it adopted its draft scheme which was promptly discussed by the Council, and after modifications was forwarded to the First Assembly of the League. The Assembly, after further amendment, then adopted the Statute of the Permanent Court of International Justice, and opened its Protocol of Signature on 16 December 1920. It decided that the Statute would come into force as soon as it was ratified by the majority of the members of the League. This process was completed by the beginning of September the next year, and the Statute then came into force. The first election of judges took place in 1921, and the Court was formally inaugurated in January 1922. The first case to come before the Court—an advisory opinion—was filed in May, 1922, and the first contentious case was instituted a year later.[18]

Thus was the concept of a permanent international judicial organ translated into reality. On the other hand, the concept of compulsory jurisdiction was not yet accepted into international practice.

THE PERMANENT COURT OF INTERNATIONAL JUSTICE

Despite Article 14 of the Covenant, the Permanent Court, which was in existence from 1922 until the dissolution of the League on 18 April 1946, was strictly speaking not an organ of the League. The fact that a State was a Member of the League did not automatically make it a party to the Statute of the Court, although, as laid down in the Statute, it could participate in the elections of the judges, and had to bear its share of the Court's expenses. This meant that what is sometimes known as the "international judicial community", i.e. the States which are parties to the Statute, was not identical with the international political community organized in the League. All members of the League were *qualified* to become parties to the Statute, but so too were other States provided certain conditions were fulfilled. Furthermore, under given conditions even States which were not parties to the Statute could litigate their differences with other States before the Court, whether as applicants or as respondents. The Court was created to serve the whole international community. Not for nothing was its seat established at The Hague, alongside the Permenent Court of Arbitration, and not at Geneva. The Court never became "tainted" with the "Geneva spirit".

Yet the Court was closely connected with the League—so close in fact that its fortunes were undoubtedly tied to those of the League, and it could not survive the disappearance of the League. This meant that developments in the general international situation, which prevented effective action on the political level by the League, could not leave the Court unaffected, and that the progressive disintegration of the post-War political system had a direct impact on the Court. That was inevitable. On the other hand, that bond made possible solutions to some of the problems which had prevented the earlier establishment of any permanent general international judicial organ. For instance, the difficulty over the composition of the Court was neatly solved by confiding the election of the judges to the two principal organs of the League, the Council and the Assembly, an ingenious device which ensured not only the presence of the Great Powers on the Court, but also a balanced Court from the point of view of representation on it of the principal legal systems and the major political trends in the world. This tie also overcame difficulties in financing the Court's expenses. All this has now been taken over by the United Nations, and will be described more fully in the following chapters.

Although, as stated, the concept of the compulsory settlement of all, or certain types of, international disputes was not incorporated into either the League Covenant or the Statute, the general political climate of the early period of the League lent encouragement to the idea that States should voluntarily take upon themselves more precise obligations for submitting disputes to the Court. That objective was further facilitated by the Statute of the Court, and even more so by its actual practice. Nevertheless, the fundamental principle which had underpinned the international arbitrations of the nineteenth century, that the consent of the litigating States is the *only* basis for the exercise of jurisdiction, remained firmly enshrined as the *only* basis for the exercise of jurisdiction by the Permanent Court. The many, and far-reaching, changes which in the course of time international practice has assimilated, have never departed from that fundamental principle.

The Permanent Court, after an experimental and tentative start, also made tremendous advances in international judicial procedure. This is above all thanks to the permanence of the institution. Using as its point of departure the principles of procedure in the domestic courts (especially the highest courts) as well as international arbitration experience, international judicial procedure is today a completely autonomous institution of international law and practice having only superficial resemblances to domestic legal procedure. The Court's procedure became crystalized by 1936 with the adoption of the last version of the Rules of Court. Together with the Statute these Rules were taken over, virtually unchanged, by the United Nations and the present Court (see Appendices 1 and 2). How these procedures were developed and applied by the Permanent Court is now a matter of historical and professional interest. Naturally, there is a continuous process of development to meet the constantly changing requirements and patterns of international life and experience, and in later chapters of this book the attempt will be made to describe their essential features as they are today, for only in 1972 did the present Court promulgate a series of major amendments to the Rules of Court.[19]

It is of greater importance to try and evaluate—or more accurately re-evaluate—the work of the Permanent Court, because now, with the passage of time, its achievements can be looked at more dispassionately and from a distance. What can be learned from its experience, that will be of value today in understanding the potentialities for, and the limitations on, the international judicial function?

The judicial statistics of the Court (see Appendix 4) show that in the 18 years of its effective life, from 1922 to 1939, a total of 66 cases was brought before it. Thirty-eight were contentious cases and 28 advisory cases. Of those, 12 were later settled out of Court. In the fifty-four cases left for decision the Court delivered 27 advisory opinions (all at the request of the League Council) and 32 judgments (two cases were pending when the Second World War silenced the Court). There were in addition a number of substantive pronouncements couched in the form of orders. This gives an average of nearly four cases filed per year, and a slightly smaller number of major judicial pronouncements—figures considerably in excess of anything experienced by international arbitration.

What were these cases about? What were the realities of the disputes with which the Permanent Court was called upon to deal? For as a matter of form by far the greater part of them superficially dealt with technical questions of law, indeed mostly the interpretation of treaties. But let us not confuse the form with the underlying causes of the disputes.

Their subject-matter, as their political context and background, varied. But looing back on these affairs we may notice some interesting, and perhaps unsuspected, features. For example, a great deal of the Court's concrete business emerged from the tensions—which in time played a major role in the course of events leading to the outbreak of the Second World War—between Germany and Poland [20] and between Lithuania and Germany and Poland. [21] Other controversial aspects of the 1919 peace settlement also were brought before the Court [22] as well as some arising out of the Middle Eastern settlement with Turkey. [23] The Council of the League was even not averse to referring to the Court for advisory opinion so explosive an issue as the proposed customs union between Austria and Germany—which the Court, some seven years before Hitler brought the *Anschluss* about to force, held to be incompatible with certain agreements embodied in the peace settlement of 1919. African affairs, too, occupied it—a harbinger of later events. [24] The Court, naturally, also had a certain amount of work to do in resolving other disputes, some of them quite serious, such as that relating to the sovereignty

over Eastern Greenland, and occasionally to give advice on the operations of
the International Labour Organization. On the other hand, it was rare for
disputes arising out of sudden, and perhaps unpremeditated, incidents un-
related to a more general political background to be brought before the
Court. [25] It seems that this type of quarrel may on the whole be more
amenable to diplomatic settlement which will avoid raising the legal questions
of principle, and acute issues of national prestige, which a reference to the
Court must encounter. Many people think that the mere existence of the
Court makes it easier for States to settle this type of dispute without recourse
to the Court: it forces them to consider the legal aspects dispassionately, and
to plan their diplomatic steps accordingly.

We may also observe, in the experience of the Permanent Court, that both
the United States and the Soviet Union manifested towards the Court attitudes very similar to those which they later manifested in the period of the
United Nations. Thus, the United States, itself not a member of the League,
signed the Statute of the Court, but the Senate refused to consent to its
ratification. On the other hand, a judge of United States nationality was
always a member of the Court. The United States was not involved, either
directly or indirectly, in any litigation during that period. The Soviet
Union did not go quite so far even as the United States. It rejected the
competence and authority of the Court in a concrete case referring directly to
its own affairs; [26] it never signed the Statute of the Court, and never concerned itself to have a judge of Soviet nationality on the bench. This latter
aspect was changed after 1945. The formal reason for aloofness of this
character is that these Powers (except the Soviet Union from 1934) were not
members of the Geneva organization: but there is reason to believe that
behind the formal attitude there existed more profound considerations related to fundamental policies of the two great Powers which, after 1945, were
to appear as the two most powerful nations on earth.

How, then, is the work of the Permanent Court to be assessed? One of the
difficulties here is to lay down the appropriate measuring rod. The real significance of the work of an International Court cannot be based on mere statistics, or be determined merely by the formal consideration that its *ipse dixit*
enjoys the formal status of being a final and binding settlement of the dispute
before it. In fact very little of its final and binding settlements of the disputes
brought before it survived the turmoil of the Second World War and its
aftermath.

Let us take another look at the Court's judicial statistics, and relate them
to the general developments of the political situation. We find that of the
66 cases brought before the Court, well over two thirds, 50 of them, were
filed in the period 1922-32, in the heyday of the League. In the five year
period 1924-8 alone, when Franco-German *rapprochement* was at its closest
in the era of the Locarno agreements (1925), 24 new cases were filed, an

average of nearly five per year, which itself is considerably higher than the annual average over the whole period. No new cases were filed in 1929, the year of the major economic crisis. This indicates the dependence of the idea of international litigation upon the existence of some modicum of general pacification and stability and relaxation of international tension. After the Nazis came to power in Germany in 1933, 16 new cases were filed in the seven years 1933-9, a sharp falling off in the Court's activities. This is not accidental, and some disputes of that period were actually litigated only after the Second World War.

Writing in 1944, a former judge of the Court, Manley Hudson, doubted if the Permanent Court had fulfilled a role as a "great bulwark of peace" (had the League of Nations?), though he recognized that some of the cases with which it dealt could have led to serious complications had they been allowed to fester. He thought that the Court's bolstering of the structure of peace had been accomplished more through the confidence it had inspired in its methods and the encouragement which it had given to the extension of the law of pacific settlement. [27] But placing the concrete—isolated—cases in the broader context of the general political situation may show that what the Court, as the other organs of the League (and often in co-operation with them) really succeeded in doing, was for a time to keep a tense situation under some form of control. Given other political conditions, the League would have enjoyed greater long-term success, and the Court with it. As things were, the major disputes with which the Court dealt were connected with that very situation which sparked off the Second World War. None of the skills of statesmanship and diplomacy available at the time succeeded in avoiding that disaster, and it is too much to expect more of the Court.

In addition to any purely political evaluation of the work of the Court within the context of the various procedures for the settlement of international disputes, it is generally recognized that it made a very significant contribution to the development of international law. [28] This is an indirect contribution to the maintenance of international peace, of no mean value, and may be set against the failure of the League of Nations (in contrast to the success of the United Nations) [29] in this field.

The real significance of the experience of the Permanent Court seems to lie in a different direction. From its experimental beginnings it established the point that a permanent international judicial organ is both feasible and necessary, even without going so far as to be accompanied by any true compulsory jurisdiction. The real measure of its worth is not to be found in the number of cases decided by it (though that is by no means to be belittled) or in its contribution to the development and clarification of the law (a by-product of the activity of all courts in all legal systems), but in the wide-ly-held satisfaction at its existence. When the League disappeared and the United Nations took its place it was never suggested that the Court had outlived its usefulness and could well be disbanded. On the contrary: the major concern was to increase its effectiveness and to strengthen its ties with the world political organization, and if too much could not be achieved in this direction, then at least to ensure that the judicial activities could be resumed at the point they had been broken off in 1939. It was never seriously suggested that the Court is unnecessary, or that it had failed in its primary mission, or that its organization was fundamentally faulty, even in quarters which for various reasons were critical of some of its decisions, or of the manner in which States sometimes invoke the judicial function. [30]

The experience of the Permanent Court, its dispassionate and unhurried consideration of the issues brought before it, the high standards of personal integrity and professional competence, and worldly wisdom, of its members, the fact that the judicial pronouncements were endowed with strong moral authority in addition to their formal finality—all these constituted an intangible asset on the positive side of the balance-sheet. They provided the foundations for the reconstituted system of international adjudication after the dust of the Second World War had started to settle.

CHAPTER II

THE UNITED NATIONS AND THE COURT

Article 7 of the United Nations Charter establishes the principal organs of the United Nations. These include the General Assembly, the Security Council, the Economic and Social Council, the Trusteeship Council, the International Court of Justice and the Secretariat. Article 92 states that the Court shall be the principal judicial organ of the United Nations, and that it shall function in accordance with the annexed Statute, based upon the Statute of the Permanent Court, which forms an integral part of the Charter. Article 1 of the Statute repeats that the Court is established as the principal judicial organ of the United Nations, and that it shall function in accordance with the provisions of the Statute. These Articles contain—and emphasize—the general provisions setting forth the position of the Court within the Organization. The Charter also deals with the execution of the Court's decisions, and the General Assembly arranges for the payment of the Court's expenses.

The ambiguity characteristic of the relations between the League of Nations and the Permanent Court of International Justice has now been replaced by clarity. The Court is a principal organ of the United Nations and its Statute, no longer a separate international treaty, is an integral part of the Charter.

Let us briefly see how this has come about, and what are its implications.

THE WAR AND THE SAN FRANCISCO CONFERENCE (1945)

Whatever may have been the original intentions of its founders, the Permanent Court, in the course of its existence and in the light of its accumulated experience, came to discharge three distinct functions, two of them primary, and envisaged in its Statute, and the third, not originally contemplated, secondary. The outbreak of the War, of course, temporarily put an end to all these activities.

Its two primary tasks were, as mentioned in the previous chapter, to decide disputes between States, and to render advisory opinions in response to requests from the Council of the League (it could also render opinions at the request of the Assembly, but in fact the Assembly never made use of this right). The decisions were given independently of action by the League, whereas the advisory opinions represented the Permanent Court's participation in the political activities of the League, and waxed and waned in sympathy with the political fortunes of the League.

Its third function, much less known, was quite different. It was to nominate umpires, presidents of arbitral commissions and of other tribunals, and similar offices. Normally these appointments were made by the President of the Court at the request of a State, but occasionally the whole Court might be consulted, and on the first occasion, as far back as 1923, the whole Court gave its approval. This has come to be known as the "extra-judicial activity" of the Court, since it is not mentioned in the Statute, and no firm rules have been promulgated to regulate the manner of its performance. It meets several international requirements. For instance, it provides a simple way of overcoming difficulties in States' agreeing on the identity of a third arbitrator, which might lead to the frustration of an agreement for arbitration. It also forms the basis for a special arbitration procedure incorporated in certain types of agreements, especially agreements on important economic matters, in which one of the parties is not a State, and therefore cannot have access to the Court itself (which is only competent in disputes between States). International practice has shown that there is need for a form of arbitration in which the President of the Tribunal can be appointed by an independent and respected international official such as the President of the International Court. This is in order to meet between the gap between the area of public law and the area of private law, and to place governments and entities which are not governments on some sort of equal basis in the procedural sense. One of the best-known transactions of this type was the Anglo-Iranian Oil Company's Concession Agreement of 1933 (which later, in 1951, came up before the new Court in international litigation proper), which had been negotiated through the good offices of the Council of the League.

The question which arose during the Second World War was whether there was still use for an international judicial organ performing all or some of these functions and, if so, was an instrument fashioned on the lines of the Statute of the Permanent Court satisfactory for these purposes.

After thorough examination both on the technical and professional level, and on the highest political level, an affirmative answer was given to those questions. There was apparently little disposition, at least among the Western Allies, to doubt the necessity for an international organ resembling the Permanent Court. The real problem which faced them appears as one of method, but underlying the question of method were important political issues. The problem of method was posed as whether to continue the Permanent Court in existence with necessary changes in its Statute, or whether to re-organize the international judicial system and make it an integral part of the general international political organization which would be set up after the War was won. The political problems for which this was the procedural manifestation were of two kinds. The first, and the more important, related to the attitude towards the future international judicial organ of those members of the anti-nazi coalition, above all the Soviet Union and the United States, which between the Wars had stood aloof from both the League and the Permanent Court. The second, which, it seems in retrospect, may have been given undue prominence, related to the position of the Axis Powers which, on the contrary, having participated in the work of the Permanent Court would, as parties to its Statute, technically have a say in its future—this included *all* the Axis Powers. These problems themselves were both closely connected with the changes in the pattern of international relationships which began emerging during the War, and which were given their first formal recognition in the differences between the major political alignments of the United Nations in comparison with those of the League (substitution of the Soviet Union and the United States for Great Britain and France as the major political influences in the Organization).

Interest in the future of the Court as a matter of immediate political concern began to revive about the middle of 1942 when both the British and the United States Governments on the one hand, and the South American Governments (through the Inter-American Juridical Committee) on the other, expressed approval in principle for the resumption of the machinery of international judicial activities after the War. The four leading Allied Powers, China, the Soviet Union, the United Kingdom and the United States, in the Moscow Declaration of 30 October 1943 on General Security, recognized the necessity of establishing a general international organization for the maintenance of international peace and security, though nothing was said publicly at that stage about the Court. A little earlier, in May, the British Government took its first concrete steps, by calling together an Informal Inter-Allied Committee of some twelve experienced international lawyers from among those who were available in London. These were asked to prepare an informal report which would not be binding on their governments, but which could be of use to the authorities in due course. The report which the Committee presented early in 1944 is the first comprehensive re-examination of the issues connected with the Court that had taken place since the outbreak of the War, and in the history of international adjudication it is an important document. The Committee, which did not question the necessity for *a* Court, reached the conclusion that the Permanent Court had on the whole worked well, and that its Statute could be retained as the basis for the general structure of the future Court. It did not think that the Court should be reconstituted as an integral part of any future international organization. In the Committee's view, it was preferable to retain the Court as an independent international organism, but one always standing at the disposal of the Organization. It also found that the policy issues involved in the question whether to maintain the Permanent Court in existence as such, or whether to establish an entirely new Court, were outside its province.[1]

In October, 1944, matters were carried a stage further, when the same four Governments, now called the Sponsoring Powers, concretized their ideas on the future general political organization and published them in the so-called Dumbarton Oaks Proposals for the United Nations.[2] Included in these was definite recognition that the International Court should be the principal judicial organ of the Organization, that all members of the United Nations should *ipso facto* be parties to the Statute of the Court, which would form part of the Charter, and that non-members could become parties to the Statute on conditions to be laid down by the General Assembly upon the recommendation of the Security Council. But on the vexed question of whether to keep the Permanent Court in existence or to create a new Court, and whether, in the latter event, the Statute of the Permanent Court could still serve as a basis, the Dumbarton Oaks Proposals were non-committal, though preference was expressed for keeping the general lines of the old Statute.

It was by now clear that further work of a technical nature was required before the political conference, due to meet in San Francisco in April, 1945, and at which the Charter was to be finally drafted, could profitably take the matter up. Both the Informal Inter-Allied Committee and the Dumbarton Oaks Proposals made it plain that comprehensive re-examination of the terms of the Statute was needed, despite their clear preference for making as few changes as possible. Accordingly, the four Sponsoring Powers decided to convene a full Committee of Jurists in Washington, at which all the United Nations could participate, to prepare the ground for the San Francisco Conference. Forty-four States took part in the work of this Committee, at which the Permanent Court was also represented. It decided to retain the existing Statute, amending it slightly, and at the end of its labours it left three major questions open: *(a)* the form in which to state the Court's mission as the principal judicial organ of the new Organization; *(b)* how to conduct the elections of the judges; and *(c)* to what extent should the jurisdiction of the Court be compulsory. Politically, this latter had now become the most significant issue, because behind it lay the more fundamental problem of whether recognition of the compulsory jurisdiction of the Court for all or certain disputes should be the condition *sine qua non* of membership in the United Nations. Such a question had not arisen, and could not arise, for the League of Nations so long as the Court was not one of its organs and the members of the League not *ipso facto* parties to its Statute.[3]

In this form the question came before the San Francisco Conference itself, where it was discussed in detail in Committee IV/1.[4] In these discussions—in which again the Permanent Court was represented by two of its Judges—it became clear that while a majority of the smaller and medium powers were in favour of making some acceptance of the compulsory jurisdiction of the

Court a condition for membership in the United Nations, the major Powers, on which the prime responsibility for maintaining the Organization would rest, and especially the Soviet Union and the United States, were not prepared to accept so far-reaching an innovation in international practice. Therefore the underlying basis on which the Permanent Court had worked, that the consent of the States concerned gives it jurisdiction to deal with a concrete case, was retained. With this out of the way there was little real difficulty in establishing the Court as a principal organ and the principal judicial organ of the United Nations, or in deciding to create in effect a new Court for this purpose. However, the relevant provisions of the Statute were drafted in such a way as to convey that this decision would not break the chain of continuity with the past and not undo the achievements attained in the field of international justice. Therefore, in some respects the new Court, called the International Court of Justice, may be regarded as the successor of the Permanent Court, even though the United Nations as a whole is not the successor of the League. The Statute emerged from this process but slightly revised, as is apparent from Article 92 of the Charter quoted above.

After the necessary administrative steps were taken by the Preparatory Commission of the United Nations, the judges of the new Court were elected in the early meetings of the Security Council and the General Assembly in February, 1946. At the same time parallel measures for the dissolution of the Permanent Court were put in hand. On 18 April, the new Court held its solemn inaugural meeting in the presence of a distinguished gathering at The Hague. On the same day, at Geneva, the League Assembly voted itself, and the Permanent Court, out of existence.

But over a year was to elapse before the first case was to be filed in the new Court, a marked contrast to what had happened when the Permanent Court was set up in 1922. What did this portend? The answer will appear from the following chapters.

PRINCIPAL ORGAN OF THE UNITED NATIONS

Apart from Articles 7 and 92 of the Charter, Article 93 gives reality to the integration of the Court in the Organization by providing, as had been proposed at Dumbarton Oaks, that all members of the United Nations are *ipso facto* parties to the Statute, to which non-members may become parties on conditions to be determined in each case by the General Assembly upon the recommendation of the Security Council. The underlying assumption is that the world political organization, already possessed of executive, deliberative and administrative organs, would be incomplete unless it possessed a fully integrated judicial organ of its own. The San Francisco records show clearly that for many the intention was in this way to place the Court in a position in which it could play an important role, alongside the other organs, in the new organization of nations for peace and security. Their idea in making the Statute an integral part of the Charter was to secure for the Court the support of all the members. Furthermore, these provisions put an end to the anomalous situation which had existed in the structure of the League, where the international judicial community was something distinct, at least in theory, from the general political organization of the international community. This was a radical innovation made by the founders of the United Nations in 1945, and its import must not be obscured by their conservatism both in matters of form, and in the concept of the underlying basis for international litigation as it had developed during the preceding century.

What are the implications of this?

The Court, as an organ of the United Nations, operates within the framework of the general objectives which the Charter lays down for the Organization as a whole, and for its individual organs. The Court's status as a principal organ imposes on it the duty of participating in the work of the Organization on an equal footing with its other organs. This was vividly expressed by one of the judges who said that the Court, "which has been raised to the status of a principal organ, and thus more closely geared into the mechanism of the U.N.O., must do its utmost to co-operate with the other organs with a view to attaining the aims and principles that have been set forth."[5] This principle of co-operation has been enunciated and acted upon by the Court in several different types of circumstances, but particularly as a ground for rejecting challenges to its competence to render advisory opinions. At the same time, recalling that it is not only a principal organ (Article 7) but also the principal judicial organ (Article 92), the Court has been insistent on maintaining one general qualification regarding this duty of co-operation. It will not co-operate with the other organs blindly, but only if it is fully satisfied that what it is being asked to do is, in the circumstances, fully compatible with its judicial character.[6] Its judicial character must be preserved at all costs. This, too, has particularly influenced its advisory competence, which, in the letter of the law, is discretionary: the Court has repeatedly stressed that in principle it should not refuse to give an opinion unless overriding considerations of judicial propriety make this imperative.[7]

The Court's status as the judicial organ also has consequences for the political organs when they have to take decisions relating to the Court. The influence of this is felt both in administrative aspects and in political aspects.

To take the first aspect, when, for instance, the Security Council has had to deal with the question of the access to the Court of States which are not members of the United Nations, the view prevailed that as the Court was a judicial organ and in consequence a non-political body, therefore the question of access to it ought not to be influenced by irrelevant political considerations.[8] To take another administrative example: when, in 1959, the

Illustration 1. The United Nations and related agencies ▶

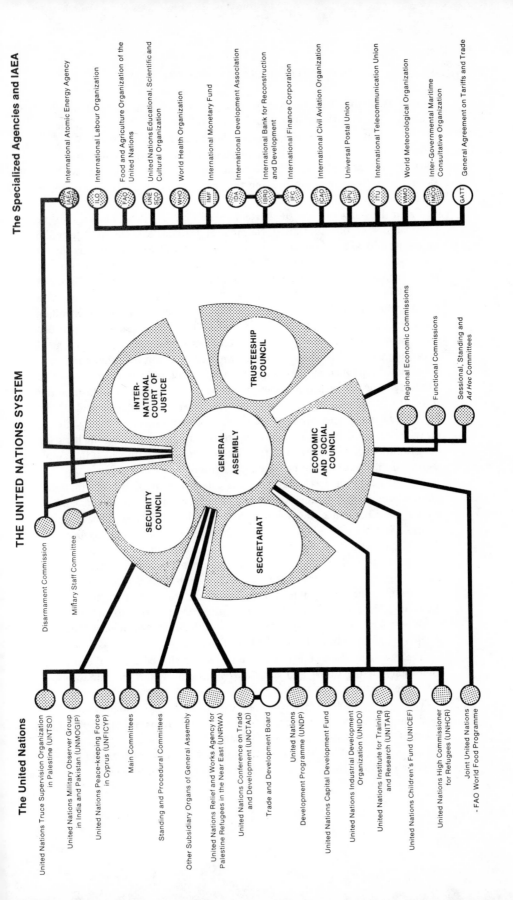

THE UNITED NATIONS SYSTEM

The United Nations

United Nations Truce Supervision Organization in Palestine (UNTSO)

United Nations Military Observer Group in India and Pakistan (UNMOGIP)

United Nations Peace-keeping Force in Cyprus (UNFICYP)

Main Committees

Standing and Procedural Committees

Other Subsidiary Organs of General Assembly

United Nations Relief and Works Agency for Palestine Refugees in the Near East (UNRWA)

United Nations Conference on Trade and Development (UNCTAD)

Trade and Development Board

United Nations Development Programme (UNDP)

United Nations Capital Development Fund

United Nations Industrial Development Organization (UNIDO)

United Nations Institute for Training and Research (UNITAR)

United Nations Children's Fund (UNICEF)

United Nations High Commissioner for Refugees (UNHCR)

Joint United Nations - FAO World Food Programme

Disarmament Commission

Military Staff Committee

INTER-NATIONAL COURT OF JUSTICE

TRUSTEESHIP COUNCIL

SECURITY COUNCIL

GENERAL ASSEMBLY

ECONOMIC AND SOCIAL COUNCIL

SECRETARIAT

Regional Economic Commissions

Functional Commissions

Sessional, Standing and Ad Hoc Committees

The Specialized Agencies and IAEA

IAEA — International Atomic Energy Agency

ILO — International Labour Organization

FAO — Food and Agriculture Organization of the United Nations

UNESCO — United Nations Educational, Scientific and Cultural Organization

WHO — World Health Organization

IMF — International Monetary Fund

IDA — International Development Association

IBRD — International Bank for Reconstruction and Development

IFC — International Finance Corporation

ICAO — International Civil Aviation Organization

UPU — Universal Postal Union

ITU — International Telecommunication Union

WMO — World Meteorological Organization

IMCO — Inter-Governmental Maritime Consultative Organization

GATT — General Agreement on Tariffs and Trade

General Assembly had to examine certain matters relating to the Judges' pensions, its Legal Committee insisted that full weight should be attached to the circumstance of their election and the character and requirements of the office of Judge as expressed in the Statute, and this view prevailed over a less constructive attitude of the General Assembly's Administrative and Budgetary Committee, approaching the matter exclusively from an administrative standpoint.[9]

From the point of view of substantive political activities, the fact that the political organs of the United Nations tend to make a sharp distinction between political problems and legal problems—there are some who say that at times too sharp a distinction is drawn—furnishes an explanation for the phenomenon that, unlike the League's practice, Court procedures have not been invoked by the Security Council or the General Assembly in the exercise of their functions relating to the pacific settlement of a dispute pending before them between two or more States. They have requested advisory opinions seeking legal advice on the consequence of decisions, and in general respecting guidance to them on their own actions. [10] On the other hand, care has always been taken by these organs, on receipt of advisory opinions, not to adopt operational decisions which could be taken to cast doubts upon the authority of the Court. Nevertheless, the fact remains that several of the Court's judgments and advisory opinions, as well as orders indicating interim measures of protection, have not been fruitful in terms of laying the basis for the resolution of the political difficulties in connection with which they were requested. Illustrations will be found in Chapter VI.

The decisions of 1945 regarding the establishment of the International Court of Justice did not signify the end of political interest in its role, and on several occasions since the matter has been the subject of debate in the General Assembly. In addition, in specific cases, especially of treaty-drafting, the United Nations as well as conferences convened under its auspices have faced great difficulties provoked by strong desires to confer jurisdiction in concrete cases arising under the treaties being drafted, and equally strong opposition to that. This, indeed, is a factor that has dominated the work of the United Nations in the field of the codification of international law, and it nearly wrecked the most important of the codification conferences, that held in 1968-9 on the codification of the law of treaties. [11]

Three debates have taken place on what might be called the political philosophy of the Court and the Court's position within the framework of the United Nations.

The first occurred in the General Assembly of 1947, on an item on the need for greater use by the United Nations and its organs of the International Court of Justice. This was the first debate of this character since the end of the Second World War. Moreover, it took place as the so-called Cold War was entering its initial stages. While it showed a very general feeling of regret and concern at the indifference shown in recent years for arbitral and judicial methods for the pacific settlement of international disputes, this feeling was not universally shared. Particularly important were the statements then made by the Soviet Foreign Minister Andrei Vyshinsky, demonstrating the negative attitude of his country towards the Court. The resolution then adopted recommended greater use of the Court, but as a practical matter had no direct impact.[12]

The second occasion was in connexion with the drafting of the Declaration on Principles of International Law concerning Friendly Relations and Co-operation among States in accordance with the Charter of the United Nations. This matter occupied the General Assembly and a special inter-sessional committee from 1963 until 1970. In connexion with the principle that States should settle their international disputes in such a manner that international peace, and justice, should not be endangered, the question of judicial settlement was discussed, especially in 1966 and 1967. The debate brought out the widespread mistrust of the role of judicial settlement in the present international situation. It also drew attention to widespread dissatisfaction at certain features of the International Court itself, especially its composition, and at the present state of general international law, and it was impossible to insert in the declaration any specific reference to the Court itself.[13]

The third debate commenced in 1970 (and at this time of writing is still continuing), the subject being a review of the role of the International Court of Justice. The sponsors' original aim was to have an expert study of the matter conducted under General Assembly auspices. There was strong opposition to this, but the debate in the General Assembly between 1970 and 1972, as well as an important series of written observations by Governments, covered a wide range. The reports of the Sixth Committee of the General Assembly are thus of particular value as a mirror of the present-day attitudes of Governments vis-à-vis the Court. A number of comments on the Court's procedure were made, and some account was taken of them by the Court in connection with its 1972 revision of the Rules of Procedure.[14]

The fact that the Court is one of several principal organs means that it exists on a par with them, being neither in a position of inferiority nor in one of superiority. Consequently, it does not exist as a general "constitutional Court" of the United Nations. There is no duty on anybody to seek its opinion on the legal issues when questions of the meaning of the Charter arise. In fact, it was decided at the San Francisco Conference that each organ of the United Nations would be free itself to interpret the Charter as and when circumstances require. This does not *prevent* the Court from giving its opinion on these matters when it is asked to do so in due form. This has been applied in practice in two ways. Thus, when the President of the Security Council, the representative of the Ukraine, once explained that the Court could not be regarded as a kind of court of appeal from the decisions of the General Assembly or the Security Council, no member of the Council dissented. [15] On the other hand, the General Assembly has occasionally sought the advice of the Court on the constitutionality of action it has already decided to take, or which it is proposing to take, and has acted on the advice received.[16] Against this may be set the complicated developments in South-West Africa situation (see p. 132 below). This case indicates that in very special circumstances the General Assembly will not permit the fact that a case is *sub judice* in the International Court to prevent it from exercising its own responsibilities under the Charter. But this is a controversial matter, on which the last word has not yet been said.

Generally speaking it can be asserted, then, that the other organs have shown awareness that the special character of the Court imposes on them an attitude of caution towards the Court, and obliges them not to embroil it directly in issues in which the political aspects in truth predominate. Perhaps this attitude was not fully held in the early years of the United Nations, before it had become clear that judicial techniques could not advance the solution of truly political problems. However, it is now increasingly realized that, in the words of a Staff Study prepared for the United States Senate in 1955, "a judicial determination of a dispute comprised primarily of political facets may not contribute to a solution of the underlying problem. This leads to the conclusion that it is much more realistic to allow political considerations full sway." [17]

The fact that the Court is the principal judicial organ means that it is the only judicial organ directly established by the Charter, but this does not mean that it is the only judicial organ that may be established either by the United Nations as an organization, or by its individual members. Article 33 of the Charter, which enumerates the various methods for the pacific settlement of international disputes, includes arbitration, judicial settlement, or other peaceful means of the parties' own choice: the principle that the parties are free to choose their own methods of peaceful settlement is firmly enshrined. Parallel to this is Article 95 of the Charter which spells out that nothing in the Charter shall prevent the members from entrusting the solution of their differences to other tribunals by virtue of agreements already in existence or which may be concluded in the future. In fact the United Nations has been instrumental in establishing other tribunals including, for example, the United Nations Tribunal in Libya, the powers and functions of which were later transferred to the Italian-Libyan Mixed Arbitration Commission. [18] Mention here may also be made of the United Nations Administrative Tribunal established for the express purpose of adjudicating disputes between members of the Secretariat and the Organization, arising out of their contracts of service. [19]

The position of the Court, as the principal judicial organ of the United

Nations, can therefore be briefly summarized. Within the framework of this highly political organization the Court, although an integral part of the Organization, stands in a special, and somewhat apart, position, as is indeed appropriate for a court of justice. It is not composed of the representatives of States. It reacts to the initiatives of States and other organs in a spirit of co-operation, but has no power of initiating action itself. The political organs, for their part, and the States represented on them, have on the whole evinced care not to allow completely extraneous political factors to influence decisions which they have been called upon to make in relation to the Court. They have equally, on the whole, tried not to embroil the Court in the intractable political problems which face them daily.

In so far as prior to the San Francisco Conference some anxiety was expressed lest too close an association of the Court with the Organization might impair its standing and its ability to perform its judicial function dispassionately, it can fairly be said that nothing has occurred since to justify apprehensions of that nature. This does not mean, however, that world political trends, themselves reflected in the United Nations, have left the Court unaffected, but that is another matter.[20]

THE COURT AND THE SPECIALIZED AGENCIES

The United Nations does not exist alone in the world of the organized international community. It stands in the centre of a complicated system of international organizations, established by inter-governmental agreement and having wide international responsibilities in economic, social, cultural, educational, health and related fields. The Charter makes it possible for these organizations to be brought into formal relationship with the United Nations by means of agreements, called "Relationship Agreements", to be approved by the General Assembly. These are called Specialized Agencies, and they form part of the United Nations family. They today include the International Labour Organization (I.L.O.), the Food and Agriculture Organization (F.A.O.), the United Nations Educational, Scientific and Cultural Organization (UNESCO), the International Civil Aviation Organization (I.C.A.O.), the World Health Organization (W.H.O.), the International Bank for Reconstruction and Development (I.B.R.D.), the International Monetary Fund (I.M.F.), the International Finance Corporation (I.F.C.), the International Development Association (I.D.A.), the Universal Postal Union (U.P.U.), the International Telecommunication Union (I.T.U.), the World Meteorological Organization (W.M.O.), the Intergovernmental Maritime Consultative Organization (I.M.C.O.) and, for some purposes, the International Atomic Energy Agency (I.A.E.A.). Most members of the United Nations are members of most of these Specialized Agencies which, while being autonomous and independent organizations, are at the same time subject to certain overriding controls of the United Nations itself. One of the matters which the United Nations controls, through the General Assembly, is their relations with the Court.

The International Court, as the principal judicial organ of the United Nations, also serves these organizations in a similar capacity. The ties between the Court and the Specialized Agencies are regulated in in the Relationship Agreements. [21] The contacts between the Court and these Agencies are spread over three dimensions.

Firstly, many of the constitutions of the Specialized Agencies, unlike the Charter of the United Nations itself, contain a provision to the effect that disputes between members arising out of the application or interpretation of the Constitution may be referred to the Court. This, in fact, is a normal compromissory clause, and provides the basis for contentious litigation. The first instance of this occurred in 1972, in the *ICAO Appeal* case (p. 159 below).

Secondly, Article 34 of the Statute of the Court empowers the Court to request public international organizations (whether or not Specialized Agencies in the technical sense), to furnish it with information relevant to cases before it. The Relationship Agreements contain undertakings by the Specialized Agencies to furnish information so requested. [22] The Court has occasionally made use of this facility, not limiting its approaches only to Specialized Agencies, and of course the Organizations approached have all furnished replies. These include the International Labour Organization and the Organization of American States.

Thirdly, Article 96 (2) of the Charter, which deals with the right to request advisory opinions, empowers the General Assembly to authorize the Specialized Agencies to request advisory opinions on legal questions arising within the scope of their activities. All the Specialized Agencies, with the exception of the Universal Postal Union (which has an internal system for settling legal disputes), are now authorized to request advisory opinions, the Relationship Agreements specifying which organs of the Specialized Agencies may initiate the request. This authorization does not extend to questions concerning the mutual relationships of the United Nations and the Special-ized Agencies, an aspect left to the exclusive competence of the Economic and Social Council in exercise of its general role of supervisor and co-ordina-tor of the Specialized Agencies: moreover, whenever any Specialized Agency decides to request an advisory opinion, it has to inform the Economic and Social Council of its action.

Contrary to early expectations, this has not led to any marked increase in the judicial business of the Court. Only two Specialized Agencies have availed themselves of their right to request advisory opinions, UNESCO and the Intergovernmental Maritime Consultative Organization. [23] As expected, in dealing with these requests the Court has followed the same principles that it enunciated in relation to the United Nations itself: in particular it has re-asserted its duty to co-operate in the activities of the organizations concerned while preserving the strictly judicial character of its own actions.

It is therefore appropriate to regard the Court not merely as the principal judicial organ of the United Nations but as the principal judicial organ of the Specialized Agencies, indeed of the whole United Nations structure.

EXECUTION OF THE COURT'S DECISIONS

As has been seen in the previous chapter, the international arbitral procedure of the nineteenth century came as a matter of course to include in every arbitration agreement an implied obligation that the decisions of the arbitral tribunal would be executed in good faith. This is also a fundamental principle of the law governing international litigation before the International Court. When the international community was not organized on the political level, no ready-made machinery existed, or indeed could exist, for compelling a recalcitrant party to comply with the terms of an award it did not like. But when the League of Nations was established, opportunity was taken to insert in Article 13 of the Covenant a stipulation to the effect that in the event of failure to carry out a decision of the Permanent Court, the Council should be empowered to propose what steps should be taken to give effect to it. Instances of this were very rare, and in fact the problem of the execution and enforcement of the decisions of the Permanent Court did not appear to be a serious one. Since the jurisdiction of the Court was based on the consent of the parties, it may be assumed that they consent in advance to carry out the judgment.

These ideas have been taken over into the Charter of the United Nations.

The basic principle, that the decision of the Court is binding, final and without appeal, is enunciated in Article 59 of the Statute, and that is because it relates to the functioning of the Court as such. This is supplemented by two important provisions which, having broader political implications, are contained in the Charter.

The first is found in the first paragraph of Article 94, which lays down shortly and simply: "Each Member of the United Nations undertakes to comply with the decision of the International Court of Justice in any case to which it is a party". States which are not members of the United Nations but which become parties to the Statute of the Court, and States which are not parties to the Statute of the Court but which are parties to litigation before the Court, have to give a corresponding undertaking before they are admitted to the Court.

The second appears in paragraph two of that Article: "If any party to a case fails to perform the obligations incumbent upon it under a judgment rendered by the Court, the other party may have recourse to the Security Council, which may, if it deems necessary, make recommendations or decide upon measures to be taken to give effect to the judgment." The underlying implication of this provision is that if failure to comply with a decision of the Court creates a new political problem, the Security Council is given wide powers to deal with the resultant situation. This type of situation would not be unlike that which several years ago confronted the Federal authorities in Little Rock.

Although the damages awarded to the United Kingdom against Albania in the *Corfu Channel* case (£ 843,947) have not been paid over—the only instance, so far as is known, of complete failure to comply with a final judgment of the Court—the competence of the Security Council has not yet ever been invoked in order to secure compliance with a judgment. On the other hand it was invoked, in 1951, by the United Kingdom in an attempt to secure compliance by Iran with the interim measures of protection (the international term for interim injunction) indicated by the Court, in the early stages of the Anglo-Iranian dispute, in order to preserve the object of the litigation pending its outcome. However, the Security Council showed little enthusiasm for this procedure, which led to no concrete result.[24] In fact, the efficacy of this provision depends upon the general ability of the Security Council to carry out its responsibilities for the maintenance of international peace. That, in turn, depends upon the unanimity of the five Permanent Members. Their inability to reach agreement on major political issues is the fundamental reason for the failure of the Security Council to face up to the challenge which was presented to it by the United Kingdom in 1951.

THE COURT'S FINANCES

The expenses of the Court are borne by the United Nations in such manner as the General Assembly decides. [25] These expenses include, besides the normal running costs of the institution, the salaries of its members and staff, and their pensions.

The estimate of expenditure is included in the annual budget approved each year by the General Assembly (by a majority of two thirds), after detailed scrutiny by the Advisory Committee on Administrative and Budgetary Questions, and the Fifth (Administrative and Budgetary) Committee of the General Assembly. Frequently a member of the Registry Staff is in attendance in order to furnish any necessary explanations. The Court's accounts are also submitted to external audit in accordance with the normal United Nations financial and accounting procedures, and ultimately approved by the General Assembly.

The members of the Court are each entitled to an annual salary of $ 35,000. On top of this, the President receives a special annual allowance of $ 8,400, and the Vice-President when acting as President $53 *per diem* up to a maximum of $5,300 *per annum*. Each judge *ad hoc* is entitled to a special allowance of $67 *per diem*. In addition, travel and subsistence allowances are payable in accordance with the appropriate U.N. regulations. [26] All these salaries, allowances and the pensions (of the members of the Court and of the Registrar) are free of all taxation, by Article 32 of the Statute. The Registrar receives a salary equivalent to that of an Under-Secretary in the United Nations Secretariat, and the members of the Registry staff are graded according to the grades in force in the Secretariat.*

The members of the Court are entitled to pensions in accordance with regulations made by the General Assembly. In principle, a member of the Court who has ceased to hold office and who has reached the age of 65 years is entitled after five years of service to a retirement pension for the remainder of his life. If he has served a full term of nine years, this will amount to one half of the annual salary, with proportionate increases or decreases according to the length of his service. Provision is also made for disability pensions and pensions for widows and children. As in the case of the salaries, the pension have been repeatedly adjusted since 1946 to account for the decrease in the value of money. [27]

Income attributable to the Court includes contributions to its expenses by States not members of the United Nations, income arising from the application of Staff Assessment under the United Nations Tax Equalization Scheme, applicable to the Registry staff, and introduced in 1949 to take the place of national income taxes in cases where United Nations salaries are tax free, income arising from sale of publications and other miscellaneous sources. States which are parties to the Statute but which are not members of the United Nations are assessed by the United Nations procedures (through the Committee on Contributions and the General Assembly), and pay a fixed percentage of the Court's annual expenses. States which are not parties to the Statute, but which are involved in contentious litigation before the Court, are assessed by the Court which applies the same principles, but on a *pro rata* basis for the Court's expenses in the period during which the case was before it.

The present arrangements for financing the Court are an improvement on those used for financing the Permanent Court, when difficulties arose in collecting the contributions due from States which, being parties to the Statute, were not members of the League. On the other hand, when in 1966 the General Assembly refused to vote certain supplementary estimates

---

* While this book was in the press, proposals for a substantial upwards revision of these honoraria were laid before the General Assembly.

required to meet unforeseen expenses occasioned by the *South West Africa* case, fear was expressed lest this would endanger the independence of the judges.[28]

In the period 1946-1971 the total audited expenses of the United Nations aggregate at $3,078,652,952, of which those incurred on behalf of the Court (the only principal organ of the United Nations which is accounted for separately in the Financial Reports) amounted to $21,758,490, or under 1% (in recent years there has been a considerable drop in the percentage of the Court's expenses in the total outlay of the United Nations). In the same period the income attributable to the Court is placed at $1,212,998. (Details are found in Appendix 6 on p. 221.)

CHAPTER III

THE JUDGES

In the previous chapters we have attempted to describe the growth of the idea of international adjudication and the place of the International Court as an institution among the organs existing for the settlement of international disputes by peaceful means. Let us now turn to the Court itself. Who are the men in whose hands is confided the power to decide international legal disputes? How do they reach their position?

The Court consists of fifteen judges, each of a different nationality, elected independently by the Security Council and the General Assembly. They serve for a term of nine years (commencing from 6 February following their election) and are eligible for re-election. One third of their number retires each three years. Occasional vacancies in their ranks, caused for example by the death or resignation of a Judge, are filled in the same way, a person elected at an occasional election taking office immediately and serving only for the unexpired portion of his predecessor's term. The process by which these elections are conducted is complex, and unavoidably so.

THE JUDGES' QUALIFICATIONS

All political societies face a delicate problem when they come to determine how their judges are appointed. The international society is no exception. The natural aspiration of those having power to appoint judges in whom they have confidence, persons sympathetic to their political and social aims and ideals, is not always reconciled with equally natural desires for an independent judiciary (though it must not be assumed that there is an unbridgeable gulf between the two); and conflicts between those having political power and the judiciary are always painful episodes. In Western legal systems this type of problem is largely overcome by a tradition of good faith coupled with a delicately balanced system of checks and counter-checks in which the representative political institutions (the Parliaments) usually have a say. But ultimately, in most countries, the responsibility for the appointment of the judges rests with the executive branch of the government. The difficulty in the international field is that international political life is conducted on an entirely different basis, and there is no executive as such responsible to an

electorate for the proper conduct of its affairs. In the last resort the choice of
the international judge is, as is the choice of a domestic judge, a political
operation, in which the attempt has been made to impose some limitations on
the free play of political aspirations. But in international affairs the nature of
that political operation is fundamentally different from what it is in the
domestic arena.

These differences are reflected in the provisions of the Court's Statute
regarding the qualifications of the judges.

These qualifications are of two distinct kinds—those of a personal
character and those of a more general character.

The requirements of a personal character are set forth in Article 2, by
which the Court shall be composed of a body of independent judges elected
regardless of their nationality from among persons of high moral character,
who possess the qualifications required in their respective countries for
appointment to the highest judicial offices, or are jurisconsults of recognized
competence in international law.

There is no international machinery for ascertaining that the candidates
possess these qualifications in fact, although, as we shall see, certain safeguards have been inserted into the Statute and others have been developed in
international practice in order to maintain the high standards of professional
competence required of the judges. This aspect is left to the good sense of the
individual States. Most of them have an interest in seeing that the Court is
composed of highly qualified persons and that the reputation of the Court as
a whole should remain high. That interest does not only derive from the
possibility, however slight it may be as a matter of political reality (keeping in
mind that the Court can only decide cases when the parties consent that it
should, as will be described in the next chapter), that they themselves may
become involved in litigation before the Court, whether as applicants or as
respondents. It is also connected with the natural desire of all States that
authoritative pronouncements on questions of international law should be
made by as "strong" a Court as it is possible to create.

REGIONAL DISTRIBUTION OF SEATS

The more general requirement appears in Article 9 of the Statute, by which,
at every election, the electors are directed to bear in mind not only that the
persons to be elected should individually possess the qualifications required,
but also that "in the body as a whole the representation of the main forms of
civilization and of the principal legal systems of the world should be assured."
That requirement introduces the political factor into the composition of the
Court.

That formula itself is a refined version of the cruder principle of "equitable geographical distribution" which the Charter lays down as the governing principle for the allocation of elective seats in most of the organs of the United Nations. The formula has been in common use since 1920 for the international legal organs, and is found, for example, also in the Statute of the International Law Commission. Both these formulas rather assume that the world is neatly divided into a number of clearly defined regions and forms of civilization (the division itself being both comprehensive and static), each of which has competent organs capable of negotiating with its partners. But the realities of the international situation are quite different, and the assumption has little justification. In practice, two sets of problems beset the elections of the judges. The first concerns the manner in which the places on the Court will be allocated *to* the main forms of civilization and the principal legal systems of the world; and the second concerns the manner in which, after the primary allocation has been made, the positions will be shared *within* the main forms of civilization and the principal legal systems of the world. This latter aspect obliquely introduces the factor of the nationality of the individual candidates.

These problems are resolved partly by a series of "understandings" which have either been negotiated diplomatically or which have emerged *de facto* in the United Nations: but in the last resort, if real contest ensues, the answer can only be given through a trial of political strength in the electing organs. These understandings are essential both for the successful functioning of the Court, and for the smooth conduct of the elections. The membership of the Court must reflect the international community as it is, and not in an idealized form.

The first of these understandings apparently is that each one of the five permanent members of the Security Council—China, France, the Soviet Union, the United Kingdom and the United States of America—may always have a judge of its nationality on the Court.[1] This is the modern form of the answer to the demand of the Great Powers for presence on any permanent international judicial organ—one aspect which the Hague Conference of 1907 was unable to solve in the absence of an organized international political community, and which was only solved, along approximately similar lines, by the League of Nations. The first serious challenge to this principle was in 1956, when a Japanese candidate offered stiff competition to one of Chinese nationality, but ultimately the traditional arrangement prevailed. However, at the election of 1967 the candidate presented by the national group of the Nationalist Chinese Government withdrew, and for the first time since 1946 one of the permanent members of the Security Council did not have a national of its own among the members of the Court. With the solution in 1971 of the problem of Chinese representation in the United Nations, it is to be assumed that in due course this problem will right itself and the basic principle will be reinstated.

The existence of this tradition means that in fact only ten seats are available for distribution among the rest of the world. When the United Nations was first established, it had 51 members: today there are 135 members together with three other States which are parties to the Statute without being members of the United Nations. Competition for the remaining places on the Court has therefore become progressively keener.

Little in the way of overt understanding regarding the distribution of these ten seats is apparent, and it is likely that such understandings as may once have existed are unable to withstand the new pressures which built up after the first large-scale admission of new members in 1955, and the second large-scale admission of new members since 1960. Following those events, the relative strength of the different groupings inside the United Nations has altered radically. It is possible to see in the results of the initial election of 1946 a reflection of an inter-regional understanding. Adopting the customary United Nations nomenclature, that election gave the following regional distribution: Afro-Asia, 1; Western Europe, 2; Eastern Europe, 2; Latin America, 4; British Commonwealth (British territories), 1. The distribution lasted until 1951 when, after a bitter fight (in which one of the most experienced members of the Court was not re-elected), Western Europe lost one of its seats to the Afro-Asian group. That distribution lasted until 1957, when Western Europe was able to regain its seat at the expense of the East European seat held by a judge of Yugoslavian nationality. There have since been further changes, and by 1966 the representation by geographical groupings has come to parallel the distribution of seats on the Security Council itself. Furthermore, this has to a great extent decentralized the nomination process in the sense that there is reluctance to interfere with decisions of the recognized organs of the regional groups. In addition, the facility enjoyed by the national groups to nominate candidates of a nationality other than their own is frequently used to signal political support and is not necessarily an indication of a purely professional evaluation of the candidate. All this notwithstanding, when, as is often the case, the regional groupings themselves are unable to reach clear decisions on their own candidates, the elections can become very fierce. These changes are further illustrated by Tables I-III which show respectively the distribution of seats by continents (since 1922), by regional groups (since 1946), and by nationality of the judges (since 1922). Full particulars of the composition of the Permanent Court and of the present Court are given in Appendix 3.

Competition is thus keen within the groups, and the absence of internal regional cohesion may lead to a change in inter-regional distribution (as occurred in 1951, 1957 and 1963-6). Here less is known about the understandings, except that in general the Latin American group will try to ensure that one member comes from Central America (a tradition which was not followed in 1972). The fluctuation in intra-regional distribution is well

TABLE I

DISTRIBUTION OF SEATS BY CONTINENTS

	1922	1931	1946	1952	1955	1958	1961	1964	1967	1970	1973
Africa			1	1	1	1	1	2	2	3	3
America (North)	1	1	2	2	2	1	1	1	1	1	1
America (South)	2	3	4	4	4	4	4	2	2	2	2
Asia	2	2	1	2	2	2	2	3	4	3	3
Australia						1	1	1			
Europe	10	9	7	6	6	6	6	6	6	6	6
Total	15	15	15	15	15	15	15	15	15	15	15

TABLE II

DISTRIBUTION OF SEATS BY REGIONAL GROUPS
(Excluding Permanent Members of Security Council)

	1946	1952	1955	1958	1961	1964	1967	1970	1973
Africa	1	1	1	1	1	2	2	3	3
Asia		1	1	1	1	2	4	3	3
W. Europe and others	3	2	2	3	3	3	2	2	2
E. Europe	2	2	2	1	1	1	1	1	1
Latin America	4	4	4	4	4	2	2	2	2
	10	10	10	10	10	10	11*	11*	11*

* There was no judge of Chinese nationality on the Court in these periods.

illustrated by the history of the so-called West European and Others representation on the Court since 1946—a history which is typical also for other regions except for the cohesive group of European Socialist States. The original West European seats were held by two judges from the northern part of the continent—Belgium and Norway. In 1951 the Belgian seat was lost, and when it was regained by the group in 1957 it went to Greece, thus giving a more balanced distribution. In 1960 an Italian candidate put up stern competition and took the seat away from Scandinavia, but the Western European representation became unbalanced. Matters have since improved, and apart from the British and French judges, Spain and Sweden secure a reasonably balanced representation of this continent.

Apprehension is frequently expressed that unless care is taken, the general criterion of Article 9 will clash with the personal qualifications required by Article 2, leading to a lowering of the standards required for the Court as a whole. On the other hand there is equal danger in exaggerating the possibility of discrepancy. Having regard for the primary purposes for which the Court exists, it seems to follow that the emphasis may rightly be placed on

TABLE III
NATIONALITY OF JUDGES

Country	P.C.I.J.	I.C.J.	Country	P.C.I.J.	I.C.J.
Argentina		1955-64	Lebanon		1964-—
		1973-—	Mexico		1946-52
Australia		1958-67			1955-73
Austria	1931-36		Netherlands	1922-45	
	(Deputy-Judge)		Nigeria		1967-—
Belgium	1931-45	1946-52	Norway	1922-30	1946-61
Brazil	1922-30	1946-55		(Deputy-Judge)	
Canada		1946-58	Pakistan		1954-61
Chile		1946-55			1964-73
China	1922-30		Panama		1959-64
	(Deputy-Judge)		Peru		1961-70
	1931-45	1946-67*	Philippines		1967-—
Colombia	1931-42		Poland	1931-40	1946-—
Cuba	1922-46		Portugal	1931-36	
Dahomey		1970-—		(Deputy-Judge)	
Denmark	1922-30		Romania	1922-30	
Egypt**		1946-65		(Deputy-Judge)	
El Salvador	1931-45	1946-59		1931-45	
Finland	1931-36		Senegal		1964-—
	(Deputy-Judge)		Spain	1922-45	1970-—
	1938-45		Sweden	1936-37	1967-—
France	1922-45	1946-—	Switzerland	1922-30	
Germany	1931-45		U.S.S.R.		1946-—
Greece		1958-67	U.K.	1922-45	1946-—
India		1952-53	U.S.A.	1922-45	1946-—
		1973-—	Uruguay		1952-61
Italy	1922-45	1961-70			1970-—
Japan	1922-45	1961-70	Yugoslavia	1922-35	1946-58
				(Deputy-Judge)	

*   See note 1 on p. 183 below.
** Also known as United Arab Republic and Arab Republic of Egypt.

Article 9. Taking that as the point of departure, obviously it is most desirable that the individual judges should be reasonably competent in the theory and practice of international law (an expression which is broad enough to include both persons who have had practical experience of international law in the course of a diplomatic career and those whose qualifications are for the most part academic or whose experience is more secluded). However, in order to ensure a properly balanced Court for the purposes of Article 9, it is permissible to depart from that test provided in that event that the persons elected are qualified to hold the highest judicial offices in their own countries. In fact there are usually found amongst the members of the Court at any given moment judges who are highly qualified and experienced international lawyers as such, judges who have had considerable diplomatic experience at a high level of responsibility (including one or two former Foreign Ministers), and judges whose main experience has been in domestic judicial and administrative activities. It is not necessary that every judge be highly familiar with the whole of contemporary international law, but out of a Court of fifteen judges there should be no difficulty in finding a sufficient number of judges who can speak with authority on all the problems which arise. The practical exercise of the judicial function undoubtedly requires a high level of statesmanship and practical wisdom in addition to knowledge of the law, and this mixture of talents is generally speaking adequate and meets the international requirements.

Yet the question is being asked with increasing insistence whether the prevalent distribution of seats is fully satisfactory. With the emergence of a numerically strong group of African Powers in the United Nations, this question has become more acute. There does exist apprehension lest the prevalence of political factors (too powerful to be ignored) may make it difficult to maintain the high standards of professional qualifications required. As a solution to this problem, the suggestion is frequently heard that a slight increase in the size of the Court from the present fifteen members ought to be contemplated. It is not believed that this would make the Court too unwieldy, and although to effect such an increase would require a formal amendment of the Statute (Article 3), an amendment which could only be achieved by the procedure laid down for the amendment of the Charter itself, it is to be hoped that proposals of this nature will receive the constructive attention they deserve in the near future.[2]

The rather complicated system by which candidates are nominated and elected is designed to ensure that the double test laid down by the Statute is applied in practice. In this connexion, it is obvious that the primary responsibility for attaining the desired standards rests with those who *nominate* candidates, especially when they have reasonable prospects of seeing their nominees elected. For the electors can only perform *their* task in the light of the objective situation placed before them. Their role is limited to choosing from among the candidates presented.

NOMINATING CANDIDATES

In an attempt to ensure that the candidates will possess the desired personal qualifications, the Statute adopts the principle not of direct nomination by the governments desirous of putting candidates forward, but of indirect nomination, by existing or specially constituted "National Groups" in each country. The original idea, when the Statute was first drafted in 1922, was that the national groups of four persons chosen by a country as its members on the panel of the Permanent Court of Arbitration (see p. 16 above) would nominate candidates for the Permanent Court of International Justice. Where a country was not a party to the Hague Convention, it was supposed to constitute a national group along the same lines. As a further check on the candidates' qualifications, the Statute recommended each of these groups to consult with its highest court of justice, its legal faculties and schools of law, and its national academies and national sections of international academies devoted to the study of law.

When the Statute was revised in 1945, there was a strong move to alter these provisions, on the grounds that in fact the system had not worked as intended, and that the same results would be attained by direct nomination by governments, especially if they would undertake a series of consultations such as were enjoined on the national groups. But in the end it was decided to retain the previous system. However, out of the present total of 138 parties to the Statute (including the non-members of the United Nations), it is understood that no more than 71 are parties to the Hague Convention of 1907. This means that in fact the nominations are in very many instances made by specially constituted nominating colleges.

At least three months before the date of the election, the Secretary-General of the United Nations communicates with the national groups (through the Foreign Minister of each country), and invites them to undertake the nominations. Each national group may nominate not more than four persons, of whom not more than two may be of their own nationality; and in no case may the number of candidates nominated by a group be more than double the number of seats to be filled.

On receipt of the nominations, the names, in alphabetical order, are presented to the General Assembly and the Security Council, by whom the actual elections are conducted. Only the persons on these lists are eligible for election, save in the case of a complete deadlock between the Security Council and the General Assembly. In addition to the list, the Secretary-General customarily circulates biographical details of the candidates. This is a useful practice which enables the electors to make their choice in full knowledge of the qualifications of the persons chosen.

Although there may, at times, be an element of artificiality in the nominating process, especially since, in the present circumstances, a ready-made national group does not exist for many members of the United Nations, the decision of 1945 to retain the existing system was wise. The International Court is the only principal organ of the United Nations which is composed of individuals not directly representing States. While it is true that a person is elected judge not only on the basis of his personal qualifications but also having some regard to his nationality, the present nominating system, if conscientiously applied, does offer the best possibility of ensuring that the candidates will be duly qualified.[3]

THE ELECTIONS

As stated, the judges are elected for a period of nine years. For the Permanent Court, all the judges were elected simultaneously for each nine-year period, and elections accordingly took place in 1921 and 1930, those due to be held in 1939 being postponed on account of the War. In 1945 a fundamental change was introduced, when it was decided that five of the judges would retire each third year, the initial choice of three, six and nine year terms being made by lot. As a consequence, the whole bench of fifteen judges was elected in February, 1946, and since then partial elections of five judges a time have been held in the sessions of the General Assembly of 1948, 1951, 1954, 1957, 1960, 1963, 1966, 1969 and 1972. The proposal for this change was made by the Washington Committee of Jurists, which felt that the previous system presented serious drawbacks principally on the ground that while it preserved continuity *during* the nine-year period, it did not maintain it *beyond* the nine-year period. It was thought that the new system would therefore overcome that deficiency, while allowing for reasonable change in the personnel of the Court each three years.[4] On the other hand, the San Francisco Conference rejected proposals to alter the system of elections, by entrusting them to the General Assembly alone. Accordingly, the League system has been retained, and judges are elected by the General Assembly and the Security Council, which proceed "independently of each other".

To be elected, a candidate has to receive an absolute majority of votes in each of these two organs. In the General Assembly, States parties to the Statute which are not members of the United Nations (there are today three States in that category) participate on a footing of equality. In the Security Council, no distinction is made between the permanent and the non-permanent members (i.e. the so-called "veto" does not apply).[5] But although the permanent members do not now have any privileged position, they are able to ensure the election of candidates of their own nationality—something which, as has been emphasized, is essential for the successful functioning of the Court—though it is doubtful if they can today do much more than that. Nor does it appear that the non-permanent members of the Security Council (they are ten in number) secure any particular advantage for themselves through their double votes, although they may be able to influence the outcome should a contest develop between two regions over a single seat. Experience has shown that on the whole, apart from the candidates of the nationality of the permanent members, the General Assembly is able to have its way in the end.

The Statute also contains elaborate provisions to overcome a deadlock between the two organs, but there has been no need to apply them yet. The prolonged phases through which an election may go before it is clear that a deadlock is really developing are usually sufficient to allow the normal processes of diplomacy to bring about a solution.

How are the elections conducted? As stated, the two organs proceed independently of each other. This means that the results of the voting are not communicated until both organs have completed their meetings, and only then is a comparison made between the two sets of results. It does not mean that the individual States do not know the results in one or other organ. The two sets of elections are carried out by secret ballot in separate public meetings, but the results are announced after each ballot. The meetings of each organ continue until the *exact* number of candidates to fill the vacant places has received the required majority, and balloting will be continued in each meeting until that result is attained. As soon as the two lists are complete, they are formally communicated to the other organ, and candidates whose names appear on both lists are formally declared elected. One meeting may therefore have an indefinite number of ballots. If places remain to be filled after the first meetings, the process continues for a second and a third meeting of each organ, and again each of the meetings continues for as many ballots as may be necessary. As the process of counting the ballots in the General Assembly naturally takes a long time, the meeting itself may be adjourned for as much as twenty-four hours, and although that is a matter of the personal convenience of the delegations, it is at the same time useful in permitting further consultations between delegations for the eventuality that no candidate will receive the necessary majority.

Only after three meetings have been held in this way, with still not all the vacant places filled by both the Security Council and the General Assembly, will the machinery for resolving the deadlock be put into operation. This machinery consists of a joint conference of three members of each of the Security Council and the General Assembly for the purpose of choosing by absolute majority one name for each seat still vacant, for submission to the Security Council and the General Assembly for their acceptance. If the joint conference is unanimous it may choose a person whose name does not appear on the original list of candidates. As a final safeguard, if the joint conference is unsuccessful, the judges already elected are empowered, within a period to be fixed by the Security Council, to fill the vacant seats by selection from among the candidates who have obtained votes either in the Security Council or in the General Assembly, the eldest judge (and not the President) having a casting vote in the event of a tie.[6]

An occasional vacancy created by the death or resignation of a judge is filled by the same process. Such elections take place during the next session of the General Assembly following the creation of the vacancy, the person elected taking office immediately.[7] Occasional elections have been held in 1951, 1953, 1954, 1957, 1959, 1960 and 1965 and even if a triennial election is due at the same time, they are kept distinct, both as regards the nomination and as regards the election.

It goes without saying that the whole process of election is accompanied throughout by a considerable amount of diplomatic negotiation which frequently commences even before the nominating phase. Sometimes an individual who wants to become a judge will himself start by canvassing his chances on his own account: the results of that phase will enable him to open negotiations with his own national group. Sometimes a government will initiate its diplomatic overtures well in advance—as much as a year or two. It is not unknown for a candidature to go forward to election without real chance of immediate success, simply to provide a jumping-off point for a sustained diplomatic effort leading to a renewal of the candidature at a later date with better prospects. The reaction to these early steps is important for the nomination phase, for it enables all concerned (including the candidate himself) to assess the probabilities. After the list of candidates is published, and especially after the session of the General Assembly begins, the diplomatic contacts become much more intense, and there is little doubt that at times a delegation is instructed to vote for a given candidate in return for promises of support on another matter of close concern to it, whether its own candidature in another election or a matter of substantive concern. It is difficult to see why such bargains should be deprecated (except out of an exaggerated regard for legal purism), because both the General Assembly and the Security Council are purely political bodies and it is not expected of them, or of the States of which they are composed, to exclude political considerations when they come to perform the very important function of electing the judges. These diplomatic contacts are also valuable in maintaining the desired professional standards of the Court. Through them, influential governments are able to indicate discreetly their view that a given candidate is or is not qualified for the duties, and there is reason to believe that this too is a factor which influences the final outcome of the elections.

CASE STUDY—THE ELECTIONS OF 1960

The operation of the whole process may be demonstrated by the elections of 1960, when both an occasional vacancy caused by the death of the United Kingdom judge, and five vacancies caused by the normal retirement of five serving judges, had to be filled.

The United Kingdom judge died on 8 May 1960, and on 31 May the Security Council decided, in accordance with normal practice, that the election to fill the vacancy would be held during the fifteenth session of the

General Assembly. Five candidates were nominated (three of them of United Kingdom nationality, but two of these intimated that they did not wish to be considered for election). At the 915th meeting of the General Assembly and the 909th meeting of the Security Council, held on the afternoon of 16 November 1960, the remaining candidate of United Kingdom nationality was elected virtually unanimously. (Normally, the occasional elections are practically uncontested, but instances have occurred when the contest was severe.)

Immediately after disposing of the occasional election, the two organs proceeded to the regular election. The five retiring judges were of Norwegian, Pakistani, U.S.S.R., U.S.A., and Uruguayan nationality, and four of them were candidates for re-election. Twenty-six candidates were nominated, and it is interesting to see their distribution by regions. For the two seats being vacated by nationals of permanent members of the Security Council, two U.S. nationals (including the sitting judge) and three Soviet nationals (also including the sitting judge) were nominated by various national groups, but three of these (including the two sitting judges) withdrew their nominations, leaving one candidate from each of these two Powers, and their election was virtually uncontested. For the remaining three places, held respectively by Western Europe, Latin America and the Afro-Asian group, the candidates were divided as follows: Afro-Asia (one of whom withdrew), 5; Western Europe, 8; Eastern Europe, 1; Latin America, 6; Miscellaneous (Switzerland), 1. It will be noticed that for each of the three groups represented by the retiring judges, *intra-regional* competition was keen.

At the 915th meeting the General Assembly proceeded to hold its first ballot, at which two candidates, the American and the Soviet, received the necessary majority. After a procedural discussion a second ballot was held, at which the Japanese candidate only received the necessary majority and, it being already late, the meeting was suspended for twenty-four hours. In the meantime, the Security Council had continued its 909th meeting and on the first ballot had given the necessary majority to the American, Soviet, Italian, Paraguayan and Japanese candidates. At the end of the day it too suspended its meeting for twenty-four hours.

When the meetings were resumed the next afternoon, the General Assembly held its third ballot, at which no candidate received the necessary majority. At the fourth ballot it gave the majority to the Peruvian candidate, and at the fifth to the Italian candidate. As a result, four of the five places had been filled by the two organs, but the Latin American vacancy remained unfilled. The meetings were then both terminated and the two organs immediately reconvened in new meetings for the purpose of filling the remaining vacancy. At the 910th meeting of the Security Council, which began late in the afternoon on 17 November, the Peruvian candidate received the necessary majority on the first ballot. The General Assembly also held one ballot at its

916th meeting, which convened at the same time, and the same person received the majority. In that way the election was completed.

We have mentioned that this election was characterized by keen *intra-regional* competition. How did this find expression? The main competitive pressures were felt in the Latin American group, between Peru and Paraguay, and in the Afro-Asian group, between India, Pakistan and Japan, but the fact that the General Assembly required five ballots to elect a West European candidate also indicates the difficulties which existed there. The procedural discussion in the 915th meeting of the General Assembly was initiated by India in an attempt to improve the chances of the Indian candidate, after the first ballot had shown how the wind was blowing.[8] But it is believed that the unexpected point of order which was raised by India caused some resentment which found immediate expression in the second ballot at which the Japanese candidate was elected, thus putting an end to Indian (and Pakistani) hopes. As for the Latin American candidate, although the Paraguayan candidate started with more support from the Latin American group than his Peruvian rival, it seems that his candidature did not attract sufficient support outside Latin America, possibly because it was felt that his professional standing was not quite sufficient. When it became apparent that he would not obtain a majority in the General Assembly, the Security Council withdrew its support for him and transferred it to the Peruvian candidate. It was the easier for the Security Council to do this, as the rivalry was a purely internal one and did not affect the inter-regional distribution of seats on the Court.

THE INDEPENDENCE OF THE JUDGES

The Statute does not content itself with the general provision of Article 2 that the judges shall be "independent", but proceeds to clothe it with other provisions to give it reality.

The underlying principle is that in the exercise of their judicial functions, judges are to act independently of any instructions received from their governments. This principle is incorporated in the solemn declaration, required to be made in public by every judge before he takes up his functions, in the following terms: "I solemnly declare that I will perform my duties and exercise my powers as judge honourably, faithfully, impartially and conscientiously."[9] No member of the Court may exercise any political or administrative function, or engage in any other occupation of a professional nature, any doubt being settled by the Court.[10] This means that any member of the Court who, immediately prior to his election, was in the service of a government or international organization has to resign his office on his election. It is also believed that if he possesses financial holdings which could lead to a conflict of interest, he should divest himself of those holdings.[11] No member of the Court may act for one of the parties in any case before the Court, and if, before he became a member, he had previously advised one of the parties, or had served as a member of a national or international court or commission of enquiry or in any other capacity in connection with the case, he has to stand down and refrain from participating in the decision of that case by the Court. Again, any doubt is to be settled by the Court. [12]

Judges are granted security of tenure during their term of office (but have no right to re-election), and are offered attractive financial terms and pension rights. A judge can only be dismissed if, in the unanimous opinion of the other members, he has ceased to fulfil the required conditions. [13] In principle, every judge is supposed to participate in each case unless he is on leave [14] or is prevented by sickness; but if the President considers that for some special reason one of the members should not sit in a particular case, or if one of the members himself reaches that conclusion, he may be excused from participation. [15]

These provisions seem to have worked reasonably well in practice, and no instance is known, whether from the history of the Permanent Court or in that of the present Court, in which doubt has been cast on the independence of the Court as a whole, or of any one of its members.

THE PRESIDENT

The Court elects by an absolute majority of votes its President and Vice-President, who each hold office for three years, and these elections take place following each triennial partial election of members of the Court. [16] The President is responsible for directing the work of the Court and for its proper administration. He also performs important diplomatic and representative functions, both *vis-à-vis* the Netherlands Government as host to the Court and in relation to others and to the organs of the United Nations, and if necessary he will represent the Court in the meetings of the General Assembly. When the Court is not sitting, the President has extensive powers to make orders for the procedure in pending cases. He directs the Court's deliberations, and is *ex officio* a member of the drafting committee unless he does not share the majority opinion, when his place shall be taken by the Vice-President, unless he is ineligible for the same reason, when the senior member of the committee shall preside. However, if the President is not a member of that Committee, the draft shall nevertheless be discussed with him before it is submitted to the Court, and if he proposes amendments which the drafting committee does not find it possible to adopt, it shall submit those proposals to the Court together with its own draft. The President and the Vice-President are also *ex officio* members of the Court's Chamber of Summary Procedure. It is therefore not surprising that provision has to be made to ensure at the seat of the Court the continuous discharge of the duties of the office of President either by the President or by the Vice-President.

The President signs all formal orders, judgments and advisory opinions and other formal texts emanating from the Court, his action being counter-signed by the Registrar. This is for purposes of authentication and does not commit the signatories to their contents. [17]

In return for their onerous duties, the President and the Vice-President (when he is acting as President) receive a special non-pensionable allowance (see p. 41 above). [18]

The President and Vice-President take precedence over all the other judges. After them, judges elected at the same time take precedence according to seniority of age, those re-elected retaining their original precedence. In public sessions of the Court, the Vice-President sits to the President's right, and the other judges take their seats to his left and right in order of precedence. In the closed deliberations of the Court, the judges vote in inverse order of precedence, as is usual in judicial bodies. [19]

If the President is the national of one of the parties to a contentious case before the Court, he has to abstain from acting as President for that case, and will hand over his duties to the Vice-President or, of he is unable to act, to the next senior judge who is not disqualified. [20]

Very frequently the "extra-judicial activities" of the Court (see p. 28 above) are confided to the President, and in carrying them out he will observe the same principles.

JUDGES *AD HOC*

What happens when one party to a case has a judge of its nationality on the Court, but not the other? Several solutions are possible: the nationality of the judges could be ignored on the ground that they do not "represent" States; or the "national judge" (or judges) could be asked to stand down; or, when only one party has a national judge, the other party could be entitled to appoint a judge of its own for the occasion. The answer given by the draftsmen of the Statute is a combination of the first and third solutions.

Firstly, a judge is not disqualified from sitting in a case merely because he is a national of one of the parties. The Statute lays this down specifically.[21]

Secondly, whenever in any litigation the bench does not include a judge having the nationality of one or both of the parties, then those parties may each choose a judge, who shall take part in the decision on terms of complete equality with his colleagues. Such judges are known as judges *ad hoc*, and a judge *ad hoc* may be appointed not only to equalize the situation when the bench already includes a judge of the nationality of one of the parties, but also when it includes no judge having the nationality of *either* of the parties.

But if the Court finds that there are several parties in the same interest and that none of them has a judge of its nationality upon the Bench, it provides for those parties acting in concert to choose one judge *ad hoc*. So far the Court has adopted a formal attitude in the few instances in which this problem has arisen. [22]

These provisions have given rise to controversy, principally on the grounds that they distort the "international character" of the international magistrature and that they conflict with the principle that no man should be judge in his own cause. [23] From the theoretical point of view this is undoubtedly true. But as we have seen, the notion of "national arbitrators" is deeply rooted in the practice of international arbitration, and indeed the facility to appoint them is probably a *sine qua non* for the success of the whole idea. The important thing for ensuring third-party judgment is not that national arbitrators or judges should disappear, but that the balance in the tribunal should be held by neutral judges. This is the conception which has been incorporated in the Statute, for in practice the decision is rarely likely to be influenced by the views of the judges having the nationality of the parties who, in the nature of things, tend to cancel each other out. The justification for the presence especially of judges *ad hoc* is to be placed on more general and psychological grounds connected with the nature of international relations and the special function performed in that context by international litigation: it is not to be sought in any strained concepts of legal theory, with which, indeed, it may conflict.

What is the role of these judges *ad hoc*? It is sometimes said that they perform a useful function in supplying "local knowledge and a national point of view", and objection is then taken that if the parties cannot do that in their pleadings, so much the worse. But clearly, it is not their function to continue the pleadings in the Council Chamber. Rather their task would seem to be more to participate in the formulation of the judgment than to influence the actual decision (except, perhaps, when the division in the Court is very close). It has to be remembered that a State is not only interested in the operative part of a judgment: and even when the decision goes against it the wording of the reasons of the judgment may be of no less significance for it. Once the pleadings are closed, the parties have no further opportunity of bringing their points of view to bear on the Court, and it rests with the judge or judges *ad hoc* not to continue to plead their countries' cases (that would be virtually impossible), but to represent their countries' interests in the actual wording of the decision. If their role could, then, be more accurately designated as that of assessors, the grant to them of the status of judge represents a concession to diplomatic susceptibilities.

In most cases in which they have been appointed, judges *ad hoc* have voted in favour of their countries' point of view and have appended a dissenting opinion of their own if the majority decided against it. Indeed, so preva-

ELECTION OF FIVE MEMBERS OF THE INTERNATIONAL COURT OF JUSTICE

ELECTION DE CINQ MEMBRES DE LA COUR INTERNATIONALE DE JUSTICE

ELECCION DE CINCO MIEMBROS DE LA CORTE INTERNACIONAL DE JUSTICIA

BALLOT PAPER   BULLETIN DE VOTE   CEDULA DE VOTACION

Representatives are requested to place an (X) to the left of the name of the candidates for whom they wish to vote.

Les représentants sont priés de mettre une croix (X) a gauche du nom des candidats pour lesquels ils désirent voter.

Se ruega a los señores representantes poner una cruz (X) a la izquierda del nombre de los candidatos por quienes desean votar.

☐ ARMAND-UGON, Enrique C. (Uruguay)

☐ BARROS JARPA, Ernesto (Chile)

☐ BARTOS, Milan (Yugoslavia)

☐ BUSTAMANTE Y RIVERO, José Luis (Peru)

☐ CASTRÉN, Erik (Finland)

☐ FERNANDES, Raúl (Brazil)

☐ FLOR, Manuel Elicio (Ecuador)

☐ GUGGENHEIM, Paul (Switzerland)

☐ HACKWORTH, Green H. (United States of America)

☐ JESSUP, Philip C. (United States of America)

☐ KAECKENBEECK, Georges (Belgium)

☐ KLAESTAD, Helge (Norway)

☐ KOJEVNIKOV, Feodor I. (Union of Soviet Socialist Republics)

☐ KORETSKY, Vladimir M. (Union of Soviet Socialist Republics)

☐ MATINE-DAFTARY, Ahmad (Iran)

☐ MORELLI, Gaetano (Italy)

☐ NISOT, Joseph (Belgium)

☐ PAL, Radhabinod (India)

☐ PETRÉN, Sture (Sweden)

☐ PRODJODIKORO, Wirjono (Indonesia)

☐ SAPENA PASTOR, Raúl (Paraguay)

☐ SØRENSEN, Max (Denmark)

☐ TANAKA, Kotaro (Japan)

☐ TROLLE, Jørgen (Denmark)

☐ TUNKIN, Grigory I. (Union of Soviet Socialist Republics)

☐ ZAFRULLA KHAN, Sir Muhammad (Pakistan)

Illustration II – Reproduction of Ballot Paper

lent is this that one may be tempted to speculate whether a judge *ad hoc* is not expected to act in this way, and whether it is not in the long-term interests of the Court as an institution that he should do so. The reason is that having regard to the fragile foundations of international adjudication, the presence of a judge *ad hoc* on the bench, and the inclusion of his dissenting opinion in the text of the judgment itself, lends reality to the dictum that justice must not only be done but that it must be seen to be done. It makes it easier for a government to decide to entrust its affairs to the International Court.

Although judges *ad hoc* display a clear tendency to find in favour of their countries, this is by no means so marked in the case of national judges, and there have been some notable instances of national judges finding against their own countries even in cases of major importance. The best known is Lord McNair's rejection of the British Government's contentions in the *Anglo-Iranian Oil Co.* case, but this is far from being a unique instance. On the other hand, there has been no case of a national judge or a judge *ad hoc* dissenting from a majority decision in his country's favour.

Judges *ad hoc* have to possess all the personal qualifications required of the titular judges, and any doubt is to be settled by the decision of the Court. They also have to make the same solemn declaration. On the other hand, they are *appointed*, and are not subject to any form of international election. They need not be nationals of the State appointing them, and indeed instances have occurred in which one or both judges *ad hoc* themselves came from "neutral" countries. They sit supernumerary to the titular judges taking part in the case, which means that the bench may include up to seventeen judges. They take precedence after the titular judges.

The failure or unwillingness of a State to exercise its right to choose a judge *ad hoc* does not obstruct the Court in trying a case. States sometimes agree between themselves that no judges *ad hoc* will be appointed.

The Court normally sits in its full composition subject to leave of absence, sickness, etc., but in no circumstances may the number of titular Judges taking part in a case fall below nine. [25] The number of judges who participate in a case is not unduly large considering the nature of the issues that come before the Court, though it is larger than is customary for the supreme courts of the common law countries.

CHAMBERS OF THE COURT

The Statute also makes it possible for the Court to sit in smaller chambers. Three types of chambers are envisaged.

The first is the Chamber of Summary Procedure, which the Court must set up each year. This now consists of the President and the Vice-President *ex officio*, and three other judges together with two substitutes. The object is to maintain in existence a small court especially attuned to the speedy despatch of business. However, hitherto States have shown no disposition to avail themselves of this facility, and during the whole of the combined existence of the Permanent Court and the present Court, only one case was ever referred to the Chamber of Summary Procedure, and that was in 1924.[26]

The second type is the so-called special chamber, consisting of three or more judges as the Court may determine, for dealing with particular categories of cases: labour cases and cases relating to transit and communications being mentioned as examples. Since 1946 the present Court has never formed one of these chambers, nor has it been requested to do so. However, during various discussions on the role of the Court which have taken place in the General Assembly and in learned societies, some interest has been shown in this institution, and revisions made in the Rules of Court in 1972 are certainly designed to breath new life into it.[27]

The third type is the so-called *ad hoc* chamber. By an amendment made to the Statute in 1945, the Court may at any time form a chamber for dealing with a particular case, the number of judges being determined by the Court with the approval of the parties. This too is an institution which has never been used, and the recent discussions on the role of the Court have encouraged belief in the potentialities of this concept. The *ad hoc* chambers were hardly mentioned in the 1946 Rules of Court, but the 1972 revision introduced important substantive and procedural provisions, designed to facilitate recourse to this kind of tribunal in appropriate circumstances. [28]

The Rules of Court envisage a relatively simplified procedure for all cases being heard before chambers. Special provisions also exist regarding the choosing of judges *ad hoc* in all the chambers, as well as for the appointment of assessors to sit with the judges.[29]

THE REGISTRAR AND THE REGISTRY

The Court has its own officials who are recruited specially and who are technically not part of the United Nations Secretariat. The Statute confers on the Court power to appoint its Registrar and such other officers as may be necessary.

The Registrar, who is elected by secret ballot and by an absolute majority of votes from among candidates proposed by members of the Court, serves for a period of seven years and is eligible for re-election provided that his candidature is again proposed by a member of the Court. A Deputy-Registrar is appointed in the same way. The other officers of the Court are appointed by the Court on the proposal of the Registrar.

The Registry Staff consists of not more than 30 officials, who form a highly trained cadre which can be supplemented whenever necessary by temporary assistance. Their duties have been officially classified under four heads, which in fact overlap: judicial, diplomatic, administrative and linguistic. They are specified in greater detail in the Court's Instructions for the Registry. Apart from the Registrar and Deputy-Registrar, the other officers are accorded the usual diplomatic titles.[30]

DIPLOMATIC PRIVILEGES

The members of the Court and the Registrar, when engaged on the business of the Court, enjoy full diplomatic privileges and immunities. In addition, the agents, counsel and advocates of the parties before the Court, and the Court's officials, enjoy the privileges and immunities necessary to the independent exercise of their functions. The details are regulated in an exchange of notes between the President of the Court and the Minister for Foreign Affairs of the Netherlands of 26 June 1946, which was approved, and slightly supplemented (with the consent of the Netherlands) by the General Assembly in its Resolution 90 (I) of 11 December 1946.

A question which lay unresolved for many years during the existence of the Permanent Court related to the relative precedence of the members of the Court and the diplomatic corps accredited to the Queen of the Netherlands. In 1971 it was agreed by the Dutch Government that the President of the Court takes precedence over the heads of the diplomatic missions, including the Dean of the Diplomatic Corps, who himself is immediately followed by the Vice-President of the Court. Thereafter, the precedence proceeds alternately between Heads of Mission and the members of the Court, each according to his own seniority. Despite some isolated objections, this arrangement has been generally accepted, and there is much relief that an old difficulty has been removed.[31]

HOW THE COURT WORKS

Considering the arguments of the parties, appraising the evidence produced by them, establishing the facts and declaring the law applicable to them— the definition by the Court of how a judicial organ works, in an advisory opinion of 13 July 1954.

CHAPTER IV

JURISDICTION

By "jurisdiction" we mean the power or authority of the Court to render a binding decision on the substance, or merits, of a case placed before it. The International Court receives this power only from the consent of the States concerned that it should so act. Neither the Charter of the United Nations, nor any general rule of present-day international law, imposes on States the obligation to refer their legal disputes to the Court. The San Francisco Conference rejected all proposals to make some compulsory jurisdiction over certain defined types of disputes a condition for membership in the world Organization.

Although the San Francisco Conference did not accept the principle of compulsory adjudication as a condition for membership in the international organization, it did accept the *political* principle that as a general rule legal disputes should be referred by the parties to the Court, in accordance with the provisions of its Statute. This appears in Article 36, paragraph 3, of the *Charter*. On the other hand, the general principle that the Court's jurisdiction depends on the consent of the parties is equally clearly enunciated in Article 36, paragraph 1, of the *Statute*: "The jurisdiction of the Court comprises all cases which the parties refer to it and all matters specially provided for in the Charter of the United Nations or in treaties or conventions in force."

The fact that the Court obtains jurisdiction to decide a concrete case only from the consent of the States concerned means that the decision to have recourse to the Court is, in all cases, a deliberate political decision.

The Court has defined in clear terms its role in the settlement of international disputes by peaceful means: ". . . the judicial settlement of international disputes, with a view to which the Court has been established, is simply an alternative to the direct and friendly settlement of such disputes between the Parties; . . . consequently it is for the Court to facilitate, so far as is compatible with its Statute, such direct and friendly settlement."[1] Article 33 of the United Nations Charter contains a general obligation on the members to seek a pacific solution of their disputes and enumerates a number of methods of achieving that aim, the choice of which is left to the parties themselves. They include judicial settlement, and the present Court has warned against hampering the free play of that provision by, for instance, drawing strict legal conclusions from actions and positions taken by parties with a view to resolving their disputes.[2] Such an attitude is not to be regarded as expressive of undue modesty on the part of the Court: it is rather a fair assessment of the place in diplomatic techniques of the judicial settlement of international disputes, and it serves notice that the Court will not make excessive claims for its particular brand of pacific settlement, while at the same time adhering firmly to the duties imposed upon it by its Statute.

But to say that the jurisdiction of the Court depends upon the consent of the States concerned, can, through an excess of brevity, be misleading. There are a number of ways in which States can give their consent, and some of these are undoubtedly moving in the direction of true compulsory jurisdiction. As a result of this probably most States have accepted the jurisdiction of the Court in one way or another, even if for only very limited types of dispute. The Court has facilitated the development of this process. Some of these ways will now be described more fully (while avoiding technicalities), because it is only through the advances in the techniques of conferring jurisdiction on the Court that the practice of international adjudication can make any headway at all.

A COURT FOR STATES

The first thing to be stressed is that only States may be parties in cases before the Court.[3] This excludes as parties to litigation both intergovernmental organizations, on the one hand, and individuals on the other. This is a matter of deliberate choice. The Court has been established to decide disputes between States, and not for other purposes. What this means is that the Court's procedures can only be set in motion by governments in exercise of the responsibilities entrusted to them, and that the judgment, the res judicata, itself can only be directly and formally binding upon States. This does not mean that the interests of an individual can never be the subject of international litigation: to the contrary. But before the Court can deal with such a case the individual's government has to take it up and make of it an international claim in accordance with international law (espouse the claim in the exercise of its right of diplomatic protection of its citizens, to use the technical expression). When that happens, the litigation is conducted exclusively between the two governments concerned, and the individual has no locus standi in the Court itself. Both the Permanent Court and the present Court have seen several instances of this.[4]

The fact that only States may be parties in litigation excludes the possibility that the United Nations, Specialized Agencies, and other international organizations may be parties in litigation, whether with other international organizations or with States. This rule originated in the idea that only States possess international personality, and the San Francisco Conference refused to change the traditional basis. However, it inserted a provision into the Statute not only entitling the Court to request relevant information from international organizations, but also entitling those organizations to submit information to the Court on their own initiative.[5] Since that idea itself is not an accurate description of present-day international law, the perpetuation of the traditional concept of international litigation is criticized. This criticism has gained in strength since 1949, when the International Court itself explained that the United Nations possessed international personality, and thus was entitled and able to advance international claims on the diplomatic plane against States, whether or not members of the Organization.[6]

As far as concerns disputes between organizations, these are now partly covered by the authorization conferred on the Economic and Social Council to request advisory opinions on legal questions concerning the mutual relationship of the Specialized Agencies and the United Nations. This is, however, little more than a residual power, as in fact close co-ordination between these different organizations is maintained through existing United Nations machineries, both on the political level and on the Secretariat level, and the possibility of conflict between them is in fact remote. (Legal disputes of such a nature as to justify recourse to the Court are also politically unlikely, seeing that for the most part the membership of the United Nations and of most of the Specialized Agencies is the same.)

As for disputes between a State and an international organization, this is the kind of matter that if it is of sufficient general interest might form the subject of a request for an advisory opinion, although there are serious limits on the ability of this procedure to resolve concrete conflicts in which States are involved.

All States, whether or not they are members of the United Nations, may be parties in litigation with other States. The Court is established as a World Court. States which are not members of the United Nations may become parties to the Statute of the Court, on a footing of complete equality with the members of the United Nations, if they accept the conditions laid down by the General Assembly on the recommendation of the Security Council. Four States have done this—Switzerland, Liechtenstein, San Marino and Japan (before becoming a member of the United Nations in 1956). States which are not parties to the Statute may also be parties in litigation if they accept the conditions laid down by the Security Council in its Resolution 9 (1946) of 15 October 1946. In brief, the effect of this resolution is to place such States in a position of equality, as far as concerns the obligations deriving from recourse to the Court including the obligation imposed by the Charter as regards the carrying out of the Court's decision, with the States parties to the Statute.[7] Now that the United Nations is to all intents a truly universal organization, the question of access to the Court by States not parties to the Statute has lost much of the practical importance it once might have had.

The fact that a State—whether or not a member of the United Nations—is a party to the Statute means that it is *qualified* to be party in litigation. It does not mean that it has agreed to confer jurisdiction on the Court. To confer jurisdiction is a separate act altogether, which has to be directed specifically towards a defined, or ascertainable State, in respect of a defined, or ascertainable type of, dispute.

HOW JURISDICTION IS CONFERRED

There are two basic ways, and many variations, by which jurisdiction to decide contentious cases is conferred on the Court or, to put it more conveniently, by which a title of jurisdiction may be created. The first is by specific agreement between two or more States. The second is by unilateral declaration emanating from a State, accepting the jurisdiction of the Court for defined types of legal disputes, in accordance with a special procedure contained in the Statute. This is sometimes called the compulsory jurisdiction—a phrase which is misleading to the extent that it causes the voluntary nature of the acceptance of the jurisdiction to be overlooked. Another form of compulsory jurisdiction exists whenever a treaty, whether multilateral or bilateral (or a collateral instrument), dealing with a given topic contains a so-called compromissory clause providing that disputes arising out of that treaty shall be referred to the Court.

There are no formal requirements for an international agreement conferring jurisdiction on the Court, and the Court has deliberately kept this aspect elastic as part of its general policy of facilitating recourse to the judicial organ. The important thing is that the Court should be satisfied that the parties are in agreement that it should decide the case, and not how that agreement is expressed. In fact this question will only arise if one of the parties should challenge the jurisdiction of the Court on the ground that no such agreement exists, a process for which a special procedure is established.

At least four systems of conferring jurisdiction on the Court by way of international agreement can be distinguished.

Firstly, two or more States may conclude a special agreement (*compromis*) referring to the Court a defined issue (see p. 87 below). This is similar in substance to the early type of a special agreement to submit a dispute to arbitration, but is now usually considerably simplified in form owing to the existence of the elaborate provisions of the Statute and Rules of Court governing all the procedural aspects. Although the special agreement was a relatively common method of conferring jurisdiction on the Permanent Court (no less than 11 cases were so brought before it), it seems to be falling out of use now, and only five cases have been decided by the present Court on this basis.[8]

Modern diplomatic requirements have introduced a refinement into the special agreement which also should be noticed. This consists in a formal agreement between two States that a dispute exists and that it should be settled by the Court, without, however, defining the precise point in dispute, and leaving it to one or other of the parties to concretize it unilaterally. This manner of conferring jurisdiction originated in Latin America. Its value is that through the agreement to invoke Court procedures, the later unilateral reference to the Court cannot be castigated as an inimical act. On the other hand, by not defining accurately the substance of the dispute, it may prevent the Court from reaching a conclusive decision, as in the *Asylum* case (p. 128 below). Two cases have come before the Court in this way.[9] This development in diplomatic techniques—which could be combined with the power of the Security Council to recommend judicial settlement—was only made possible by the fact that a permanent international judicial organ is in existence: it is inconceivable for *ad hoc* arbitration.

A second method of conferring jurisdiction on the Court is by a compromissory clause in a multilateral treaty according to which any disputes arising out of the application or interpretation of the treaty may be referred by any of the parties to the Court. This, too, originated in nineteenth century arbitral practice. Here the scope of the disputes that may be referred to the Court is defined in advance by reference to the treaty, while the number of States who can be potential litigants is limited to the actual parties to the treaty.

In the practice of the League of Nations, and in the early practice of the United Nations, a compromissory clause of this nature was included almost as a matter of course in most multilateral conventions of general character drawn up under the auspices of the international organization, and there must by now be hundreds of these agreements still in force. However, in recent years a change of sentiment is to be noticed. According to a view which is being advanced with insistence by the Soviet Union, the inclusion of procedural rules for the settlement of disputes in treaties dealing with substantive matters could jeopardize the efficacy of the substantive provisions by making it difficult for States to accept the obligations of the Convention. This clash of principle came to a head in the Geneva Conference on the Law of the Sea of 1958, and the solution which was then adopted consisted in placing the provisions conferring jurisdiction on the Court in a separate protocol which States are free to accept or reject at will.[10] This development may be regretted. However, there is little doubt that it accurately reflects contemporary international realities, including the fact that an important group of States, headed by the Soviet Union but not confined to its Allies, are not willing to agree in advance to submit undefined disputes to judicial settlement.

Despite the large number of treaties containing compromissory clauses of this nature, they have not proved to be a fruitful source of business for the Court, and in fact it seems that this type of dispute is on the whole well suited to the normal diplomatic processes of adjustment. However, these in turn may be able to operate more efficiently when the Court exists in reserve, so to speak, should all other methods fail. Only eight cases have come before the Court on the basis of this type of title of jurisdiction. Four of them related to the problems of decolonization of the African continent, two were a consequence of the tension between India and Pakistan aggravated by the independence of Bangladesh, and two, relating to the legality of nuclear tests, were partly based on the General Act for the Pacific Settlement of International Disputes, first adopted in 1928. [11]

The third manner in which jurisdiction can be conferred is through a bilateral treaty, which may be a bilateral treaty on some specific topic containing a general compromissory clause of the type mentioned, or one in which the arbitration or judicial settlement of disputes is the very substance of the agreement (such as a Treaty of Friendship, and the like). Here the scope of the litigation is limited to the two parties to the treaty and materially, by the terms of the treaty. This too is a system which originated in nineteenth century arbitration practice. It was greatly encouraged by the League of Nations and the Permanent Court, and has continued to be popular in the present time, and there are undoubtedly hundreds of these clauses in existence conferring jurisdiction on the Court. But here, again, this has not turned out to be a fruitful source of judicial business, probably because most of these treaties are in force between pairs of States which are likely to be able to settle their disputes amicably and through normal diplomatic processes, and the real value of the Court is as an instance of last resort when the diplomatic processes are unsuccessful. [12] It is indeed significant that a number of cases which originated in this way have been ultimately settled out of court and the judicial proceedings discontinued. [13]

Finally, and this is a particularity of judicial procedure proper (it being almost impossible for *ad hoc* arbitration procedure), the International Court recognizes that as it is concerned with the substance of the agreement that it should exercise jurisdiction, and not with the form in which it is expressed, the consent may be given informally even after the proceedings have been started. The commonest example of this is when the respondent pleads to the case on the merits while formally refusing to recognize the title of jurisdiction invoked by the applicant State. Once the issues on the merits have been joined, the respondent State cannot be heard to deny the jurisdiction of the Court. This kind of tacit agreement is a useful system for perfecting the jurisdiction of the Court when, for any reason, the case in the course of the pleadings extends beyond the strict letter of the title of jurisdiction.

This form of conferring jurisdiction achieved some prominence in 1948 as a result of the manner in which the Court held that it had jurisdiction in the

Corfu Channel case, and during the fifties a number of attempts were made to bring cases before the Court by means of a unilateral invitation to the respondent to confer jurisdiction on the Court, contained in an application instituting proceedings. Most of these cases were instituted by the United States in connection with various claims against the Soviet Union and its Allies arising out of incidents involving American military aircraft, but two cases were also instituted by the United Kingdom against Argentina and Chile relating to the disputed sovereignty over the Falkland Islands. [14] In none of these cases did the respondent State accept the invitation, and in the absence of any jurisdiction whatsoever, the Court ordered the cases to be removed from the list. The fact that these attempts were made, and that the practice of the Court permits them, is nevertheless significant and demonstrates new possibilities in opening up ways of access to the Court. For its part, the Court will satisfy itself that what it is being asked to do is compatible with its status and that its essential characteristics as a judicial organ are not being impaired.

JURISDICTION BY UNILATERAL DECLARATION
(THE COMPULSORY JURISDICTION)

The most noteworthy advance in the techniques of conferring jurisdiction on the Court introduced by the Statute of the Permanent Court, and maintained by the Statute of the present Court, is the possibility which it contained of conferring jurisdiction over legal diputes, as defined in the Statute, by means of unilateral declaration. This is today frequently called the compulsory jurisdiction or the system of the optional clause (it being optional for States to make such a declaration), and it is embodied in Article 36, paragraph 2, of the Statute as follows:

"The states parties to the present Statute may at any time declare that they recognize as compulsory *ipse facto* and without special agreement, in relation to any other state accepting the same obligation, the jurisdiction of the Court in all legal disputes concerning:

a. the interpretation of a treaty;
b. any question of international law;
c. the existence of any fact which, if established, would constitute a breach of international obligation;
d. the nature of extent of the reparation to be made for the breach of an international obligation."

Such declarations may be made unconditionally or subject to reservations which are not incompatible with the purposes of the optional clause. Reciprocity is inherent in the system, and where two declarations are in different

terms, jurisdiction exists only to the extent they coincide. They may be limited or unlimited in time. No questions of form are prescribed, but as a matter
of procedure they have to be deposited with the Secretary-General of the
United Nations, and take effect immediately.

It will be noted that the description of "legal dispute" for which jurisdiction can be conferred in this way is virtually identical with that which
appeared in Article 13 of the Covenant of the League of Nations (see p. 20
above).

The introduction of this type of jurisdiction in 1922 was a great innovation in international practice, and time was required before diplomatic techniques could adjust themselves to it. It was not until about 1930 that the
Great Powers of the League of Nations finally decided to translate the
abstract principle into the language of reality by themselves making declarations under the optional clause, but they did so only in a half-hearted way by
recognizing the jurisdiction subject to many reservations and safeguards. The
effect of this was to reduce its scope within limits somewhat narrower than
seem to have been originally contemplated. This led a great number of other
States to follow in their footsteps, and it has been estimated that at its height,
in 1934, there were in force 42 declarations accepting the compulsory jurisdiction of the Permanent Court, this being the equivalent of 861 bipartite
agreements. [15] In eleven of the cases of which the Permanent Court was seised
such a declaration was invoked as the title of jurisdiction, ten of them
occurring after 1930. Clearly this was a method of conferring jurisdiction on
the Court of growing importance, and it was taken over, virtually unchanged
(save in some technical details) when the Statute was revised in 1945.

The kinds of reservations and exclusions which are made in these declarations fall into a number of common patterns, and most of them are reasonable. They include, for instance, reservations limiting the jurisdiction to disputes arising after a given date, to disputes for which a solution is not reached
through diplomatic means or for which the parties have not agreed on some
other method of settlement, excluding disputes relating to events occurring in
time of war, and so on. Occasionally, individual States have inserted special
conditions appropriate to their particular international situation. [16]

A common form of reservation excludes disputes which come within the
domestic jurisdiction of States. This is not strictly necessary, as if the subject
of the dispute comes within the domestic jurisdiction of States it cannot be a
legal dispute governed by international law and therefore in the nature of
things cannot come within the scope of the compulsory jurisdiction. The
League Covenant excluded from the competence of the League disputes
arising out of a matter which "by international law is solely within the
domestic jurisdiction" of a party, [17] and in this form it was taken over into
the compulsory jurisdiction. However, in the equivalent provision of the
United Nations Charter the words "by international law" have been omitted

(although they appeared in the original Dumbarton Oaks Proposals). [18] This has led some countries, headed by the United States of America (on the insistence of the Senate), to exclude from their acceptances of the compulsory jurisdiction of the present Court disputes with regard to matters essentially within their domestic jurisdiction *as determined by themselves*. [19] Such a subjective reservation largely vitiates the acceptance of the compulsory jurisdiction because, as in the case of the early arbitration treaties which were illusory to the extent that they conferred a power of unilateral determination concerning the justiciability of a dispute after it had arisen (see p. 17 above), it deprives the Court of the power of determining whether it has jurisdiction, although that power is expressly conferred on it by the Statute. For that reason the view is now widely held that a reservation in these terms is incompatible with the purposes and objects of the compulsory jurisdiction, and that effect cannot be given to it. [20]

The fact that the United States has accepted the compulsory jurisdiction in this extremely restricted manner, and that the Soviet Union has not accepted it at all (a striking parallelism with the attitude of the former Great Powers in the period 1922-29), is probably responsible for the fact that acceptance of the compulsory jurisdiction is today confined to a relatively small number of States. Out of the international judicial community of 138 members, the compulsory jurisdiction is accepted by only 46 of them. [21] Never in the joint history of the Permanent Court and the present Court has the percentage of members of the organized international community having accepted the compulsory jurisdiction been so low. This is a regrettable fact which runs in series with the attitude of a number of powerful and influential States which are only prepared to recognize the jurisdiction of the Court by express agreement relating to a defined dispute. Despite this unfavourable political atmosphere, this compulsory jurisdiction is probably the most important single source of contentious judicial business for the Court today. Indeed, of the 60 cases brought before the Court since 1946, it was the basis of jurisdiction invoked in 14 of them, including some of the politically most important (*Fisheries, Anglo-Iranian Oil Co., Right of Passage* and (partly) *Nuclear Tests*). [22]

The significance of the compulsory jurisdiction ought not to be measured solely by the number of States which have accepted it, or by the number of instances in which it has been invoked (although the increase in the frequency of its invocation is a factor to be noted). The chief importance of the system is psychological. It is a useful instrument for disseminating the idea that judicial settlement of international disputes is both possible and desirable. If States are agreed, on the political level, to have recourse to the Court, the fact that they have both accepted the compulsory jurisdiction may make it unnecessary for them to take any further steps in order to bring their dispute before the Court thus, from the political point of view, greatly facilitating recourse to the Court. There is reason to believe that something like this occurred in the diplomatic phase of the Fisheries dispute between the United Kingdom and Norway, which was decided by the Court in 1951. On the other hand, if the political agreement is not present, the respondent State may well challenge the jurisdiction of the Court, which will then proceed to decide, on the basis of law, whether the dispute comes within its acceptance of the compulsory jurisdiction so as to oblige it to recognize the jurisdiction in the concrete case. Experience has shown that the Court will display the maximum of prudence and judicial caution in dealing with that type of situation, and not allow the existence of the system of the compulsory jurisdiction to be abused in such a way as to compel a State to submit to the jurisdiction when it is clearly not obliged to do so.

CONTINUITY OF JURISDICTION BETWEEN THE PERMANENT COURT AND THE PRESENT COURT

Most of these different systems of conferring jurisdiction became established for the Permanent Court, and when it was decided, at San Francisco, to liquidate that Court and establish a new Court in its stead, the question arose of the future of the various treaties and agreements in force conferring jurisdiction on the Permanent Court, and of the various declarations recognizing its compulsory jurisdiction. It was decided to make every effort to keep these instruments in force, at least as between the States parties to the new Statute, in order to maintain continuity in the domain of international justice and to prevent the reorganization from adversely affecting the achievements in this sphere.

To that end, two stipulations were inserted into the new Statute. The first provides that declarations accepting the compulsory jurisdiction of the Permanent Court which were still in force should be deemed, as between the parties to the new Statute, to be acceptances of the compulsory jurisdiction of the new Court for the period which they still had to run and in accordance with their terms. The second states that whenever a treaty or convention in force provided for reference of a matter to the Permanent Court, the matter should, as between the parties to the new Statute, be referred to the new Court. [23] The Court has given an unexpectedly narrow interpretation to the first of these provisions, by holding that it only applies to the original members of the United Nations and not to members admitted subsequently, unless these had given some other indication that they were willing to recognize the Court's compulsory jurisdiction. [24] As to the second of these provisions, the Court has been more emphatic in asserting its jurisdiction if the treaty as treaty had been continuously in force and both States were parties to the 1945 Statute when the proceedings were instituted. [25]

INTERIM MEASURES OF PROTECTION

A special provision appears in the Statute giving the Court power to indicate, if it considers that circumstances so require, any provisional measures which ought to be taken to preserve the respective rights of either party. As this is likely to be a matter having political implications, the Court is under the duty of giving notice of the measures which it suggests not only to the parties, but also to the Security Council. [26] This power enables the Court to take steps roughly equivalent to the interim injunction which domestic courts are frequently empowered to issue pending the final determination. A request for an indication of such measures may be made at any time in the course of the proceedings, and the Court will normally only accede to the request if there is the possibility that the object of the litigation will be prejudiced by the action of the respondent State—for example if there is a danger that economic assets which are the object of the claim may be lost. An order indicating measures of protection will remain in force so long as the Court is dealing with the case, unless previously revoked.

The present Court has dealt with seven requests for interim measures. In *Anglo-Iranian*, in a period of great tension, it indicated interim measures, but the respondent Government did not acknowledge the jurisdiction of the Court (its preliminary objection was later upheld), and the Security Council, in which political considerations predominate, was unable to take any effective steps in the matter. [27] In *Interhandel* the Court upheld its jurisdiction to indicate interim measures even though its jurisdiction was going to be contested, but found that there was no need for them at the time. [28] In *Fisheries Jurisdiction*, the Court made two orders, substantially identical, in which it again upheld its jurisdiction to indicate interim measures despite respondent's intimation that it did not recognize the Court's jurisdiction and that in its view interim measures would be unnecessary. [29] A similar attitude was followed in *Nuclear Tests*. [30] In *Pakistani Prisoners of War* the request was withdrawn after the hearing. [31]

As this power is exceptional, the Court is strict in insisting upon the observance of the proper procedure. It will not give general instructions to the parties to abstain from any measure capable of exercising a prejudicial effect on the subject-matter of the case or which might bring about an aggravation or extension of the dispute, unless the power to indicate interim measures is expressly invoked. In this connection it has to be recalled that the Court as such does not have the direct responsibility for the maintenance of international peace. That responsibility is expressly confided in the Security Council by Article 24 of the Charter. [32] On the other hand, the Court is entitled to rely on the general good faith of the parties not to exacerbate a dispute with which it is dealing.

DISPUTES OVER JURISDICTION
(PRELIMINARY OBJECTIONS)

A' State against which legal proceedings are instituted is not obliged auto-matically to accept the title of jurisdiction invoked by the applicant State. If it considers that it has good reason, it may challenge the jurisdiction of the Court to determine the merits, or it may challenge the admissibility of the suit or of a claim made in it. For this purpose a special procedure—the preliminary objection procedure—exists. The State making use of this right is, however, obliged to accept the decision of the Court on the question of jurisdiction. This follows from the obligation imposed by the Charter on all parties to the Statute to comply with the decision of the Court (see p. 39 above), and it is possible to say that as regards the decision on jurisdiction to determine the merits, true compulsory jurisdiction does exist.

It has been seen (p. 18 above) that already nineteenth century arbitral procedure had reached the position that disputes over the jurisdiction of an arbitral tribunal should normally be settled by the tribunal itself and not be referred back to the parties, unless the arbitration agreement provided other-wise. When the Statute of the Permanent Court was drawn up specific power was inserted enabling the Court to decide on all disputes concerning its juris-diction, and this has been taken over into the present Statute unchanged. [33] This being a specific power conferred on the Court, any submission to the jurisdiction which purports to override it would probably be held to be inconsistent with the Statute, and effect would not be given to it.

The inclusion of this provision in the Statute, coupled with the perma-nence and universal quality of the international judicial organ, was an innova-tion, and a few years were required before it could be fully assimilated into the diplomatic and judicial practice. The main features of the preliminary objection procedure are that if a party—and in very exceptional circumstances the applicant State may challenge the jurisdiction [34]—wishes to contest the Court's jurisdiction or the admissibility of the claim, it must do so *before* it pleads to the merits. If it decides to raise that kind of challenge, the proceed-ings on the merits will be suspended until the question of jurisdiction is decided. This is a categoric rule. [35] Then the question of jurisdiction is first pleaded in complete independence of the main proceedings (indeed, normally the parties' roles are reversed, the respondent on the merits appearing as the applicant on the objection), [36] in the form of a case within the case. Further-more, these proceedings are interlocutory, and as such are not finally decisive of the legal merits of the action. The meaning of this has recently been usefully elucidated by the Court. The issue is substantive inasmuch as it may decide the whole affair by bringing it to an end, if the finding is against jurisdiction. The essential legal point involved is that a party should not have to give an account of itself on issues of merits before an international tribunal which lacks jurisdiction or whose jurisdiction has not yet been established. On the other hand, a jurisdictional question may have to touch upon the merits, or at least involve some consideration of them. [37]

The Court has several possibilities open to it. If it decides that the objection is well founded, the proceedings will come to an end. If it decides that the objection is unfounded, the proceedings on the merits will be resumed. The same result will follow if the Court decides that in the circumstances the objection does not possess an exclusively preliminary character. That would leave the party concerned free to take it up again later, probably as a defence to the merits. These choices are spelled out in the 1972 amendment of the Rules of Court. The possibility may also exist that the Court has an inherent power to postpone any decision on objections which are closely related to the merits, until the merits. This type of decision was first made by the Permanent Court in reliance on the Statute, and was later incorporated into the Rules of Court of 1936 and 1946. [38] The rewriting of the Rule in 1972 may not necessarily imply the abandonment of this option. Furthermore, the Court has now definitely held, after the 1972 Rules were promulgated (and this removes doubts that might have existed), that while it is to be desired that objections to the jurisdiction should be put forward as preliminary objections for separate decision in advance of the merits, the Court must always be satisfied that it has jurisdiction and must if necessary raise the issue *proprio motu.* [39] This enables the respondent State to argue to the merits and raise the objections not as *preliminary* objections, obliging the Court to decide upon them before it decides on the merits proper.

Broadly speaking, preliminary objections fall into three categories. One type argues that the title of jurisdiction invoked by the applicant State simply does not exist, for instance that it is a treaty, or a declaration accepting the compulsory jurisdiction, which is not yet in force or which has terminated or is for some reason or other void. Clearly, this kind of objection is the most remote from the merits. Indeed, normally it has no direct connection with the merits. Another category of objection does not contest the existence of the title of jurisdiction as such, but argues that the concrete dispute does not come within its scope. For instance, if jurisdiction is accepted only as regards disputes arising after a certain date, the argument that the concrete dispute arose before that date should be raised as a preliminary objection. Examination of this type of examination may be inseparable from the merits, but how the Court will deal with it will depend on all the circumstances of the case, all variants appearing in the combined practice of the Permanent Court and the present Court. This is not an easy matter.

The third category is not really an objection to the jurisdiction at all, but is normally treated procedurally in the same way. Accepting the jurisdiction of the Court, it argues that the claim is inadmissible, usually on the ground that some rule of general international law has not been complied with—for instance the substantive conditions of the law for the exercise of the right of diplomatic protection.

Preliminary objections are a prominent feature of the work of the Court. In the Permanent Court, objections were raised in 13 cases, being upheld in three, rejected in eight (one of which was subsequently discontinued), and in two cases the main proceedings were broken off before the Court gave its decision on the objection. Since 1946, objections have become more frequent. Up to the end of 1971, preliminary objections had been raised in 18 cases (of which, incidentally, nine had been instituted in reliance on the compulsory jurisdiction), with the following results. In seven cases they were dismissed; in seven (four of them compulsory jurisdiction cases) upheld (one after joinder to the merits); in two cases the main proceedings were discontinued before the Court decided on the objection; in one the applicant State recognized the objection as being well-founded and discontinued the main proceedings; and in one, where the objection was purely technical, it was withdrawn and the proceedings on the merits resumed. One of the cases in which the Court found it was without jurisdiction was of major political significance—the *Anglo-Iranian* case—and this has thrown the problem of preliminary objections into sharp relief. In another case—*South West Africa*— after the Court had dismissed a series of preliminary objections to the jurisdiction it found that the claim was inadmissible, and dismissed it. That created a political storm. In five pending cases—*Fisheries Jurisdiction, Nuclear Tests* and *Pakistani Prisoners of War*—in which the respondents all intimated their unwillingness to recognize the jurisdiction, the Court called for the issue of jurisdiction to be pleaded first. [40] In *Fisheries Jurisdiction* the Court upheld its jurisdiction, the respondent not appearing, in an unusual procedure which does not fall into the normal preliminary objection pattern. The other cases are pending on the jurisdictional issue.

Coupled with the growing frequency with which the Court's jurisdiction is challenged is another factor, namely, that nowadays it is rare to be challenged on a single, simple, ground. Instead, multiple objections, falling into all the categories previously mentioned, are put forward. Of the 18 cases in which preliminary objections have been raised since 1946, only four raised a single objection. Cases have occurred in which as many as six distinct objections, some of them further subdivided, have been advanced. When this happens, and especially when the objections relate both to the jurisdiction and to the admissibility, the nominally interlocutory proceedings are liable to assume a somewhat different character, and frequently it will be difficult to unravel the objections from the merits, even if the encroachment is only oblique. It would be an over-simplification to regard a judgment declining jurisdiction given in those circumstances as being necessarily a merely technical matter, or to assume that because of the objections the Court has been prevented from making an effective contribution to the settlement of the dispute. It may be

that the issues which were discussed and decided by the Court in the preliminary and to some extent procedural form of a preliminary objection were
in fact issues which exacerbated the political situation and made the settlement of the dispute more difficult. Many people, for instance, regard the
decision in the *Anglo-Iranian* case as being a more valuable contribution to
the final settlement of that dispute than a decision dismissing the objections
and resuming the case on the merits would have been; and it is believed that
there have been other instances in which the formal decision of the Court
declining jurisdiction has in fact assisted the parties in reaching an agreed
solution of their difficulties.

Impatience is often expressed at the prevelance of the practice of raising
preliminary objections and at the apparent frequency with which the Court
has accepted them. But such impatience is misplaced. A State—as any private
litigant—is fully entitled without abusing the due process of law to adopt any
tactics allowed by the law to prevent judgment being given against it. Every
State is entitled to intimate, through the preliminary objection procedure,
that is not willing for a concrete dispute to be decided by the Court—its
subjective willingness being something quite different from its objective legal
obligation to submit to the jurisdiction, on which the Court will pronounce
itself in the decision on the objection. Every State has the right that the
existence of that obligation be judicially determined before it takes issues
with the applicant on the merits. Cases can even be conceived in which a
respondent Government may be constitutionally obliged, or because of a
domestic situation be politically compelled, to have its obligation to accept
the jurisdiction of the Court judicially established. This result can only be
attained by raising preliminary objections, and the judicious handling of them
by the Court will be useful in assuaging local opinion. And so long as the
international community is not prepared to accept the principle of compulsory jurisdiction as such, the Court is certainly justified in the prudence
and circumspection with which it deals with questions of its own jurisdiction,
and in its refusal to attribute to States intentions which they themselves have
not clearly formed.

In addition to the parties' right to ask for a decision on the question of
jurisdiction, the Court has an inherent power to raise on its own initiative the
question whether it has jurisdiction to do what the parties are asking it to do.
This power is sparingly used in contentious cases, and when the parties are in
agreement about submitting a case to the Court, it is more likely that what
the Court itself might raise is not so much a question of jurisdiction in the
formal sense, as whether it would be proper for the Court, as a Court of
international justice, to give the decision requested. There were some
instances of this in the Permanent Court. Since 1946, although individual
judges have occasionally recalled the existence of this power, and indeed
duty, of the Court to satisfy itself that it can do what it is being asked to do,

the Court did not invoke this power until the *ICAO Appeal* and *Fisheries Jurisdiction* cases in 1972.

APPEALS TO THE COURT

Provided that it has jurisdiction, under the principles already described, the International Court of Justice may act as an instance of appeal from other international judicial or quasi-judicial tribunals. The first case of this kind to come before the International Court of Justice was the *ICAO Council* case—where India appealed to the Court a decision of the ICAO Council on complaints by Pakistan, jurisdiction arising under the terms of the ICAO constitution—the 1944 Chicago Air Agreement. The Court took the opportunity to explain that in this type of case, the appeal to the Court must be regarded as an element in the general régime contemplated by the basic agreement, and that the provision for judicial recourse gives member States, and through them the organ in question, the possibility of ensuring a certain measure of supervision by the Court over the decisions of the organ in question which can be appealed. To that extent, the treaty enlists the support of the Court for the good functioning of the Organization. [41] This is a useful clarification of the principles on which the Court will entertain appeals from jurisdictional or quasi-jurisdictional organs within the United Nations context. It is a further illustration of the general policy of the Court to co-operate with the other organs in the implementation of United Nations policy—using here the term "United Nations" in its broadest sense.

ADVISORY COMPETENCE

The principle underlying the advisory competence is that qualified international organs are entitled to ask the Court for an opinion on legal questions, that opinion itself not constituting *per se* a "decision" with which anyone is legally bound to comply. In a number of national legal systems the Executive has power to request the Supreme Court to render an advisory opinion of this nature: though other legal systems tend to look askance on the idea of a Court rendering advisory opinions, on the ground that it distorts the true function of a Court of law, which is to render binding decisions on disputes (for instance, in 1793 the United States Supreme Court refused to give an advisory opinion to President Washington). [42] The introduction of this idea into the Covenant of the League of Nations was thus a controversial innovation.

After considerable hesitation and experimentation, the main lines of the international advisory practice were clarified by the middle thirties. Its features include the following: *(a)* the right to request advisory opinions should be retained by organs of international organizations, which would be expected to weigh the interests of the organization as a whole before making the request; *(b)* although the advisory jurisdiction opened up new ways of access to the Court, its existence should not be taken to authorize the surreptitious introduction of compulsory jurisdiction to decide concrete disputes between States by devious means; *(c)* the Court, in the exercise of its discretion to render advisory opinions, would remain faithful to its character as a court of justice, and as the supreme international tribunal, incorporating into its advisory practice such of the basic principles of its contentious jurisdiction as were appropriate; *(d)* subject to this, the *procedure* for dealing with advisory matters would be assimilated as far as possible to that for dealing with contentious matters. Indeed, the main difference, from the procedural point of view, between the two classes of case is that in advisory matters there are technically no "parties" and no binding "decision": the role of individual States in advisory cases is essentially that of supplying "information"—an *amicus curiae* function so to speak.

Since the organs authorized by the Covenant to request advisory opinions were the Council and the Assembly of the League alone, on which only States were represented, it follows that the advisory competence did not constitute any departure from the basic nature of the Court, as a tribunal established by and for States. Only States, collaborating in the duly qualified organs, could initiate an advisory case. The difference between access to the contentious jurisdiction, and access to the advisory jurisdiction, is that in the first type of case a State could go to the Court on its own responsibility, while for the second it required the concurrence of other States, expressed in the form of a resolution requesting the Court to give the opinion. Suggestions are sometimes heard that certain individuals, for instance the Secretary-General, might be empowered to request an advisory opinion, but these have not been acceded to. It is also sometimes suggested that individual States, or at least pairs of States, might be authorized to request advisory opinions. This, too, has so far been rejected, for to accept it would surely mean to make possible the substitution of the advisory jurisdiction for the contentious—a real distortion of the true function of the Court.

The San Francisco Conference approved the patterns of advisory practice as they had developed previously. It contented itself with a few technical and drafting changes which have, however, had the effect of accentuating the differentiation between the advisory and the contentious competences. This has been carried further by the general developments in United Nations forms of activity as they have evolved in the last twenty-five years, under the heavy pressures of the times.

Accordingly, the Charter grants the Security Council and the General Assembly the right to request an advisory opinion on "any legal question". It

further extended the right to request advisory opinions to other organs of the
United Nations and Specialized Agencies which, so long as they are so
authorized by the General Assembly, may request advisory opinions on legal
questions arising within the scope of their activities. [43] At the same time the
Statute confirms that the Court "may give"—i.e. has a discretionary power—
an advisory opinion on any legal question at the request of any duly authorized body. [44] All the principal organs of the United Nations (excluding the
Secretary-General), and the Specialized Agencies are now authorized to
request advisory opinions (as explained on p. 38 above): in addition the
Interim Committee of the United Nations, and the Committee for Review of
Administrative Tribunal Judgments, have been so authorized. (See Appendix 5 for the particulars of the authorizations given.)

The real changes occasioned through San Francisco and which influence
the advisory work of the Court since 1946 are of a political and institutional
(or constitutional) character. They relate to the manner in which the different organs of the United Nations and the Specialized Agencies operate, in
comparison with the League's organs, and the scope of their activities. This
accounts for the great hesitations, and indeed perplexities, which are to be
found in all discussions, political and academic and professional, regarding the
advisory competence. In the League, unanimity, or virtual unanimity (i.e.
excluding the parties) was the rule for the adoption of substantive decisions,
and a simple majority was required for the adoption of procedural decisions.
The Council never decided clearly whether a decision to request an advisory
opinion was substantive or procedural, but in an early advisory opinion the
Permanent Court explained that the votes of the parties should not be taken
into account in ascertaining whether there is unanimity, [45] and that was the
practice commonly adopted both by the Council and by the Assembly. It
does not seem that the Permanent Court ever gave an advisory opinion against
the *opposition* of one of the parties: however, in one case it exercised its
discretion not to give an advisory opinion when a State directly concerned,
which had not been invited to participate in the discussion in the Council,
categorically refused to take part in the examination of the question by the
Court. The Court found that to answer the question would be substantially
equivalent to deciding the dispute between the parties, and in the absence of
the necessary consent held that it should not do so. It also pointed out that
the case involved an enquiry into the facts, for which the collaboration of the
two parties was essential. [46]

But in the United Nations, the unanimity rule has been completely
abandoned. In the General Assembly the most that is required is a two-thirds
majority (and even this is doubtful in present practice). In the Security
Council a majority of nine out of the fifteen members is sufficient (subject to
the so-called veto, and this, too, is problematic). This has meant that the
decision to request the advisory opinion can—indeed has—been taken in the

teeth of strong opposition, even of those States directly concerned, and in the Security Council despite the abstention of its permanent members. The Court has not regarded this as an obstacle to its giving the requested opinion. But it may be one of the factors which has prevented the Court's advisory work from becoming a decisive element in the political evolution of a given issue.

In the early fifties, the General Assembly several times decided to request advisory opinions on matters directly connected with the Cold War. These decisions were reached despite strong opposition of the Soviet Union. Although the Court decided that it should answer the question thus put to it, these attempts to invoke Court procedures in the sensitive political areas of Soviet-U.S. relations were no more successful than corresponding attempts to invoke contentious procedures. On the other hand, the advisory procedure has sometimes been useful in obtaining authoritative answers to legal questions of general international concern. Illustrations can be seen in the questions about the capacity of the United Nations to advance international claims in respect of damages it has suffered, about the effect of objections to reservations to multilateral conventions, about the binding character of awards rendered by the Administrative Tribunals, and about the legal obligations of States arising under Security Council decisions relating to Namibia. Such cases could not have come before the Court but for the advisory procedure.

The combination of the two factors—that a request for an advisory opinion may be adopted despite politically important opposition and that the advisory opinion itself is not formally "binding"—became an element of great importance in the protracted, and as yet unfinished, dealings of the General Assembly, the Security Council and the Court with the twin problems of *South West Africa* and *Namibia* (see p. 132 below). Here the United Nations organs have been trying to put "teeth" into the advisory procedures, despite serious structural weaknesses which have been revealed since 1946.

In United Nations history, fourteen requests for advisory opinion have been made—one by the Security Council, ten by the General Assembly, one by the Committee for Review of United Nations Administrative Tribunal Judgments, one by the Governing Body of UNESCO and one by the Assembly of the Intergovernmental Maritime Consultative Organization.[47] These opinions have always been formally "adopted" in some appropriate form by the requesting organ and in many cases this has been the end of the matter. However, in a number of politically controversial cases important States which opposed the request for the opinion refused to accept it subsequently, and finally different policy decisions had to be taken. This has not enhanced the authority of the advisory process, nor the general standing of the Court itself.

In one respect, the United Nations has broken new ground. That is in the employment of the advisory procedure a part of the machinery for judicial

review of the decisions of the Administrative Tribunals. This was first introduced by the International Labour Organization when it inherited the
Administrative Tribunal of the League of Nations. That Tribunal was
established in 1927 to deal with disputes between the members of the Secretariat and the Organization arising out of the contracts of service. In 1946,
when the Statute of the Tribunal was revised and the Tribunal converted into
the I.L.O. Administrative Tribunal, a provision was inserted empowering the
Governing Body, if it wished to challenge a decision of the Tribunal confirming its jurisdiction, or if it considered that a decision was vitiated by a
fundamental fault in the procedure followed, to submit the question of the
validity of the decision to the International Court for an advisory opinion. No
similar provision appeared in the Statute of the United Nations Administrative Tribunal which was established in 1949. Difficulties subsequently arose
and in 1955 it was decided to institute a form of review, along similar lines to
that of the International Labour Organization. For this purpose a Special
Committee was created, and authorized to request advisory opinions on the
initiative of any member State, the Secretary-General or a person in respect
of whom a judgment has been rendered by the Tribunal. That Committee,
which is composed exclusively of the representatives of States, has the limited
function of deciding, in a *prima facie* way, whether there is any substantial
basis for an application to request an advisory opinion.

These provisions do not have the effect of setting up the Court as a court
of appeal from the decisions of the Administrative Tribunals. That means that
it is not empowered to rehear the case. Its task is more limited, namely to
review the procedure or the decision of the Tribunal and to give an opinion
on the legal issues which thereby present themselves. [48]

Two of these cases have come before the Court (see p. 144 below). Their
significance is that in principle the Court does not regard replying to them as
incompatible with its judicial function, and that it was capable of adopting a
sufficiently flexible procedure for the individuals' contentions to be brought
before it.

CHAPTER V

HOW A CASE IS TRIED

Procedure in the International Court is governed for the most part by the Rules of Court, and in a number of details by the Statute itself. But these procedural requirements are little more than a framework to guide those responsible for the conduct of a case. It would not be appropriate for an International Court to attempt to regulate its procedure in the precise and detailed fashion which is necessary for domestic tribunals. Litigation in an international court—and especially in the International Court of Justice— cannot be approached on the same basis as litigation in a domestic court. Suggestions to model the International Court's procedure more closely on that of the Supreme Court of the United States or of the Judicial Committee of the Privy Council in London overlook essential features of international litigation. The litigants are sovereign States not lightly accepting outside inter- ference in their conduct of their affairs. The legal relations of States are of an extreme complexity. The issues involved are normally of great moment. The preparation and presentation of such cases require time and patience; and the argumentation has to be developed in a way that will be convincing to the majority of a non-homogeneous body of fifteen judges, each the product of a different legal culture. Furthermore, the Court's very power and authority derive from those litigants themselves, and they are few, actually and potentially, not millions. In the light of this, the general approach of the Court is to interfere as little as possible, subject to the Statute and to the more flexible Rules, in their presentation of their cases by the parties before it. Moreover, subject to the general control exercised by the Court, the parties are free to propose procedural modifications to suit their particular circum- stances, although instances of this are rare.

There are three characteristic features of the Court's procedure. The first is the sharp division of a case into two distinct phases of the written pleadings and the oral pleadings. Although the Court might accept differences in the *quantity* of pleadings in each of these two phases, the Statute insists on the maintenance of the two phases themselves.[1] Secondly, it is rare, though not entirely excluded,[2] for the Court to give directions as to the contents of written pleadings, although as will be seen (p. 98 below) the Court may be stricter in controlling the contents of oral pleadings. This is above all a reflec- tion of the fact that the litigants before the Court are sovereign States.

Thirdly, noteworthy is the complete secrecy which attends the deliberations of the Court itself. No word of these has ever reached the public. This stands in sharp contrast to the essentially public character of the pleadings themselves. The rule of judicial secrecy is so strictly kept that no judge is ever obliged to indicate how he voted, though he is free to do it by means of a separate or dissenting opinion, should he so desire (see p. 106 below).

It is proposed now to demonstrate how a case is tried by reference to a case—the *Right of Passage* case—which occupied the Court from the end of 1955 until the middle of 1960. In one form or another that case raised most of the kinds of problems which are encountered in international litigation. The modifications made by the 1972 Rules of Court will also be indicated.

THE *RIGHT OF PASSAGE* CASE: BACKGROUND

In the Indian Peninsula are situated the three districts of Goa, Daman and Diu. In 1955 these were Portuguese territory. Daman also included two enclaved parcels, Dadra and Nagar-Aveli, at the time entirely surrounded by Indian territory. It was in respect of communications between these enclaves and Daman and between each other that the question of a right of passage in favour of Portugal through Indian territory arose. Commencing in 1950, India had been trying to annex all those districts, in pursuance of its policy of expelling the last vestiges of European colonialism from the Peninsula. In 1954, an internal insurrection overthrew Portuguese authority in Dadra and the enclaves, and in the light of the tension produced by those events in the neighbouring Indian territory, the Indian Government then suspended all passage over its territory to and between them. That suspension had remained in force, and it prevented Portugal from restoring its authority. At that point the legal dispute between the two countries crystallized.

In 1954 Portugal was not a member of the United Nations and not a party to the Statute of the Court. The only way in which it could then have brought its dispute with India before the Court was by making an appropriate agreement with India. Portugal's application to become a member of the United Nations was first submitted in 1946, but the Security Council and the General Assembly only completed their action on that request on 14 December 1955. Portugal at no time requested to become a party to the Statute without being a member of the United Nations.

India had accepted the compulsory jurisdiction of the Permanent Court by a declaration of 28 February 1940 which excluded from the jurisdiction disputes with regard to questions which by international law fall exclusively within the jurisdiction of India; and the acceptance was limited to disputes arising after 5 February 1930—the date upon which India had first accepted the compulsory jurisdiction—with regard to situations or facts subsequent to that date (this was a common form of reservation). That declaration had remained in force in accordance with the arrangements contained in the present Statute for preserving continuity in the administration of international justice (see p. 74 above). On 19 December 1955, five days after becoming a party to the Statute, Portugal deposited with the Secretary-General of the United Nations a declaration accepting the compulsory jurisdiction of the present Court. That declaration contained the following condition, which was subsequently to play an important role in the *Right of Passage* case:

"3. The Portuguese Government reserves the right to exclude from the scope of the present declaration, at any time during its validity, any given category or categories of disputes by notifying the Secretary-General . . . and with effect from the moment of such notification."

Three days later, on 22 December 1955, the Portuguese Minister at The Hague filed with the Registrar an application instituting proceedings against India.

THE INSTITUTION OF THE PROCEEDINGS

Cases may be begun in two ways, by special agreement or by application. The choice is a matter for the States concerned, the Statute not stating when one or other method shall be employed.

A special agreement both confers jurisdiction on the Court and defines the question which the Court is requested to decide. For example, the special agreement of 29 December 1950 between France and the United Kingdom stated:

"The Court is requested to determine whether the sovereignty over the islets and rocks (in so far as they are capable of appropriation) of the Minquiers and Ecrehos groups belongs respectively to the United Kingdom or the French Republic."

In such cases, the Court's judgment will normally consist of a formal answer to the precise question.

But when the case is introduced unilaterally, by application, the situation is different. The application has to include certain obligatory contents, such as an indication of the two parties and the subject of the dispute. It must also specify as far as possible the provision on which the applicant founds the jurisdiction of the Court, state the precise nature of the claim, and give a succinct statement of the facts and grounds on which the claim is based, these being further developed in later pleadings.[3]

Accordingly, the Portuguese application defined the subject of the dispute as concerning "the right of Portuguese officials and nationals, as well as foreigners authorized by Portugal, to cross India on their way between the Portuguese territory of Daman and the Portuguese enclaved territories of Dadra and Nagar-Aveli, and between each of the two last-mentioned territories." It was stated that Portugal, to whom the right unquestionably belonged, had claimed and continued to claim it, and that India had opposed and continued to oppose its exercise. That was the dispute submitted by Portugal to the verdict of the Court.

This was followed by a succinct statement of the facts and a summary of the law applicable. The jurisdiction of the Court was specified as founded on the compulsory jurisdiction, and the Court was formally petitioned to recognize and declare the Portuguese right of transit and the violation by India of its international obligations arising out of the right, and to adjudge that India must put an immediate end to the *de facto* situation by allowing Portugal to exercise its right of passage.

The application was in the English language. It stated that the Minister had been appointed Agent for the purposes of the case by the Portuguese Government, and that his address for service was the Portuguese Legation in The Hague.

OFFICIAL LANGUAGES

The official languages of the Court are French and English. The parties may agree to use one or the other language exclusively, in which case the judgment too shall be delivered in that language. In the absence of agreement, each party is free to use whatever official language it prefers. The Court may also authorize a language other than English or French to be used by a party, but in that case an English or French translation has to be attached. If a party conducts its oral pleadings in a language other than English or French, it must make its own arrangements for the interpretation into one of the official languages.[4]

In the present case, there was no agreement between the parties regarding language. The Portuguese written pleadings were in French (other than the application) and those of India in English. In the oral pleadings, the Portuguese used exclusively French but the Indian delegation used both languages. The authoritative text of each of the eight orders and the two judgments given in this case was English.

REPRESENTATION OF THE PARTIES

The person in whose hands is entrusted the formal representation of a party in international litigation is called the Agent. He, of course, may be assisted in the pleadings by counsel and advocates, and other experts who may be required. The Court, however, has now reserved the right itself to determine the number of counsel and advocates who will address it in the oral phase.[5]

The status of Agent is roughly equivalent to that of a head of a special diplomatic mission, and he must be authorized to bind his country. As far as the Court is concerned, it is assumed that a person who is appointed Agent is fully authorized to represent his country, and frequently full powers are conveyed to the Court (although this is not an absolute requirement). In that capacity, he has to sign every important document relating to the case, and he has to confirm every important and binding statement made in his government's name in the course of the proceedings.

There are no formal qualifications for the position of Agent. States exhibit two tendencies, either to appoint a high-ranking member of their diplomatic service (for example, their Ambassador or Minister at The Hague), or the Legal Adviser (or one of his subordinates) of the Ministry for Foreign Affairs, but this is not invariable, and occasionally a practising lawyer is appointed.

An application should be signed by the Agent, and if he is not the accredited diplomatic representative of his country at The Hague, that diplomatic representative has to authenticate the signature on the application. The respondent government should appoint its agent when acknowledging receipt of the application, or as soon as possible thereafter, although these provisions must not be read too literally in the event that the respondent Government, not acknowledging the jurisdiction of the Court, should decline to appoint an Agent or otherwise be represented before it—a step which is sometimes taken for political reasons.[6]

In the present case, Portugal appointed its Minister at The Hague as Agent together with the Director of the Faculty of Law in the University of Lisbon. India appointed its Attorney-General as Agent, and the Legal Adviser of its Ministry of External Affairs as Assistant Agent.

Similarly, there are no formal qualifications for counsel and advocates. These are frequently chosen from experienced members of the national bar, but in addition there has grown up over the years a small group of international lawyers, drawn mainly from the legal professions of England, France, Belgium and Switzerland, who have specialized in pleading cases in the International Court. Both parties availed themselves of the services of such men in the present case. Thus, in addition to the Agents, there pleaded for Portugal in one or other phases the late Professor Bourquin of Geneva (who had pleaded in many cases before the International Court) and Professor Pierre Lalive, also of Geneva; and the Indian Agent was assisted by Sir Frank Soskice, former Attorney-General of England, Maître Henri Rolin of Brussels (who had commenced his career at the international bar in the Permanent Court), Professor Guggenheim of Geneva (who, in addition to having pleaded in several cases, had also once served as judge *ad hoc*), and Professor Waldock of Oxford (who in 1973 became a member of the Court), who had also pleaded in a number of other cases. Two strong teams were to be ranged against each other.

It is being asserted with increasing frequency that the cost of litigation in the International Court is disproportionately high, and it is even suggested that this is one of the explanations for the general decline in judicial business since 1946. While it is impossible to establish the accuracy of these views, it is noteworthy that a number of procedural amendments introduced in 1972 were deliberately designed to reduce the expense of litigation. Other measures, including the possibility that some of the expenses of the parties might be borne by the United Nations, are currently under study.

STEPS FOLLOWING THE INSTITUTION OF THE PROCEEDINGS

As soon as the application was handed to the Registrar, he had to carry out a number of statutory duties.

Firstly, after assigning the case a number and opening a folio in the Court's general list (this case was No. 32), he must forthwith communicate the application to all concerned. This includes first of all the respondent Government, and secondly the members of the Court.[7] Standing arrangements exist for the direct transmission of communication to the Minister of External Affairs in New Delhi. However, after Agents have been appointed, they are the sole channel of communication for all matters connected with the case, at an address for service selected by them in The Hague.[8]

Secondly, all members of the United Nations have to be notified of the institution of the proceedings, through the Secretary-General, and all other States entitled to appear before the Court. For this purpose the application (or special agreement) is translated into the other official language, printed, and certified copies are sent off. The object of this communication is to serve general notice to all governments of the institution of the proceedings, and what they are about, so as to enable them to consider whether they wish to intervene in the case. Also for more general political reasons, it is important that governments should have exact knowledge of cases pending in the Court.

The Statute grants two possibilities of intervention. Whenever a State considers that it has an interest of a legal nature which may be affected by the decision, it may submit to the Court a request for permission to intervene at any time up to the opening of the oral proceedings. The application for permission to intervene is given the same wide circulation as the original application instituting proceedings. The Court decides by judgment whether to admit the application, and if so arrangements are made for the intervening State to file appropriate proceedings. The first instance of this occurred in *Nuclear Tests*.[9] By another provision, whenever the construction of a convention to which States other than those concerned in the case are parties is in question, those States are to be notified forthwith: they have the right to intervene, and if they do so the construction given by the judgment will be equally binding on the intervening States. [10] One instance of this occurred in the Permanent Court and one in the present Court. The same principle is applied, by analogy, to determine what States are to be invited by the Court to submit information in advisory cases.

No requests for intervention, of either kind, were submitted in the *Right of Passage* case.

After these communications have been made, and the two Agents duly appointed, the next step is for the President to ascertain their intentions regarding the future conduct of the case. He does this either by correspondence or he may summon the Agents to a meeting with him. (The Agents need not always attend personally. Depending on the circumstances, their place may be taken by the diplomatic representative at The Hague.) After informing himself on this aspect the President is in a position to advise the Court regarding the proceedings, or if it is not sitting, to order the necessary steps himself. In the amendments of 1972 a subtle change was introduced and it is now provided that if the consultations with the parties held at various stages of a case reveal persistent disagreement between them on the procedure, the Court itself will decide the matter. [11]

In the present matter, the first order was made on 13 March 1956: it fixed the time-limits for the first stage of the written pleadings—15 June for the Memorial and 15 December for the Counter-Memorial.

Parties are normally granted equal time for their various pleadings, but this does not fully apply to the first round of written pleadings, because it is fair to assume that, except perhaps in cases of great urgency, before a Government decides to institute proceedings, it has carefully considered the case it wishes to present and has at least the outlines of the Memorial prepared. Indeed, since there is a close relation between the application and the Memorial, it is difficult to see how an application could be properly drafted if this were not the case.

THE WRITTEN PLEADINGS

No precise rules are laid down for the form of written pleadings, and this is a matter in which Sates are usually guided by their own national traditions and their sense of good taste. The fact that the pleadings are all ultimately published and remain on permanent record should influence the presentation of a case in the pleadings.

On the other hand, the Court's practice regulates to some extent the content of the pleadings. Thus the memorial, as the first written pleading of the applicant State is called, should contain a statement of all the relevant facts, a statement of law and submissions. Copies of all relevant documents should be annexed. The first written pleading of the respondent State on the merits of the case is called the counter-memorial. This should contain more: —an admission or denial of the facts stated in the memorial, additional facts if any, observations concerning the statement of law in the memorial, a statement of law in answer thereto, and submissions. Again, copies of all relevant documents should be annexed. A document raising preliminary objections should set out the facts and the law on which the objections are based and the submissions. Copies of all relevant documents should also be annexed. If a second round of written pleadings on the merits is authorized, it consists of a reply (by the applicant) and a rejoinder (by the respondent)—these pleadings are not usual in preliminary objection or in other formal interlocutory phases. The Rules of Court prescribe that these pleadings should not merely repeat the party's contentions, but should be directed to bringing out the issues that still divide them. [12] It frequently occurs that the issues are not fully brought out until the counter-memorial is filed, for instance when that document contains a counter-claim. Even if it does not, it is only when the argument and submissions of the memorial and those of the counter-memorial are compared that it is possible to see what the case is really about, for only then does its presentation cease to be unilateral. That is why the reply and the rejoinder are usually important stages of pleading in the International Court.

The original of every written pleading is signed by the Agent and filed in the Registry together with a number of copies, now usually fixed at 150. The Registrar delivers one certified copy and a sufficient number of plain copies to the other party and circulates the document to the members of the Court and other interested persons, including governments who have been authorized to receive them. He also prepares an unofficial translation of the pleading into the other official language. Unlike the procedure in international arbitration, the parties do not communicate their pleadings directly to one another. In cases of urgency, the Court will accept a pleading sent to it by modern methods of communication such as the telegraph if it is received before the expiration of the time-limit, and then the original signed text may be filed later in the normal course. This procedure is naturally rare.

Nowadays, pleadings are normally filed by the parties consecutively, as in domestic litigation, but in cases introduced by special agreement it is possible for the parties to file their written pleadings simultaneously. This used to be the common practice in international arbitration, and its justification is the equality of States and the absence, in true arbitration, of the idea that the parties are in the formal relationship of plaintiff and defendant, or applicant and respondent. But experience has shown that this is an inconvenient mode of pleading, and modern special agreements usually specify the order in which the pleadings shall be filed.

The written pleadings are not normally made generally available until after the termination of the case. This is in order to avoid prematurely exposing them to public, and perhaps polemical, discussion which, it is considered, would not be conducive to the good administration of international justice. However, any government may apply to the Court and ask for the pleadings to be made available to it, and this will normally be granted after enquiry of the Agents. Exceptionally, and if both parties consent, the Court may authorize the pleadings to be made generally available before the termination of the case, and in that event a set will be placed in the Library of the Peace Palace at The Hague. [13]

Now let us come back to our case. Portugal filed its memorial by the date fixed. It is a relatively short document expanding the case as set forth in the application. It consists of 25 pages of text together with 54 annexes and two maps, 92 pages in all. Its submissions are slightly different from the claim as originally included in the application. The Court is asked:

"(1) To judge and declare:

(a) that Portugal has a right of passage through the territory of India in order to ensure communications between its territory of Daman and its enclaved territories of Dadra and Nagar-Aveli;

(b) that this right comprises the transit of persons and goods, as well as the passage of representatives of the authorities and of armed forces necessary to ensure the full exercise of Portuguese sovereignty in the territories in question.

(2) To adjudge and declare:

(a) that the Government of India must respect that right;

(b) that it must therefore abstain from any act capable of hampering or impeding its exercise;

(c) that neither may it allow such acts to be carried out on its territory.

(3) To adjudge and declare that the Government of India has acted and continues to act contrary to the obligations recalled above.

(4) To call upon the Government of India to put an end to this unlawful state of affairs."

With the filing of this document, the initiative passed to India. What choices were open to it?

First, it could let the case go by default, an unlikely event. Second, having now seen the applicant's case, it could decide to take issue on the merits and file its counter-memorial. Third, it could challenge the jurisdiction of the Court by raising one or more preliminary objections. India had six months in which to make up its mind. It decided on the latter course, but ran into difficulties in preparing its pleading. On 10 November 1956 the Indian Agent requested a six months extension of time to which Portugal was opposed, while trusting in the discretion of the Court to make the extension as short as required by the interests of justice. After a conference with the Agents the Court extended the time-limit by four months, expiring on 15 April 1957, by order of 27 November 1956.

Within the new time-limit India filed a pleading 78 pages long, together with 431 pages of annexes. In this, six preliminary objections were raised. The case now took on a new turn.

THE PRELIMINARY OBJECTIONS

The first objection argued to the effect that the Portuguese declaration accepting the compulsory objection was invalid on the ground that the third condition was incompatible with the Statute, the consequence being that India was under no obligation to recognize the jurisdiction *vis-à-vis* Portugal. This raised highly technical issues related to the manner in which the compulsory jurisdiction works. The second and fourth objections were connected with that argument, but they attacked the Portuguese action in bringing the case on the basis of a surprise move, before India had had any opportunity of seeing the Portuguese declaration and of availing itself of the possibility of amending its own declaration. This was an attack on Portuguese good faith, for it contained the implication that the terms of the Portuguese declaration, and particularly its third condition, were in fact tailored to suit Portugal's immediate ends in her dispute with India and were not a genuine acceptance of the jurisdiction of the Court. These three objections belong to that general category which argues that the title of jurisdiction invoked by the applicant State simply does not exist, and that the manner in which the case was instituted was invalid. They belong, therefore, to the remotest class of objection.

The third objection argued that diplomatic negotiations had not been exhausted before the application was filed, and that because of that no legal dispute existed between the parties. The fifth objection argued that the dispute related to a matter within India's domestic jurisdiction and therefore was excluded from the acceptance of the jurisdiction contained in the Indian declaration of 28 February 1940. The sixth objection argued that the dispute, if it existed, arose before 5 February 1930 and concerned facts or a situation antecedent to that date, and therefore did not come within the jurisdiction accepted by India, which was limited to disputes arising after that date. These three objections, which were intimately connected with the actual dispute brought before the Court, therefore belonged to the general category of objections which argue that the concrete dispute does not come within the scope of the jurisdiction conferred on the Court: and the third objection is of a type that in some circumstances can be regarded as an objection to the admissibility, although it was not so treated in the present case.

The effect of this document was to suspend the proceedings on the merits. These were put aside for the time being. At one time a preliminary objection was regarded as a new case which was notified to all concerned in the usual manner. But later the Court decided that it was to be regarded as an incident in the procedure: at most a general notification is made that the preliminary objections have been filed and that the proceedings on the merits are suspended, leaving it to interested governments to take steps to ascertain if they have any reason to think of intervening (in fact there is no instance of any attempt at intervention in the preliminary objection phase). Accordingly, on 16 April 1957 an order was made recording the suspension of the main proceedings, and fixing 15 June as the time-limit within which Portugal could present its written observations and submissions on the objections. These are normally the only written pleadings in a preliminary objection phase: it is an assumption that by the time preliminary objections have been filed the applicant government has had sufficient opportunity to foresee the possible objections (or at least most of them), and is ready to meet the challenge. For this reason, too, the Court usually likes to dispose of the objections after a short time-limit for the written pleading. However, the Indian objections in this case were undoubtedly long, and the case, although preliminary, correspondingly heavy, and early in May the Portuguese Agent was compelled to ask for an extension of the time-limit. India made no objection and on 18 May the time-limit was extended for two months to 15 August.

On that date Portugal filed its pleading on the question of jurisdiction. The pleading itself was 77 pages in length, to which were appended 168 pages of annexes. The submission was short: that not one of the preliminary objections was justified, and therefore that they should all be rejected and the proceedings on the merits resumed.

On 15 August 1957, with the filing of the last written pleading, the case on the question of jurisdiction reached the technical stage of being "ready for hearing". [14]

THE CASE READY FOR HEARING

There are two consequences of a case becoming ready for hearing. The first is that it is entered into the list for oral proceedings. If more than one case is ready for hearing on the same date, the order in which they will be heard is fixed either by agreement between the various parties, or by reference to their places on the Court's general list. When this phase of the *Right of Passage* case became ready for hearing, no other pending case was in the same position. However, while the hearings were taking place Switzerland filed a request for interim measures of protection in another case in which it was concerned. Such a request has absolute priority over all other cases, and the decision on it is to be treated as a matter of urgency. [15] That application was filed on 3 October. The hearings thereon took place on the 12th, and the order was made on 24 October 1957, immediately after the hearings in our case.

The Court decided to commence the hearings in the present case immediately after its summer vacation.

The second consequence of a case being ready for hearing is that no further documents may be filed except with the consent of the other party or by leave of the Court should it consider the document necessary, and the Court will decide the matter after hearing argument by the parties. [16] The Court does not like the belated submission of documents if this is avoidable, yet it is flexible and undogmatic on this aspect, treating each case on its merits. Government archives are rarely so efficiently run that all the documents in its files—especially if the case has long historical antecedents—are always easily available for the lawyers working on a case, and it often happens that new documents are discovered after a case is ready for hearing. Parties, too, usually are not too formal on these questions: it would be wholly exceptional for the result of international litigation to be dependent upon a single document not produced in good time, and as there is a general obligation on the parties to co-operate with the Court in ascertaining the true facts, a formalistic attitude is rarely likely to be helpful.

THE HEARING

In the hearings on the preliminary objection, India appeared as applicant and Portugal as respondent. It therefore fell to India to open these oral proceedings.

Unlike the written pleadings, the oral pleadings are in principle held in public, though in exceptional circumstances the public may be excluded. [17] They take place in the dignified setting of the Great Hall of Justice in the Peace Palace at The Hague. The members of the Court and the Registrar wear their judicial robes: the Agents (if they are members of the legal profession), counsel and advocates their professional or academic robes. Present are also the official recorders, interpreters and other members of the staff on duty. The speaker's rostrum is immediately facing the President: to the left of it sits the applicant government's Agent and his delegation, and to the right those of the respondent State.

At the appointed hour the Chief Usher, after ascertaining that all is ready (and in particular that the representatives of the parties are present), gives the traditional cry of *La Cour*. All rise. The judges proceed with measured steps to their seats. At a sign from the President they are seated, and the others follow. The atmosphere is subdued and forensic. The Great Hall of Justice at the Peace Palace is bigger than many court-rooms, but discreetly placed microphones carry the voices to all corners. The remarks of the President and his colleagues are immediately interpreted. Speeches, which are usually delivered from full notes if not from prepared texts (as in other United Nations principal organs), are simultaneously interpreted into the other official language of the Court.

It is the oral pleadings which have the most direct impact. The written pleadings lay the foundation—of fact and of law—on which good oral pleading can be based. One cannot fail to be struck by the close attention with which they are followed: for they have great psychological value and act as the focusing point for the work of the Court. While, clearly, there is no room for histrionic advocacy appropriate for a jury trial, the effect of intonation, of candour, of inflexion, of command of language and a cultivated presentation of the case, of mastery of complicated issues, and, where appropriate, a touch of humour, of drama, a well-timed quotation—all this is concealed in the lifeless printed version of the oral pleadings which are subsequently circulated and published. Above all, it is the oral hearings that the two parties first meet face to face. Their cases emerge from the remote tranquility of Counsel's chambers and clash head-on in the hands of highly skilled lawyers, each of whom knows the strength, and the weakness, of his own and of his opponent's cases. The pleading is strenuous. The Rules require that the oral statements shall be as succinct as possible within the limits of what is requisite for the adequate presentation of that party's contentions at the hearing. They should be directed to the essential issues that divide the parties and should not traverse the whole ground covered by the written pleadings nor simply repeat facts and arguments those contain. Furthermore in the 1972 Rules the Court has spelled out a power (previously possibly only implicit) to indicate to the parties any points or issues to which it would specially like them to address themselves as well as points or issues on which there has already been sufficient argument. This is designed above all to obviate prolixity and repetitiousness in the oral phase. [18]

The Court is careful to preserve good "atmosphere" which is essential for the proper and dispassionate consideration of the case. The style of pleading is courteous—indeed the Court is one of the few international organs in which old-style diplomatic courtesies have survived. The good custom has recently been introduced by which the President offers a formal dinner to the two Agents at which all the members of the Court and the Staff of the Registry, and of the two delegations (together with their ladies) are present. This usually happens early in the case and is important for creating those intangible mutual contacts between the parties and the Court which assist in the smooth conduct of the litigation.

The normal order for addressing the Court (unless the parties agree otherwise) is that first the oral argument of the applicant State is presented, than that of the respondent State. This is followed by the oral reply and oral rejoinder, delivered in the same order. In the course of the oral proceedings the Agents will present their "final submissions".

Witnesses and expert-witnesses as to facts or deductions are rarely called in the International Court, although the practice seems to have become more common now than it was for the Permanent Court. In three cases heard since 1946 witnesses and expert-witnesses (called by the parties) have been heard— *Corfu Channel, Temple of Preah Vihear* and *South West Africa*. In each case the procedure for this, worked out by the Court in consultation with the parties, differed in accordance with the circumstances and the function of the disputed questions of fact in the case as a whole. The Court has retained a general right to determine for each case how and when evidence shall be taken, and has exhibited a valuable capability of adapting itself to different requirements. [19] On the other hand, the Court has refused to make an inspection *in loco* in the *South West Africa* case, as suggested by the respondent and opposed by the applicants. [20]

In the preliminary objection phase of the *Right of Passage* case the hearings commenced on 23 September 1957 and, after 14 meetings, terminated on 11 October. The Indian case was presented by five persons, and the Portuguese by three. The printed record covers some 263 pages. [21]

Judges have the right to put questions to the parties and to ask them for explanations. [22] For a long while this right was rarely exercised. For instance, in our case there is no record of any interruption by any judge. This is very unlike the practice in common law courts, where judges frequently interrupt counsel. It is closer to practice in the continental courts. Considerable criticism has been levelled at the International Court for its apparent inactivity in the course of the written and oral proceedings, although not all this criticism, which sometimes fails to appreciate the delicate position of the international judge deciding a dispute between sovereign States, is justified. For the pleading is frequently an act of State, permanently on public record, and the representatives of the State (especially if they are officials in its service) may have their own reasons for pleading a case one way or another. Their case stands or falls on the ground of their own choice, and it would not be proper for any international tribunal to interfere more than is absolutely necessary for the orderly conduct of the case.

The 1968 revision of the resolution on the internal judicial practice of the Court (p. 103 below) and even more the 1972 revisions of the Rules of Court, nevertheless open the way to a more active posture by the Court, especially in the oral phase. Exchanges between the judges, asking questions or seeking explanations, and the parties have become more frequent in all hearings that have taken place since 1968.

FINAL SUBMISSIONS

It has been mentioned that certain written pleadings—including all those which have been filed in our case up to now—have to contain "submissions". In the course of the oral pleadings, usually during the two opening statements, the parties present what are commonly called their "final submissions". [23] So important are these that it is obligatory for the Court's judgment to set forth the parties' submissions.

A submission is an extremely concise statement of what a party wants from the Court, and it should be drawn up in such a way as not to recapitulate the arguments. Each submission indicates what that party considers should be the language of the operative part of the judgment (as opposed to the pleading, which explains the party's view on the relevant reasons of facts and of law in support of its submission). It shows what the party is asking the Court to decide concretely. When a case is introduced by application, the decision of the Court is given on the final submissions, but when it is introduced by special agreement that, as we have seen, defines what it is that the Court has to decide. The final submissions, therefore, are the ultimate concretization of the dispute and as such have to be regarded as an act of State. The outcome of the case will depend on their formulation, and the interpretation of the final submissions may in turn depend upon a comparison of them with the earlier submissions in the case.

For this reason, and to assist the clarity of the discussion, the Court has, in the course of its judicial experience, come to require certain attributes of the final submissions. They should be worded in the form of a positive statement: if they are worded negatively, or interrogatively, they may not provide a satisfactory basis for the decision, and the Court may not be able to give effect to them. As a statement of what a party thinks the decision should be, they should also not contain a series of arguments or propositions in support. That is the function of the pleadings. However, it has become fairly common for States to commence their submission by a series of preambles, "Whereases . . ."—in which the whole case is epitomized with the maximum of succinctness, a practice which is sometimes deprecated as not being consonant with the proper function of a submission, but which may be justified if the diplomatic role of the judicial settlement of international disputes is kept in mind. For its part, however, the Court will ignore the irrelevant parts of submissions—as it did in our case.

Furthermore, the submissions should stand in direct relation to the original statement of the claim as it appeared in the application (or preliminary objection). They do not have to be identical with it, and through the normal processes of pleading modifications, sometimes far-reaching, will appear in the shape of the case through the successive developments in the pleadings. The Court will watch this carefully, in order to guard against a change in the character of the case which might affect the basis of its jurisdiction, and in order to make sure that, by reason of such change, circumstances have not arisen in which notice should be given to third States to alert them to the possibility that they may have to apply for permission to intervene. As between the parties, however, the principle that consent to the jurisdiction can be given tacitly means that when they file submissions they are taken to accept any possible irregularities in the jurisdiction which might exist up to that stage. Submissions which "match" will normally confer jurisdiction on the Court, at least unless some clear reserve to the competence of the Court is expressed.

Having regard to their importance, the final submissions in the oral phase should be read by the Agent, and written copies, signed by him, should be communicated to the Court and to the other party. Submissions may always be modified up to a party's last statement, and the party against whom they are filed is always given the opportunity of commenting on them, even if that involves a modification of that party's own final submission.

The final submissions in our case were complicated. The direction which the case took was fixed by India. On the first four objections, and on the sixth, the submission was for the Court to declare that it was without jurisdiction broadly speaking on the grounds set forth in the preliminary objections themselves. But the submission of the fifth objection was further subdivided into five parts. Three of these were closely based on the arguments of the parties in law and in fact, whereas two raised general questions of principle, including the novel argument that in effect the Portuguese had not disclosed an arguable cause of action under international law, and therefore India had no case to answer. (This was partly based on the shortness of the Portuguese Memorial.) In reply to this, Portugal's final submissions asked for the first, second, third and fourth objections to be dismissed. On the fifth it asked either for the objection to be dismissed or for it to be joined to the merits, and the same was at first submitted as regards the sixth. Portugal went further and, claiming that the Indian argument that there was no case to answer was in fact a new objection filed out of time, objected that it was inadmissible and should be dismissed. Finally, Portugal added a new claim that the Court should recall to the parties the universally admitted principle that they should facilitate the accomplishment of the Court's task by abstaining from any measure capable of exercising a prejudicial effect in regard to the execution of its decision or which might bring about either an aggravation or an extension of the dispute. As a result of this, the original six preliminary objections had now expanded into eight distinct issues, and this gave India the right to make modifications in its final submissions. On the "no case to answer" argument, India took to the offensive and filed a new final submission calling for the rejection of the Portuguese claim. On the last issue, India was quick to point out that if Portugal wanted an interim injunction it should proceed accordingly, and it therefore asked for the submission to be rejected.

This in turn gave rise to a further reaction on the part of Portugal which modified its previous submission on the sixth objection, and now asked for its outright dismissal.

This affords a good illustration of how the direct encounter of the parties before the Court affects the issues which the Court is to decide.

INTERIM MEASURES OF PROTECTION

As we have seen (p. 75 above), a request for interim measures of protection can be filed at any time during the proceedings. That request is a formal document which initiates interlocutory proceedings of a summary character, and the decision of the Court is only given after argument. It is the Court's practice to couch its decisions on these applications in the form of an order, to which separate and dissenting opinions may be appended.

Nothing like this procedure was followed by Portugal in the present case. In fact the Portuguese government expressly disclaimed any intention of invoking the provisions of the Statute concerning the indication of interim measures of protection. In those circumstances the Court did not think that it should comply with the Portuguese request.

CLOSURE OF ORAL PROCEEDINGS

After the parties have completed their presentation of the case, the President formally declares the hearing closed. He may do this at the termination of the last hearing devoted to the case, or he may wait a few days, depending on the circumstances. Once the oral hearings are closed, no further evidence or pleading may be submitted by either party (unless the Court calls for it), and the Court withdraws to consider the judgment. The parties can now relax, and the initiative passes to the Court.

THE BENCH

The Court met for this phase of the case under the Presidency of Judge Hackworth, of the United States of America. All the titular judges participated in the hearing. As neither of the parties had a judge of its nationality on the bench, they both exercised their right to choose a judge *ad hoc*. India chose the Hon. Mahomad Ali Currim Chagla, who was then Chief Justice of Bombay and who later became his country's ambassador in Washington, and Portugal Senhor Manuel Fernandes, Director-General at the Ministry of

Justice and a member of the International Relations Section of the Upper House. At the beginning of the meeting on 23 September the two judges *ad hoc* made the solemn declaration required of all judges, Mr. Chagla having precedence (by virtue of age).

For this phase of the case the Bench consisted of seventeen judges.

THE COURT'S DELIBERATION

The following are the basic rules governing the manner in which the Court deliberates. The judgment has to state the reasons on which it is based. [24] All questions are decided by a majority of the judges present, the President* having a casting vote in the event of a tie. [25] If the judgment does not represent in whole or in part the unanimous opinion of the judges, any judge is entitled to deliver a separate opinion. [26] The Court sits in private for its deliberations, only the judges and assessors (if any) taking part, but the Registrar or his substitute is present. The President (or the Acting President) is generally responsible for the conduct of the deliberations. Each judge should state his opinion together with the reasons on which it is based, and if any judge so desires the question to be voted upon has to be drawn up in precise terms. The decision is based on the conclusions concurred in after final discussion by a majority of the judges, who vote in inverse order of precedence. No detailed minutes are prepared of these private meetings. Such minutes as there are are confidential and record only the subject of the debates, the votes taken, the names of those voting for or against, and statements made expressly for the record. [27] On that basis the contents of a judgment have been laid down. They must include a statement whether delivered by the Court or a Chamber, the date of delivery, the names of the judges participating (in the final vote), the names of the parties and their agents and representatives, a summary of the proceedings, the submissions, a statement of the facts, the reasons in point of law, the operative provisions of the judgment, any decision in regard to costs, the number of judges constituting the majority, and an indication of the authoritative text. Any judge may attach his individual opinion to the judgment, or a bare statement of his dissent. [28]

Within that framework, there has occurred a long evolution in the Court's internal procedure. The first formulation is found in the resolution regarding the Court's judicial practice adopted by the Permanent Court on 20 May 1931. This was revised on 17 March 1936, and in that form was taken over and "provisionally" adopted by the present Court in 1946. [29] That was the

---

* The term President here includes the judge acting as President for a given case (see p. 57 above).

Inaugural Meeting 1946

A signed and sealed Judgment

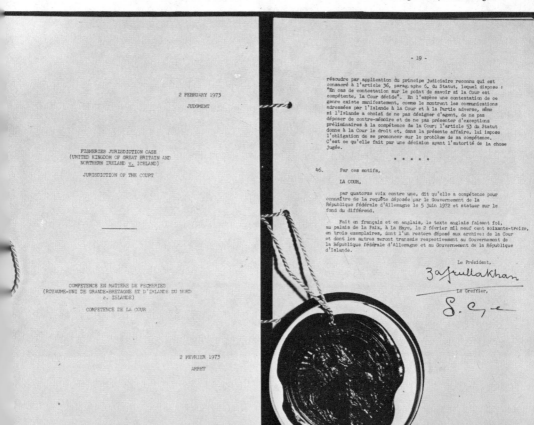

Photo: ANP Foto, Amsterdam

Regular Session of the Court 1973

The Registry Staff at work

practice which governed the deliberations in the *Right of Passage* case. Those provisions were completely replaced by a new resolution on the internal judicial practice of the Court, adopted on 5 July 1968, [30] the essential features of which will now be described.

After the termination of the written proceedings and before the hearing, the judges exchange views, normally in a private meeting of the Court, regarding those proceedings and to bring out any point in regard to which it may be necessary to call for explanations during the oral proceedings. A similar exchange of views takes place after the first round of oral pleadings. When the oral proceedings are over, and the judges have had an appropriate period for study of the case, a deliberation is held. The purpose is to examine the case as it presents itself after the hearing and to bring out the questions to be solved, but without, at that stage, proposing or debating solutions. It is the duty of the President to outline the issues which, in his opinion, will require subsequent discussion and decision by the Court, any judge having the right to comment or to call attention to any other issue or question which he considers relevant. If necessary, the texts of formulated questions will be circulated.

Following this deliberation, each judge prepares a written note, which is circulated to all the judges. This note contains the judge's views on the questions thus raised, including his tentative answers and tentative conclusion for the disposal of the case. A further deliberation then takes place. Here the judges are called upon to speak not in the order they request, as in the earlier deliberation, but in inverse order of seniority, and they must declare their views. After this, a drafting committe is appointed by secret ballot. This is a complicated matter. Two judges are elected from the members of the Court (i.e. excluding the judges *ad hoc*) whose statements and notes have most closely and effectively reflected the opinion of the Court as a whole. The President is *ex officio* a member of the drafting committee unless he does not share the majority opinion as it appears then to exist. In that case his place is taken by the Vice-President. But if he too is ineligible for the same reason, another member of the Court is elected, and the senior judge will preside in the drafting committee.

The preliminary draft of the decision is then circulated, and the judges may submit amendments. After these amendments have been considered, a draft decision is submitted by the drafting committee for discussion in the Court in first reading. After this first reading, the texts of separate or dissenting opinions are circulated. An amended draft of the decision is then submitted for second reading.

Subsequently the final vote is taken, judges voting in inverse order of seniority, and only an affirmative or a negative vote is permitted at this stage. Abstentions are not permitted. Separate voting is allowed where the issues are separable.

When all is ready, the parties are notified of the date of the public meeting at which the judgment will be delivered. [31] At the public meeting the judgment is read in its authentic text, a translation also being read of its operative clause, and signed and sealed copies of it are handed to the Agents (a further signed and sealed copy is retained in the archives of the Court). A copy of every judgment is also sent officially by the Registrar to every member of the United Nations and to every State entitled to appear before the Court. [32] The text is immediately made available to the Press.

The judgments, advisory opinions and orders are published consecutively throughout each year. At the end of the year they are collated, indexed and bound, and form a series of *Reports* similar to domestic series of Law Reports. Apart from official distribution to governments, these texts (as the other publications of the Court) are also placed on sale to the general public. [33]

THE JUDGMENT OF 26 NOVEMBER 1957

The deliberations in this phase of the *Right of Passage* case lasted from 11 October to 26 November 1957, when the judgment was delivered. In a document of 31 pages (18 devoted to the formal parts), the Court rejected the first objection by fourteen votes to three, rejected the second objection by the same vote, rejected the third by sixteen votes to one and the fourth by fifteen votes to two. The fifth, however, it decided to join to the merits by a vote of thirteen to four, and it reached the same decision on the sixth by fifteen votes to two. A declaration of dissent was made by Judge Kojevnikov, and dissenting opinions were appended by Vice-President Badawi, Judge Klaestad (with which Judge *ad hoc* Fernandes concurred) and by Judge *ad hoc* Chagla. The document as a whole is 59 pages long. In consequence, the proceedings on the merits were resumed, and new time-limits fixed.

At first sight, this was an impressive victory for Portugal. Four of the objections had been rejected by very substantial majorities, while two had been postponed. Portugal had overcome the first hurdle and was now assured that the case would be fully ventilated on its merits.

But let us see what effect this judgment had on the case. As stated, the first, second and fourth objections had related exclusively to the title of jurisdiction and the manner in which the proceedings had been instituted in reliance on it, and discussion of those issues in the pleadings and in the judgment had no direct connection with the merits of the case. Psychologically, however, these objections had undoubtedly put Portugal's good faith in issue, although this is nowhere overtly expressed in the judgment.

It was otherwise with the discussion of the other objections. The dismissal of the third preliminary objection, which argued that the filing of the application was premature because the diplomatic negotiations had not been exhausted and therefore the existence of the dispute was not sufficiently disclosed, knocked away one of the props of India's case, but this was partly compensated by the manner in which the Court dealt with the fifth objection. Here it adopted the purely formal position that the facts and their interpretation were disputed between the parties so that it could not pronounce on that objection at that stage without prejudging the merits. For that reason it found it unnecessary to examine the other questions which had arisen in regard to that objection, including the whole question of whether Portugal had produced a reasonably arguable case. This for Portugal was no light matter to have still open. Even more significant was the Court's reasoning on the sixth objection. Although in form this type of objection—that the dispute relates to situations and facts occurring before a certain date—appears highly technical, its impact on any case is in fact extremely strong, because it compels the Court to examine the dispute in all its *minutiae* so that it can establish precisely of what elements it is composed in order to relate it to the date which governs the jurisdiction of the Court in the concrete case. In so far as the date is accidental [34] this is really an artificial process, because historically the dispute developed without any direct connexion with that date, but in practice it is of considerable psychological importance. The Court had given notice that in due course it would investigate these questions closely, but decided to postpone that process for the moment on account of divergences of fact between the parties. The adjournment of these two objections enabled India to stress in all the subsequent stages that it was still contesting the jurisdiction of the Court.

What had India gained by this procedure? In the first place, by interrupting the normal course of the pleadings, it had forced its adversary to show its cards earlier than obviously was intended, as appears by comparing Portugal's memorial with its observations on the preliminary objections. The pleadings on the third, fifth and sixth objections in particular had drawn attention to a number of weaknesses in Portugal's case as a whole, and in fact made serious dents in it. India was able to exploit this in the later phases of the case.

Secondly, India had gained time—in fact something like a year if not more. A respondent nearly always wants to gain time. India was in no hurry for the Court to reach its final decision, for the case was taking place against a general political background which was changing to India's advantage. Furthermore, triennial elections were due to take place at the end of 1957, and the composition of the Court was likely to change. The effect of this was, of course, unknown in advance: but it could not be excluded that the changes would be beneficial to India, for at least it would mean that the final decision would be given by a Court different in its composition from that which Portugal had in mind when it decided to commence the proceedings.

Thirdly, the treatment of the sixth objection had raised the fundamental question of what was the precise dispute which the Court was to decide. It is tactically useful to have this kind of issue pending throughout this type of case.

THE SEPARATE AND DISSENTING OPINIONS

An opinion given by a judge who supports the view of the majority is called a separate opinion, and one given by a judge who disagrees with the view of the majority is called a dissenting opinion—a formal distinction which refers primarily to the attitude adopted by the individual judge on the final vote and the operative clauses of the judgment. The term "individual opinion" covers both types of opinion.

The system for the preparation and promulgation of judgments (as well as advisory opinions, and, where necessary, orders of substance) is a combination of the continental approach, which prefers a single judgment given anonymously in the name of the Court as a whole and without any indication of dissentient views, and the approach of the common law jurisdictions, according to which every judge is entitled to express his own opinion and to state the reasons for it, even if this means criticizing the majority and his colleagues. (Something like the continental system is followed by the Judicial Committee of the Privy Council in London.) The judgments of the International Court are themselves collective and anonymous in the sense that their author and the composition of the drafting committee remain unknown. At the same time each judge is entitled, but is not obliged, to give public expression to his own views by means of a separate or a dissenting opinion, and like-minded judges sometimes combine to write joint opinions. Usually it is possible, by a simple process of arithmetic, to work out who were the judges comprising the majority, but this is not always so. A case recently occurred in which the Court reached its decision by nine votes to five, but as only two dissenting opinions were appended there is no possibility of knowing who were the nine and who were the other three members of the five.[35]

Many people think that the right of each judge to append his own opinion is essential for the effective working of the Court. A former President of the Permanent Court of International Justice, Dr. Max Huber, stated in 1929 that this right was "a guarantee against any subconscious intrusion of political considerations," and that through its existence "judgments were more likely to be given in accordance with the real force of the arguments submitted." In 1956 he went on record as saying that he would hardly have accepted the office as judge if the Statute had not taken over the Anglo-Saxon system of dissenting opinions. A judge of the present Court has pointed out that this system "has come to be regarded as a safeguard of the individual responsibility of the Judges as well as of the integrity of the Court as an institution. . . . It precludes any charge of reliance on mere alignment of voting and lifts the pronouncements of the Court to the level of the inherent power of legal reason and reasoning." [36]

At the same time, the collective and anonymous drafting of the majority opinion has certain drawbacks. The opinion tends to be colourless and lack "character" and even cohesion, although there are exceptions, and our judgment is one of them. It is the product of compromise over words and phrases between a group of men who may be united only in their determination to reach a formally binding decision in the concrete case. but who remain in fact divided between themselves; and in such circumstances questions of semantics become of major importance. When this happens the opinion will appear excessively brief, for it will do no more than represent the common denominator of the divergent views of the judges, and exclude every redundant word. The problem which arises is the following: Should the Court strive for the largest possible majority for its decisions, at the cost of eliminating every word and thought that gives rise to controversy; or should it place the general cogency of the reasoning at the head of its concern, voting only on the operative clauses of the judgment, and leaving the reasons to the skill and energy of the individual judges? The Court has chosen the first course, and while it was probably a wise choice, it adds to the general significance of the individual opinions.

The individual opinions, whether they are separate or dissenting opinions, perform several functions. Thanks to the greater freedom of expression and emphasis enjoyed by the individual judges, many of them do no more than underpin the anonymous collective opinion of the majority, which, owing to the process by which it was put together, cannot always articulate fully and expressively the underlying principles which were applied. In other cases, the individual opinion may indicate other general underlying principles which its author believed should have been more appropriately applied in the concrete case. Such an opinion may have a value of its own in correcting any misleading impression which could be obtained from the majority opinion. The fact that certain ideas only appear in a separate opinion does not mean that the Court as a whole *rejected* them. It means nothing more than that the Court was not prepared to accept them for the purposes of its decision— something quite different. In another direction, one sometimes encounters individual opinions which flatly contradict both the underlying principles and their application by the majority and here, dependent on the author's general reputation and the cogency of his reasoning, the individual opinion may in the course of time come to be seen by enlightened and informed opinion as expressive of better law. Above all, the publication of these opinions focuses attention on the nature of the discussion in the Council Chamber. For a full understanding of the real implications of any judgment, the discerning reader will consult not merely the pleadings, which will show him how the parties presented the issues, but also the individual opinions appended to the majority judgment, which will show him the main lines of the discussion in the Court when it withdrew to deliberate on the case.

Nevertheless, there is a tendency for excessive prolixity, leading to the possibility of abuse, in some individual opinions, especially when these go beyond the limits fixed by the Court in its judgment. The *Reports* since 1946 are replete with instances of this, and of warnings against the perpetuation of this practice. Both in learned societies and in political circles considerable impatience is being expressed at what, in the view of many observers, is ultimately a demonstration of the lack of *esprit de corps* among the members of the Court and therefore of its inefficacity.

There is another factor to be noticed. The figures of the final voting by the judges are an extremely deceptive guide to the strength of the two cases. In most instances of international litigation, the balance between the two parties' cases, from the point of view of abstract legal merit, is extremely fine. Countries do not become involved in international litigation, and certainly not applicant governments, if their case is not reasonably arguable! The fact that in the *Right of Passage* case the six clauses of the operative part of this judgment were reached by extremely large majorities, in no instance less than thirteen out of the seventeen judges who sat, is no test whatsoever of the strength of the Indian objections, all of which are much more plausible than a *cursory* reading of the judgment would suggest. How, then, is this phenomenon, of the large majorities in this and other cases, to be explained? The answer is in the overriding necessity of the Court to reach a decision which will be final and authoritative. This means that in the end a *choice* must be made—a choice which must be in accordance with the professional skill and the conscience of the individual judge. The care with which the issues are sifted by the Court during its deliberations, even before the writing of the judgment is taken in hand, is designed to enable the normal processes of free and equal discussion and persuasion to take their course. The right of the judges to express their own views of the case in the form of individual opinions thus is an important residuary power, and even a stimulus to the formation of large majorities on which the ultimate acceptability of a decision will depend. A government, and public opinion, will the more easily acquiesce in a decision reached by a large majority than in one reached by a narrow majority.

Not all these aspects are fully illustrated by the Judgment of 26 November 1957, in which, the division in the Court being clear-cut, there are no separate opinions, and only three dissenting opinions. But in the second judgment, on the merits, the situation was different.

The Court reaches its decision by applying international law. In the case of the preliminary objections in the present matter, the law applied was a limited and highly technical aspect of the law governing the compulsory jurisdiction of the Court. Broader issues of this character came out in the second phase of the case, and that will therefore be the most convenient place to discuss this aspects of the Court's working.

THE RESUMED PROCEEDINGS ON THE MERITS

The Judgment of 26 November 1957 had two automatic consequences. It terminated (with the force of *res judicata*) all further judicial discussion of the first four objections, which were thereby removed from the Court's agenda. On the other hand there was no *res judicata* on the fifth and sixth objections. It also resumed the proceedings on the merits, to which the two outstanding objections were now joined. New time-limits were therefore fixed—25 February 1958 for the Counter-Memorial, 25 May for the Reply and 25 July for the Rejoinder. In January, however, India asked for a month's extension to which Portugal consented provided it could have four months for the Reply, and the dates were correspondingly refixed, by an order of 10 February 1958.

The counter-memorial was accordingly filed on 25 March. This was a document of 153 pages, to which a further 250 or so pages of annexes were added. India now, for the first time, put forward its submission on the merits. This was short and to the point. The Court was simply asked to declare that it had no jurisdiction to decide on the claim of Portugal, and, in the alternative, to declare the claim ill-founded. In that way the issues were joined without any direct complications, other than those resulting from the outstanding preliminary objections. On 25 July, Portugal filed its reply—a pleading of 190 pages together with a further 250 pages of annexed material, but there was no new submission. The Indian rejoinder was due for 25 September, but in August the Indian Agent asked for an extension of five months. This was opposed by Portugal, which was nevertheless prepared to agree to an extension of two months on the condition that the time allowed for the preparation of the oral arguments should not be less than that granted to India for the preparation of the rejoinder. The Court, without accepting that condition, by an order of 28 August postponed the date for the filing of the rejoinder to 25 November. But that was not the end of this discussion, and in October an additional extension to 25 January 1959 was requested. This required a further consultation with the parties (especially as it then looked as though the Court would have a very heavy time-table for the year 1959 and might have difficulty in hearing the case), and by an order of 6 November, that extension was granted. On 17 January a further slight extension, to 5 February, was granted after Portugal had consented, and after this long process of gestation, the rejoinder was finally filed, and the case became ready for hearing. This pleading is some 320 pages in length together with a further 660 pages of annexes.

Let us now see how this case looked when it was ready for hearing. The Court had had presented to it something like 290 pages of pleading and 462 pages of annexes by Portugal, and 550 pages of pleading together with 1,340 pages of annexes by India; and if we add the oral pleadings in the preliminary objection phase, which were still of considerable relevance, we see that by this time the *dossier* contained nearly three thousand printed pages. [37] A formidable case! And more was to come.

The written pleadings, especially the reply and rejoinder, had not succeeded in narrowing down the issues. In fact the position was very much to the contrary. What they did was to bring out two sharply differing concepts of the purpose of the case. Portugal was aiming at a decision which could protect it from the effects of the Indian policy of driving out the last vestiges of European colonization in the Indian Peninsula. India, having failed to have the Portuguese case dismissed on the formal grounds advanced in the first, second and fourth objections, now concentrated on a more complicated double objective. The first was to try and isolate the incidents of 1954 from their general political background so that at the most a decision by the Court, if unfavourable to India, would be of limited implications. The second was not merely to challenge the Portuguese conception that it enjoyed sovereignty over the various districts and enclaved areas but also the corollary of that view, namely that Portugal had a *right* of passage over Indian territory: and in that connection there was a further development in that India made a determined attempt to break the right of passage up into a number of categories. The important thing for India was, if it were to lose the case, nevertheless to try and exclude from the right of passage the armed forces which had, for the first time, been specifically mentioned in the submissions of the memorial (see p. 93 above). On the political level, India was still not in agreement with Portugal that *any* dispute between the two countries relating to the right of passage should be submitted to the Court. It was obliged to recognize the jurisdiction of the Court, but that did not mean that it had to look on the case in the same light as Portugal.

The change in date for the filing of the rejoinder affected a number of other cases. On 3 February another case became ready for hearing: on 5 February the *Right of Passage* case became ready for hearing: and on 31 March yet a third case became ready for hearing. There was no difficulty over the case which became ready on 3 February: in accordance with the normal rule that had to be heard before the later cases (see p. 95 above). It was, however, obvious from the Indian rejoinder that a considerable amount of preparatory work would be required both by the parties and by the Court before the hearings could profitably be opened. Arrangements were therefore made to take the third case before the summer vacation, and to postpone the *Right of Passage* case. In that way, incidentally, Portugal obtained satisfaction of the condition which it had made for consenting to the extension requested by India for the filing of the rejoinder, without prejudicing the position of principle adopted by the Court.

The hearings accordingly commenced on 21 September and terminated on 6 November, occupying thirty-six meetings of the Court. Five persons shared the presentation of Portugal's case, and five that of India. The printed record covers some 840 pages. Final judgment was delivered on 12 May 1960.

A triennial election had intervened between the first judgment and the second, and the term of office of the former President had come to an end. There is a rule that the President shall continue to act as such if a case is begun before a periodic election, but it has long been the practice to regard the preliminary objections and the merits as two "cases"—even when, as in our matter, some of the objections are joined to the merits. For the same reason, although by the Statute the members of the Court shall continue to discharge their functions until their places have been filled, and though re- placed shall finish any cases which they may have begun, [38] when a case is divided into two distinct phases, it is usual for the Court to sit on the second occasion in its new composition. As a result, the Court now sat under the Presidency of Judge Klaestad of Norway: two of the judges who had sat in 1957 had been replaced; there was one vacancy in the Court's ranks (which was filled only on 29 September, but that judge did not take part in the case); and one judge was absent after the first few sittings on account of sickness. The same two judges *ad hoc* continued to sit. The Court accordingly consist- ed this time of fifteen judges (the absence of two members from the bench may have had a decisive effect on the final outcome of this case).

MUST A STATE APPEAR?

It has been mentioned (p. 93 above) that theoretically India, instead of filing a Counter-Memorial, could have taken no action at all and let the case go by default. What would have happened then?

Provision is made for such an eventuality. It would have been pointless to have gone to the trouble of setting up an International Court and then to have opened the way to the complete frustration of its work by not closing this gap. Accordingly, the Statute lays down that whenever one of the parties does not appear before the Court, or fails to defend its case, the other party may call upon the Court to decide in favour of its claim. But before doing so, the Court must satisfy itself both that it has jurisdiction in accordance with the provisions of the Statute, and that the claim is well founded in fact and in law. [39] Instances of this are naturally rare, because States will not lightly risk the possibility that judgment will be given against them. It should be noted, however, that this procedure for giving judgment by default only applies if the Court is satisfied that it has jurisdiction, and if the defaulting party has been duly notified of the hearing.

In the present case, it should not be assumed that the Court would have automatically held that it had jurisdiction in the event that India failed to appear. As it happened, there was on record a note by the Swedish Government of 23 February 1956 in which that Government had stated that it regarded the third condition of the Portuguese acceptance of the compulsory jurisdiction as incompatible with the Statute, and on 5 July Portugal had replied thereto. [40] These documents had been circulated in the normal way by the Secretary-General of the United Nations, in his capacity of depositary of the acceptances of the compulsory jurisdiction. The Court would therefore in any event have had to have dealt with the issues presented by the first objection, and possibly by the second and fourth as well. It is not unlikely that some of the other objections would have been raised by the Court of its own initiative.

SETTLEMENT OUT OF COURT

Since Portugal was the applicant, Portugal could at any time have discontinued the proceedings by giving the Court notice to that effect. Before making the order recording the discontinuance, India would have first been asked if it had any objection. As applicant in the preliminary objection phase, India could likewise have discontinued the proceedings on the objections, in which event the proceedings on the merits would have been automatically resumed. [41] In addition to this, the two parties could have settled the case out of Court by agreement, and the Court would have placed this on record. [42] Instances of both these procedures are fairly common.

THE LAW APPLIED BY THE COURT

The Court being an international Court designed to serve the international community of States, the law which it applies is naturally international law. The Statute of the Court therefore contains some general directions on this aspect. According to this, the Court shall apply: (a) international conventions, whether general or particular, expressly recognized by the contesting States; (b) international custom, as evidence of a general practice recognized as law; (c) the general principles of law recognized by civilized nations; and (d) judicial decisions and the teachings of the most highly qualified publicists of the various nations, as subsidiary means for the determination of the rules of law. [43]

For theoretical reasons that enumeration has given rise to a not inconsiderable controversy. In practice, however, it is regarded as generally satisfactory, and indeed is frequently taken over into international arbitration agreements. Difficulty is nevertheless experienced on two points. The first is the word "civilized" in head *(c)* which in the view of most persons is supererogatory as well as meaningless. The second relates to the place of the so-called "law-making resolutions" of United Nations organs. This is an extremely problematical matter because to include these among the sources of law to be applied by the Court would attribute to them a status which does not flow either from the Charter or from the rules of international law itself concerning the creation of legal norms applied in international relations. This does not mean, of course, unresponsiveness on the part of the Court to the trends registered in those resolutions, and the Court is sensitive to the so-called "inter-temporal law"—the marriage of old and new law. Heads *(a)*, *(b)* and *(c)* refer to the rules of law itself. The real innovation that was introduced when the Statute was first drafted in 1920 related to head *(c)*; its purpose was to remove any danger that the Court would be unable to give a decision on the mere ground that it could find no rule of law to govern the case. [44] This useful provision enables the Court to deal with entirely unprecedented situations, and through its pronouncements to keep the law abreast of the constantly changing developments.

Head *(d)*—which refers to two distinct aspects which are not on the same level, judicial decisions and the teachings of the highly qualified publicists—is a guide to explain how the law may be ascertained. However, it is far from exhaustive. It is an interesting compromise between the two approaches—of the continental jurist on the one hand, who freely makes use of *doctrine*, theoretical literature, of publicists of repute and who attaches no formal authority to judicial decisions, and of the common law which on the whole refuses to employ the writings of publicists in this way and indeed would even tend to look askance on their citation in a pleading or in a judgment, but which gives to judicial decisions the formal authority of a binding precedent. Nevertheless, the practical difference between these two schools of thought is not so great, for on the one hand the continental jurist will tend to recognize the inherent as distinguished from the formal authority of judicial precedents, especially when the higher courts are consistent in their decisions (the French call this *une jurisprudence constante*), whereas the American and English lawyer is second to none in his ability to "distinguish" one precedent from another.

International thinking tends to prefer the continental approach in theory, and the common law approach in practice. One reason for this is that in comparison with domestic litigation, international litigation is sparse, and for a judicial system which has given about one hundred and ten substantive decisions in a period of fifty years to regard those decisions as constituting binding precedents would be little short of absurd. There are a number of other fundamental reasons for rejecting in international law the Anglo-American theory of precedents. One of these is the particularism of the international judicial system and its unintegrated character. Another is the absence of automatic enforceability in its decisions, especially advisory opinions or orders indicating interim measures of protection, and to some extent even judgments. We therefore find that the International Court has refrained from saying that it was *obliged* to follow previous judicial decisions—of itself, of the Permanent Court, or of authoritative Arbitration Tribunals—although it has been very careful not to upset established jurisprudence unless it was convinced that there was good reason. For example, in the Judgment of 26 November 1957 on the preliminary objections of the *Right of Passage* case, two previous cases are quoted, and a further three are cited in the judgment of 12 April 1960 on the merits. Writings of publicists are almost never directly cited by the Court itself. The opinions of the individual judges are, naturally, freer in this regard, and the parties' pleadings even more so. This means that the non-citation of an earlier judgment or of important works of reputable publicists in the judgment itself does not imply that the Court was unaware of them or wilfully ignored them. It could be mentioned that the experience of the International Law Commission has also shown that to cite writers by name, at all events in its final report which constitutes a collective *exposé des motifs* for decisions reached, is an extremely delicate matter. In 1966, after carefully weighing the issues, the Commission decided to omit citations from *doctrine* from its final report on the law of treaties. [45]

The use of judicial decisions as precedents is subject to one important limitation—namely that a judicial decision itself has no "binding force" except between the parties and in respect of that particular case. [46] There is, however, no real contradiction. The "decision" which is only "binding" on the parties to a particular case is found in the operative clauses of the judgment. The Court's reasoning—its statement of what it regards as the correct legal position *and why*—enters into the general storehouse of public international law. That is why the decisions of the International Court have become one of the most important repertoires today for the rules of international law, and indeed one of the law's most powerful instruments for adaptation to the constantly changing conditions.

The Court also has power, if the parties agree, to "decide a case *ex aequo et bono.*"[47] What this means is that if the parties expressly confer that power on the Court, it may lay down, in the form of a binding decision, a reasonable adjustment of the relations between the two parties, and not limit its decision to a statement of what those relations are on the basis of the law as it is. No instance has occurred of States conferring this power on the Court. The reason probably is that it is the normal function of diplomacy to bring such adjustments about, and it is not a judicial function to do so, and the normal processes of diplomacy have developed special machinery, such as conciliation and mediation procedures, to assist it.

In the merits of the *Right of Passage* case a number of significant general issues regarding the law applied by the Court arose.

One of the Indian arguments in connection with the fifth preliminary objection was, as seen, that a reasonably arguable cause of action based on the kind of legal rules which the Court has to apply had not been presented to the Court, and that in consequence there was no legal dispute which the Court could adjudicate. India further made it clear that it was not consenting to any adjustment of the situation *ex aequo et bono*. In the preliminary objection phase the Court had not considered this part of the argument, but it could not avoid doing so in the second phase. In the second part of the case India slightly changed the effect of this argument. It was no longer put forward exclusively as an argument against the jurisdiction of the Court, but rather as an argument for the dismissal of Portugal's claim on the merits. In consequence it became somewhat modified and contended that Portugal's claim was too vague and contradictory to enable the Court to pass judgment on it by application of any of the four categories of rules enumerated above. The Court dismissed this part of India's contention and explained that while there was no doubt that the day-to-day exercise of the right of passage may give rise to delicate questions of application, that was not, in the view of the Court, sufficient ground for holding that the right itself was not susceptible of judicial determination with reference to the rules which the Court is authorized to apply. This is an important observation, for it shows that if the Court has jurisdiction it will not be deflected from its judicial task by exceptional difficulties, nor will it accept the argument that there are gaps in international law.

THE FINAL SUBMISSIONS ON THE MERITS

Portugal's final submissions were filed on 6 October at the end of the first pleading by Portugal—a pleading which itself had started on 21 September and had lasted over fourteen hearings. The submissions contained forty-seven "Whereases" and five operative clauses. Two of these asked for the dismissal of the remaining objections. As for the merits, the first submission asked for a declaration by the Court that the right of passage "as defined above" was a right possessed by Portugal which must be respected by India—that is to say a right "claimed only to the extent necessary for the exercise of Portuguese sovereignty over the enclaves". The second asked for a declaration that India had not complied with the obligations incumbent upon it by virtue of Portugal's right of passage. The third was more complicated and was divided into four parts. The Court was asked to hold that certain arguments by India relating to: *(a)* its right to adopt an attitude of neutrality in the conflict between the Portuguese Government and the insurgents in the enclaved territories; *(b)* the application of various provisions of the United Nations Charter relating to human rights and the right of self-determination of peoples; and *(c)* the existence of a provisional *de facto* local government in the enclaved territories, were all without foundation: and *(d)* on an argument that the exercise of the right of passage in "present circumstances" would cause grave dangers to India's public order, either to order India to end the suspension of the right of passage or to impose conditions for the temporary suspension of the right of passage until the danger to India passed. In reply to this India's final submissions, filed on 21 October after a further eleven days of pleading by India, contained forty-five "Whereases", leading to a single submission, that the Court was without jurisdiction, and alternatively that the claim was without foundation.

It should here be noted that between the application and this final submission, the Portuguese claim had undergone one fundamental modification. In the application Portugal asked for unconditional recognition by the Court for its right of passage (p. 88 above). But now, after all this strenuous pleading, the right claimed was conditional—"only to the extent necessary for the exercise of Portuguese sovereignty": and this was coupled with a reticent acknowledgement that in certain circumstances India did have the right to suspend the exercise of the right.

India's method of pleading had not been without effect. By bringing Portugal to these conclusions, India had gone a long way towards re-insuring itself against serious long-term adverse effects of a judgment in favour of Portugal. It is good diplomacy to be content with the possible. India's handling off the case *as a whole* had succeeded, come what might, in protecting India's national aspirations from any long-term harmful effects of the Portuguese surprise move of 1955.

THE JUDGMENT OF 12 APRIL 1960

After something like five months of deliberation, broken only for the Christmas vacation, the Court delivered its judgment on 12 April 1960. This judgment is 44 pages long, 24 of which are taken up by the formal parts. Short declarations were added by President Klaestad and Judges Basdevant, Badawi, Kojevnikov and Spiropoulos; Judge Wellington Koo appended a separate opinion and Judges Winiarski and Badawi (jointly), Armand-Ugon, Moreno Quintana, and Sir Percy Spender, and Judges *ad hoc* Chagla and Fernandes dissenting opinions. The whole text is 142 pages in length. By thirteen votes to two the Court dismissed the fifth preliminary objection and by eleven votes to four the sixth. On the merits, by eleven votes to four it found that Portugal had *in 1954* a right of passage, to the extent necessary for the exercise of Portuguese sovereignty over the enclaves and subject to the regulation and control of India, in respect of private persons, civil officials and goods in general. By the narrow margin of eight votes to seven it found that Portugal did not have *in 1954* such a right of passage in respect of armed forces, armed police and arms and ammunition. By nine votes to six it found that India had not acted contrary to its obligations resulting from the right of passage of private persons, civil officials and goods in general. All the other Portuguese claims were dismissed without vote. Although both sides could cry victory—an important factor from the point of view of prestige—there is little doubt that India is the substantial victor in this case, and that if Portugal did obtain from the Court formal recognition of Portuguese sovereignty over the territories in question, the judgment effectively deprived Portugal of the means of enforcing that sovereignty.

How did the Court reach this judgment of Solomon? (That it was a judgment of Solomon the reader who is sceptical can see from the curious phenomenon of a dissenting opinion by each Judge *ad hoc*.)

The key lies in the delayed action effect of the sixth preliminary objection which, although (or perhaps because) it was dismissed, forced the Court to look very closely at the different elements of which the dispute was composed in order to decide precisely when it came into existence, and what were the facts and situations with which it was concerned. The answer to that would determine what was the dispute which the Court had to decide. The Court found that the *legal* dispute came into existence in 1954 against the background of the *political* dispute which came to a head in that year, and that the service of the Court was prayed in aid to redress the illegal situation which, in Portugal's view, flowed from India's failure *in 1954* to comply with its obligations in respect to the right of passage. That explains both the insertion of that date in the two fundamental operative clauses of the judgment, and the Court's refusal to consider all that part of Portugal's third submission on the merits which related not to the events of 1954, but to what had occurred later.

How did the Court reach its conclusion that a right of passage did exist on that date, and that it only applied to the "civilian" categories of transit?

As we have seen, specific reference to "armed forces" had appeared for the first time in the submission of the memorial, and in subsequent pleadings, the existence of the right, its historical origins going back to the earliest period of British India, was discussed not as an entity, but with reference to the different categories. The Court, after examination of the vast quantity of material placed before it (mostly of an historical character collected from various archives), reached the conclusion that the right only existed with regard to the civilian categories, and that Indian (or formerly British) permission had always been obtained for the transit of the "armed" categories. The fact that prior authorization was necessary made it impossible to say that for the "armed" categories the passage was exercised as of right.

Nevertheless, as the voting shows, it was this question which caused the major division in the Court. A swing of one vote would have produced an entirely different result. Objectively speaking the case against the breakdown of the right of passage into the various classes, as expounded in the various individual opinions dealing with this aspect, is no less persuasive than the majority opinion. The balance is truly fine.

Two major questions arise from this judgment. The first is why, having regard to the actual decision, did the Court not seek the easier way out by accepting one of the preliminary objections, most of which contain elements of plausibility not reflected adequately in the size of the majorities dismissing them. The second is what did the Court do in relation to the *real* conflict between the two countries.

It is believed that the answer to the first question is to be found in long-term considerations of judicial policy. All these objections dealt exclusively with technical aspects of the compulsory jurisdiction. The first objection (and the second and fourth, closely associated with it) broke new ground relating, as they did, to the facility which a State, a member of the United Nations, possesses by a surprise move to subject itself to the compulsory jurisdiction: the Court in effect held that the element of surprise was not an abuse of rights, basing itself on a strict interpretation of the relevant texts. [48] The remaining objections are of a kind frequently raised, and the Court has well-developed patterns of approach towards them. This approach tends towards keeping them with reasonable limits, so as to avoid creating an easy way of frustrating an obligation to recognize the jurisdiction. It was probably an inarticulate desire to remain faithful to those patterns of jurisprudence which ultimately tipped the balance in favour of the rejection of those objections.

As to the second question, by placing itself on the narrow basis of the events of 1954, the Court gave a limited decision relating to a particular incident. In this way it avoided giving judgment on a much broader political conflict of interests. This was to become clear later when, in December 1961, India proceeded to occupy the three territories, and the Security Council, before which Portugal complained, took no action on the matter.[49] The subtle tactics adopted by the Indian Government were successful in that they prevented the Portuguese initiative in applying to the Court from affecting adversely the attainment of India's political aspirations.

The attitude of the Court is a significant illustration of judicial caution, all the more striking in the light of the fact that in order to reach even its limited decision the Court had to overcome no less than six preliminary objections. [50]

By the judgment of 12 April 1960 the file in Case No. 32 was closed.

COSTS

The Court has general power to award costs, although the normal principle in international litigation is that each party bears its own costs. [51] This principle is an expression of the sovereign equality of the States at bar.

Neither party asked for costs in the present case, and no decision by the Court on that aspect was, therefore, required.

INTERPRETATION AND REVISION

The Judgment became binding on the parties with its delivery: and there is no appeal. It finally decided the issues between them with the force of *res judicata*. [52] But what could happen if difficulties arose over its implementation?

The Statute deals with that eventuality. If a dispute arises over the meaning or scope of a judgment, the Court has jurisdiction to construe it on the request of either party. Such a request may be submitted either by special agreement or by unilateral application, and the Court will decide on it by judgment. [53] This does not give the Court an unlimited power to re-open the case (for the judgment is final and without appeal), and the extent of what the Court can do by means of interpretation is in fact limited. The reason is to prevent a new dispute being submitted to the Court in the guise of a request to interpret an earlier judgment, for the jurisdiction to interpret derives directly from the Court's jurisdiction to decide the merits of the original case, and is not, to that extent, an independent jurisdiction. No encouragement must be given to its abuse, at all events so long as the international community does not accept the legal principle of compulsory jurisdiction. The present Court has had one case of interpretation (see p. 129 below).

The Court also has general power to revise the judgment, under the same conditions as to jurisdiction, if some new fact of a decisive nature which was unknown to the Court and to the party producing it (provided that such ignorance was not due to negligence) is discovered within the period of ten years from the date of the judgment. [54]

THE EXTRA-JUDICIAL FUNCTION

No question arose in this case of inviting the Court to employ its extra-judicial function to assist the parties in reaching a settlement of their dispute. However, it may be mentioned, for the sake of completeness, that India has not been averse to the use of this procedure to assist it in achieving its national aspirations. In 1949 the French Government, formally as a matter of exclusive domestic sovereignty, decided to hold a referendum in the French Settlements in India to enable the populations to decide freely on their destiny and future status, and the Vice-President (the President being a French national) was asked to appoint a group of neutral observers to supervise it. The Vice-President carried out this assignment. [55]

In practice, the President will only accede to requests of this character if he is satisfied that the parties are in agreement that he makes the appointment.

CHAPTER VI

THE WORK OF THE COURT

Before attempting to evaluate the role of the Court since 1946, a rapid survey of the cases that have come before it is required.

THE CORFU CHANNEL

On 22 October 1946 a squadron of British warships sailed through a previously swept minefield in the Corfu Channel, which separates Albania from Greece. In the course of the mission, two of the ships, H.M.S. *Saumarez* and H.M.S. *Volage*, struck mines, subsequently established to have been "recently laid", and were badly damaged. Forty-four officers and men were killed and forty-two injured. The British Government held Albania responsible and, after the failure of diplomatic negotiations to lead to a settlement, referred the matter to the Security Council in January, 1947. After a long and complicated discussion, in which one draft resolution was vetoed by the Soviet Union, the Council, on 3 April 1947, recommended that the two governments should "immediately" refer the dispute to the International Court of Justice, in accordance with the provisions of the Statute of the Court." The resolution was adopted by eight votes to none, with two abstentions (Poland and the U.S.S.R.), the United Kingdom not participating in the vote in accordance with Article 27 (3) of the Charter. During the proceedings Albania had accepted the formal invitation issued by the Council under Article 32 of the Charter inviting it to participate without vote in the discussion on condition that Albania accepted all the obligations which a member of the United Nations would have to assume in such a case. After the resolution was adopted, the President of the Council observed that although Albania could not be compelled to appear before the Court, by accepting the obligations of a member it was obliged to comply with the provisions of the Charter and the Statute (cf. p. 67 above).

On 22 May, the United Kingdom filed in Court an application instituting proceedings. In July the Albanian Government informed the Court of its view that in proceeding unilaterally the United Kingdom was not acting in conformity with the Statute, as required by the Security Council's resolution, and that accordingly Albania would be within its rights in holding that the case could not be brought without a special agreement. However, this not-withstanding Albania, accepting the recommendation of the Security Council, was prepared to appear before the Court. Yet when the time came to file the counter-memorial, Albania raised a preliminary objection which, in effect, repeated that attitude regarding the consequences of the initial irregularity of the manner in which the case had been instituted. In a judgment of 25 March 1948—the first delivered by the present Court—the objection was dismissed by fifteen votes to one, only the Albanian judge *ad hoc* dissenting, and the proceedings on the merits were resumed.

On the same day on which that judgment was delivered the parties concluded a special agreement by which they decided to put two questions to the Court. The first asked the Court to decide whether Albania was responsible under international law for the explosions which occurred on 22 October 1946 in Albanian waters and for the damage and loss of human life which resulted therefrom, and whether there was any duty to pay compensation. The second enquired whether the action of the United King-dom in sending its warships through the Corfu Channel on 22 October, and whether its later action in re-sweeping the Channel on 12 and 13 November, violated Albanian sovereignty, and whether there was any duty to give satis-faction. The Court thereupon recognized that this special agreement con-stituted the basis for the future conduct of the case.

The pleadings showed—as had also been evident in the Security Council—that there were serious divergences between the parties on questions of fact, and it became necessary for the Court to hear witnesses and experts called by the parties. This was the first occasion in which witnesses were heard in the International Court. Five witnesses and two witness-experts were called by the United Kingdom, and three witnesses and two experts by Albania, and as the differences of fact were not easily resolved, the Court decided to obtain an expert opinion on a number of contested points. Therefore, a committee of experts, consisting of senior officers of the Netherlands, Norwegian and Swedish Navies, was appointed, and when their first report did not sufficient-ly clarify matters, they were requested to proceed to the scene, there to make further investigations. Although it was never fully established who had laid the mines which had damaged *Samaurez* and *Volage*, the Court in its judg-ment of 9 April 1949 found sufficient evidence to hold that in law Albania, as the territorial State, was responsible, and was under the duty of making compensation for the consequent loss and damage. The Court also found that the passage of the British warships through the Corfu Channel on 22 October was not a violation of Albanian sovereignty, but that the minesweeping activities of November "violated the sovereignty of the People's Republic of Albania, and that this declaration by the Court constitutes in itself appro-priate satisfaction."

However, there had been no pleadings on the question of the amount of compensation to be paid—indeed Albania proceeded to argue that on a proper interpretation of the special agreement the Court did not have jurisdiction to assess the amount of compensation. In its judgment of 9 April the Court rejected that argument, and decided on a third phase of the case, limited to the question of compensation. Albania failed to present any pleadings in that phase of the case and, although duly notified, did not participate in the Court's hearing devoted to that question. This led the Court to apply the procedure for default of appearance (see p. 111 above)—the first instance of this. The question of jurisdiction had already been decided, but the figures advanced by the United Kindom were found to raise questions of a technical nature for which expert opinion was required. The Court accordingly appointed another committee of experts consisting of two senior officers of the Netherlands Navy to examine the claim. The experts reached the conclusion that the amount claimed by the United Kingdom could be taken as a fair and accurate estimate of the damage sustained, and the Court, by a judgment of 15 December 1949, gave judgment in favour of the United Kingdom for the sum of £ 843,947. [1]

The compensation awarded to the United Kingdom has never been paid. Echoes of this were to be heard in the Court later (see p. 143 below).

The incidents in the Corfu Channel—among the earliest incidents of the Cold War—had caused a great deal of tension, and this had been exacerbated by the debates in the Security Council. The Security Council by itself was unable to remove the friction and therefore enlisted the aid of the Court by recommending the parties to refer the case to it. The special agreement opened the way to proceedings which could take account of Albania's complaints against the United Kingdom (in fact Albania could always have introduced its complaints in the proceedings, by way of a counter-claim), and the Court was enabled to deliver a judgment which gave partial satisfaction to both sides. To that extent, the combination of Court proceedings with those of the Security Council may be regarded as a successful innovation, and it may perhaps be regretted that the Security Council (or the General Assembly) has not found it possible to repeat it since.

This case raised expectations in some circles that with the emergence of the Soviet Union as a major power, the earlier attitude of reserve manifested towards the Permanent Court might be relaxed, at least to the extent that the Soviet Union would be prepared to conclude special agreements for referring specific disputes to the Court. However, later developments were to show that any such hopes were premature.

MEMBERSHIP IN THE UNITED NATIONS

Article 4 of the Charter lays down how new members can be admitted to the United Nations. Paragraph 1 specifies the conditions for membership—that the applicant State shall be peace-loving, have accepted the obligations contained in the Charter, and be able and willing to carry out those obligations. Paragraph 2 indicates the procedure—that admission to membership shall be effected by a decision of the General Assembly on the recommendation of the Security Council. Both these provisions have been interpreted by the Court.

From the beginning of 1946 the Security Council had been deadlocked on the question of the admission of new members, candidates proposed by the Communist States not receiving the necessary majority of votes (at that time seven), and those proposed by the West encountering the veto. This gave rise to sharp discussions in the Security Council and later in the General Assembly which, on 17 November 1947, by forty votes to eight, with two abstentions, decided to ask the Court for an advisory opinion on the interpretation of the first paragraph. The question put to the Court was whether a member which is called upon to express itself by its vote, either in the Security Council or in the General Assembly, on the admission of a State to membership, was juridically entitled to make its consent to the admission dependent on conditions not expressly provided for in paragraph 1. In particular, could such a member, while recognizing the conditions to be fulfilled, subject its affirmative vote to the additional condition that other States would be admitted together with that State? This was designed to obtain a ruling on the "legality" of a possible "package deal", by which all outstanding applications for membership would be accepted.

The competence of the Court to give the advisory opinion was challenged on the grounds that the question was a political one and therefore fell outside the jurisdiction of the Court, that it was abstract, and that the Court is not entitled to interpret the Charter. The Court, in its advisory opinion of 28 May 1948, rejected these arguments, and then, by nine votes to six, proceeded to answer both questions put to it in the negative. But two individual opinions were given by judges forming part of the majority, and these seemed to indicate that despite the *juridical* answer, political considerations could not be regarded as irrelevant. This led to considerable confusion over what the Court had actually decided, and why. Nevertheless, the General Assembly in a resolution of 8 December 1948, recommended that each member of the Security Council and of the General Assembly, in exercising its vote on the admission of new members, should act in accordance with the Court's opinion. [2]

In practice, the Court's opinion did not mean very much because all States could fully comply with it simply by explaining their negative vote on the basis of their view that the applicant State did not meet the conditions of paragraph 1. The political problem of the admission of new members did not originate in the explanations given for the negative vote, but in the underlying political situation for which those votes were merely an expression. The request for the advisory opinion did not, and indeed could not, bring out that aspect, and the practical wisdom displayed by the General Assembly in requesting the opinion and in trying to tie its hands on the question of the "package deal" is therefore highly questionable. On the other hand, the Court's decision rejecting the challenges to its jurisdiction rests on solid and convincing grounds.

The advisory opinion, then, could contribute little towards resolving the *political* problem of the admission of new members, and a move developed in the General Assembly urging that when the Security Council made no recommendation at all, the General Assembly could decide to admit new members. Although the language of paragraph 2 of Article 4 of the Charter seems clear enough, the General Assembly decided to put the question to the Court by a resolution of 22 November 1949 which was adopted by forty-two votes to nine with six abstentions. In a brief and clear advisory opinion of 3 March 1950 the Court gave its opinion that admission to membership cannot be effected by a decision of the General Assembly when the Security Council has made no recommendation for admission, by reason of the candidate failing to secure the requisite majority or of a veto in the Security Council. The Court reached this decision by a majority of twelve votes to two. The Court summarily rejected challenges to its jurisdiction, similar to those which had been advanced in the first *Admission* case. [3]

There has been some criticism of the General Assembly in putting the question to the Court, on the ground that it did not raise a difficult point of law. That criticism is not justified. The putting of the question to the Court resulted from political considerations, and not from the difficulties of the legal question. The Court's opinion prevented extravagant claims being put forward in the General Assembly and performed a valuable function in keeping the dispute confined within given limits.

The deadlock over the admission of new members continued until the end of 1955 when the U.S.S.R. and the United States were able to agree between themselves on the means for bringing it to an end. A "package deal" was negotiated, and by a resolution of 14 December 1955, sixteen new members were admitted. The advisory opinion of 1948 had been interpreted as excluding a package deal of this sort, and many people consider that the manner in which the problem was ultimately resolved was not in conformity with the legal interpretation of the Charter given by the Court. On the other hand, there was a general relief that a solution had at last been found, and there is no serious disposition now to query its legality.

REPARATION FOR THE UNITED NATIONS

Following the assassination of Count Bernadotte, the United Nations Mediator in Palestine, in Israel, and the killing of other United Nations agents in Jordan and Egypt in the latter part of 1948, the question arose whether the United Nations could claim from the responsible governments reparation for the injuries it had suffered, and the General Assembly decided at the end of 1948 to refer a series of complicated legal questions to the Court for its opinion. The advisory opinion of 11 April 1949 is one of the Court's major opinions. In it the Court held that the United Nations has the capacity to bring an international claim against the responsible *de jure* or *de facto* government of a member or non-member State with a view to obtaining the reparation due in respect of the damage caused to the United Nations in the event of an agent of the United Nations, in the performance of his duties, suffering injuries in circumstances involving the responsibility of that State. The opinion also indicated how to reconcile claims brought on behalf of the United Nations itself and those brought on behalf of other States injured by the acts, and mentioned the safeguards necessary to protect a respondent State against the possibility that it would have to pay double damages. [4]

On the basis of that opinion, the Secretary-General made proposals for the method by which the United Nations would claim the reparation due, and after approval by the General Assembly, proceeded to present the claims against the responsible governments. None of the respondent governments contested the right of the United Nations to present these claims, although only the Government of Israel paid the damages claimed, the others contesting the basis on which they had been calculated.

FISHING IN THE NORTH SEA

On 28 September 1949 the United Kingdom filed an application instituting proceedings against Norway, on the basis of the compulsory jurisdiction, the subject of the proceedings being the validity or otherwise, under international law, of the Norwegian system of delimitation of a Norwegian fisheries zone by a Decree of 1935. Although disputes between British and Norwegian fishermen had prevailed in one form or another for several centuries, it was only since the beginning of the twentieth century, with the introduction of modern methods of fishing and the increasing economic pressures on the world's fish stocks, that Norway began to take more stringent measures to protect its own fisheries interests in the sea areas adjacent to its coast. After the decree of 1935 the dispute became more acute and there was talk of referring it to the Permanent Court, but those negotiations had not been completed when the Second World War broke out. After the War, the danger of depletion of the fish stocks through over-fishing had brought to a head a number of fishing disputes, in both the North Sea and the North Atlantic, and in other parts of the world. Indeed, these disputes have become one of the major concrete international issues now pending, although the United Nations has only been obliquely concerned with them. The *Fisheries* case was therefore partly a test-case on a matter of great and general international interest.

Before the Norwegian Decree of 1935, it had been generally believed that the base-line from which the strip of territorial sea (over which the coastal State has exclusive fishing rights) is measured is the low-tide line on the coast, with a number of special rules for dealing with bays, gulfs, estuaries and other indentations: and in such cases, if artificial base-lines should be drawn, they should be based on points on the mainland and as far as possible follow the sinuosities of the coast, even if the coast is deeply indented by fjords and lochs, as is the coast of Norway. The Decree of 1935, however, proceeded on a different principle. It laid down a series of base-points, 48 in all, many of them not being points on continental Norway at all but on rocks out at sea and visible at low tide (drying rocks, or low-tide elevations). The total length of these lines, which did not follow the sinuosities of the coast but at most its general direction, was some 600 miles. From these base-lines an exclusive fishing zone of four miles in width is claimed. This decree affected some 6,900 square kilometres of sea, in which are found important stocks of cod, saithe, haddock, halibut, plaice, herring, mackerel, seal and some types of whale.

The case was introduced in form unilaterally by the United Kingdom. But it appears that although the parties were unable to draw up a special agreement, there was diplomatic agreement to refer the dispute to the Court in this way, and the proceedings took their course without any complications. On 18 December 1951 the Court rendered its judgment in which, by ten votes to two, it upheld the Norwegian contentions. [5]

This is commonly regarded as one of the most important judgments rendered by the present Court. The issues far transcended the bipartite dispute of which the Court was seised, for since the end of the Second World War, as stated, questions of fishing rights have become a major international issue, and the implications of a judgment admitting that the new conception of base-lines on this extended scale was not contrary to international law, and even more so the reasons adopted by the Court, were general. In 1950 the General Assembly had decided to take up the whole question of the codification of the law of the sea, and the first phases of the work were entrusted to the International Law Commission. It soon became clear that the question of generalizing the rules applied by the Court in the *Fisheries* case for the delimitation of base-lines, and those applied earlier in the *Corfu Channel* case relating to the right of innocent passage through the territorial sea in general

and through straits serving international navigation in particular, would encounter major political difficulties. In the end, the United Nations
Conference on the Law of the Sea, which was in session for two months in
Geneva in the spring of 1958, succeeded in achieving agreement on these vital
aspects. [6] There can be little doubt that but for the Court's decision in 1951,
the Conference would not have been able to complete its work. The Court, in
deciding the concrete case, had expounded the principles which were applicable. Those principles were then taken up first by the International Law
Commission (with political guidance from the General Assembly and from
individual governments), and in that way generalized, and later finally approved, on the political level, by the 1958 Conference. Here is an important
instance of the manner in which the Court, by its decision on a concrete
dispute, makes a significant contribution to the develoment of international
law, which itself is the basis for the prevention, or the settlement, of other
international disputes.

To remove all doubt, it should be stated that the Court was not asked to
decide, in 1951, what is the breadth of the territorial sea recognized by
international law. That was not in issue in 1951. The sole question was the
manner in which the inner, or landward, limit of the area of territorial sea
may be fixed in cases where the coast-line presents the special features of the
coast of Norway.

For a later case about the North Sea, see p. 158 below, and for cases about
fisheries, see p. 160 below.

For a later case about the North Sea, see p. 158 below, and for cases about
fisheries, see p. 160 below.

FRENCH NATIONALS IN EGYPT

In October, 1949, France filed an application against Egypt, based on the
Montreux Convention of 1937 for the abrogation of the Capitulations, asking
for compensation for the damage suffered by a number of French nationals
and protected persons, in their persons, property, rights and interests, as a
result of measures taken by the Egyptian Government in May, 1948, in
connection with the hostilities which broke out on the termination of the
Mandate for Palestine. The proceedings were instituted after fifteen months
of diplomatic negotiations had been in vain. In February, 1950, the op-
pressive measures were lifted. In those circumstances the proceedings were
discontinued. [7]

A CASE OF DIPLOMATIC ASYLUM

On 3 October 1948 an unsuccessful military rebellion broke out in Peru at
the instigation of a political party led by the well-known Peruvian politician
Señor Victor Raúl Haya de la Torre. Judicial proceedings were thereupon

opened against him, but he managed to evade arrest, and on 3 January 1949 sought, and was granted, political asylum in the Colombian Embassy in Lima, on the basis of certain Latin American customs and conventions regulating diplomatic asylum. The next day, the Colombian Ambassador made the usual demand for a safe-conduct so that he could leave the country. This was refused on the ground that he was not charged with political offences, and a dispute ensued between the two countries. On 31 August 1949 they concluded an agreement, called the Act of Lima, to refer the dispute to the Court, but being unable to determine the terms of the reference, agreed that either party might institute the proceedings unilaterally without that being regarded as an unfriendly act towards the other. On 15 October, Colombia, on the basis of the Act of Lima, filed an application instituting the proceedings, in the course of which the Court was to render three judgments in what became technically three separate cases.

In the application the Court was asked to decide, on the basis of the various legal rules binding the parties, whether Colombia was legally entitled, for the purpose of granting the asylum, to qualify the offence as a political offence and not as an ordinary offence (for which no asylum should be granted), and whether Peru as the territorial State was bound to give the necessary safe-conduct to enable Sr. Haya de la Torre to leave the country. In the course of the proceedings, Peru submitted a counter-claim, asking the Court to declare that the grant of asylum was in violation of the Havana Covention on Asylum of 1928. In the judgment of 20 November 1950, the Court found that Colombia was not entitled unilaterally, and in a manner binding on Peru, to qualify the nature of the offence, and accordingly it rejected the Colombian demand that Peru must give the necessary safe-conduct. On the other hand, while partly rejecting the Peruvian counter-claim, it nevertheless found that the grant of asylum was not made in conformity with the Havana Convention.[8]

This judgment left things as they were. This was not the fault of the Court, but was the consequence of the manner in which the case was presented. The agreement in principle to refer the dispute to the Court did not, apparently, go so far as to include any underlying agreement about the real issues on which the Court's decision could lay the basis for the political settlement. On 20 November, the day on which the judgment was delivered, Colombia filed an application for interpretation. The purpose of this was to obtain a decision from the Court on the manner of the termination of Sr. Haya de la Torre's continued enforced residence in the Colombian Embassy in Lima. In a judgment of 27 November 1950 the Court declared the request for interpretation to be inadmissible on the grounds that no dispute as to the meaning and scope of the judgment had been disclosed, and that new questions were raised, and not questions of the meaning of statements appearing in the judgment.[9]

The next day, Peru demanded the surrender of the refugee on the basis of the judgment of 20 November, and Colombia refused on the ground that neither of the judgments had dealt with the question of the surrender. This gave rise to a new dispute between the parties, and on 13 December 1950 Colombia filed a further application asking whether or not Colombia was bound to deliver Sr. Haya de la Torre to Peru. Jurisdiction was based on the Treaty of Friendship between the two countries of 24 May 1934. Colombia was willing to have a decision by the Court *ex aequo et bono* (see p. 114 above), but Peru did not agree to this course. On 13 March 1951 Cuba, as party to the Havana Convention of 1928 the construction of which was again in question, intervened, but the admissibility of the intervention was contested.

By a judgment of 13 June 1951, Cuba's intervention was first admitted, limited, however, to the new questions that had arisen, and not covering the interpretation of the Havana Convention which had been given in the first judgment. On the merits, the Court found that it was unable to give effect to submissions of both parties asking it to declare how the judgment of 20 November should be executed, on the ground that this was a submission couched in an interrogative form which implied a political choice which only the parties were in a position to appreciate. It was not part of the Court's judicial function to make such a choice. It went on to find that Colombia was not obliged to surrender the refugee to Peru, and that the asylum itself ought to have ceased after the judgment of 20 November. [10]

This had cleared up one point, but still left outstanding the major issue of how to bring the asylum to an end. This aspect reverted to the diplomatic channel. The reason for this again was the fact that the parties had been unable to agree what was the dispute to be referred to the Court. The Court, for its part, and consistent with its usual caution, did not feel itself empowered to do any more than declare the legal position between the parties. The Court nevertheless expressed the hope that after their mutual relations been made clear the parties would be able to find a practical and satisfactory solution by seeking guidance from those considerations of courtesy and good-neighbourliness which, in matters of asylum, have always held a prominent place in the relations between the Latin-American republics. Over three more years were to elapse before Sr. Haya de la Torre was able to leave the Colombian Embassy, and the virtual stage of siege under which it had been placed was lifted.

QUESTIONS OF HUMAN RIGHTS IN CERTAIN PEACE TREATIES

Starting in 1948 the General Assembly had been discussing the observance of the human rights clauses of the Peace Treaties with Bulgaria, Hungary and Romania, which were being accused of grave violations of those provisions. The Peace Treaties each contained a clause for the settlement of disputes which provided, among other things, for the reference of a dispute to a three-man Commission of which the third member should be appointed by the Secretary-General of the United Nations in the event of disagreement. Attempts to refer the disputes to the Commissions having failed, owing to the refusal of Bulgaria, Hungary and Romania to appoint their commissioners, the question arose in 1949 whether the Secretary-General could make the third appointment. In October, 1949, the General Assembly decided to ask for advisory opinions on four legal questions: *(a)* Was the existence of disputes disclosed by the diplomatic correspondence? *(b)* If so, did the provisions of the Peace Treaties for the settlement of disputes come into operation? If the answer to those questions was in the affirmative, and if, after a delay of one month, the national commissioners had not been appointed, *(c)* was the Secretary-General authorized to proceed to the appointment of the "third" commissioner; and *(d)* if so, would such a Commission be competent? The General Assembly had adopted this resolution by forty-seven votes to five, with seven abstentions.

In its first advisory opinion of 30 March 1950 the Court answered the first two questions in the affirmative, each time by a vote of eleven to three. In its second opinion of 18 July, by eleven votes to two it answered the third question in the negative, and therefore did not consider the fourth question. [11]

As in the previous advisory opinions which originated in Cold War issues, here, too, the competence of the Court was challenged, on the ground, essentially, that if there were concrete disputes, the invocation of the advisory procedure was in fact an attempt surreptitiously to introduce a form of contentious case, and the Court was not authorized to deal with such a case in the absence of the consent of all the parties. The Court rejected these contentions in the present case. Its principal reason was that the advisory opinion as such was not binding, representing the participation of the Court in the work of the United Nations. The object of the request for the advisory opinion was to obtain enlightenment for the General Assembly, and in the present circumstances the advisory opinion would not be substantially equivalent to deciding the questions in dispute between the parties.

The General Assembly had no alternative but to take note of the two advisory opinions, and in effect dropped the matter. [12]

As in a previous case, it may be considered that here too the questions put to the Court were on the whole not difficult from the legal point of view. The disputes were rooted in a more intractable political situation which all the organs of the United Nations were unable to solve. The real significance of this experience was that it showed once and for all that the Soviet Union and its Allies were not prepared to enable the advisory procedure to be employed to handle disputes relating to the Cold War.

SOUTH-WEST AFRICA AND NAMIBIA

Questions relating to the Mandates system established by virtue of Article 22 of the Covenant of the League of Nations came before the Permanent Court in one instance only—the *Mavrommatis Palestine Concessions*—and although the Mandates system did not survive the liquidation of the League, being replaced by the International Trusteeship System set forth in Articles 75-91 of the Charter, the new Court has had before it no less than five cases to do with the legal status of the former mandated territory of South-West Africa (now known as Namibia). [13]

On 17 December 1920 the League Council conferred this Mandate on South Africa and confirmed its terms. It was what was called a "C" class Mandate, under which the mandatory had full powers of administration and legislation over the territory as an integral portion of its own territory, subject to a number of obligations, and the League was to supervise the administration and see to it that the obligations were fulfilled. Difficulties over the interpretation and application of the Mandate had appeared already in the days of the League, but they only came to a head in the United Nations, when South Africa refused to convert the Mandate into a Trusteeship agreement, despite repeated urgings by the General Assembly. In 1949 the General Assembly decided that for its further consideration of the question, the Court's opinion on a number of legal questions was desirable. On 11 July 1950 the Court gave an opinion on five questions. It found that the Mandate was still in force and that the obligations arising thereunder were still binding on South Africa; that under the Charter the territory could be placed under the Trusteeship system but that there was no legal obligation on South Africa to do so; and that South Africa, acting alone, does not have the competence to modify the international status of the territory, but that modifications in its international status could only be made with the consent of the United Nations. [14] The competence of the Court to give this opinion was not challenged.

The General Assembly then adopted the advisory opinion and commenced a long series of efforts to implement it. In the course of these efforts further questions arose of the meaning of certain passages on the 1950 Opinion in which the Court had stated that the degree of supervision over the territory by the General Assembly should not exceed that which had previously been applied by the League and should conform as far as possible to the procedure of the League Council. On that basis the General Assembly had established the Committee on South-West Africa, broadly analogous to the Permanent Mandates Commission of the Council of the League. South Africa refused to co-operate with this Committee and to submit the annual reports which had been required by the League. This deprived the Committee of information necessary to enable it to discharge its functions. Other difficulties had arisen, because it was contended that the substitution in the United Nations of the two-thirds majority for the unanimity previously current in the League implied an increase in the degree of supervision, against which the Court in 1950 had uttered a warning. In 1954 the General Assembly therefore decided to ask the Court for an advisory opinion on that question—which the Court, in its Opinion of 7 June 1955, answered in the negative. [15]

After accepting this opinion the General Assembly continued its efforts, and the next year found it necessary to ask the Court whether it would be consistent with the 1950 opinion for it to authorize the Committee on South-West Africa to grant oral hearings to petitioners (under the original Mandates system, petitioners could only submit their petitions in writing, and the question was whether oral petitions would constitute an excess in the degree of supervision). The underlying purpose in granting oral hearings was to supplement the Committee's information on the situation on South-West Africa. In its opinion of 1 June 1956 the Court answered the question put to it in the affirmative. [16]

These opinions had certainly gone a long way towards clarifying the legal situation, but being advisory opinions these were not technically binding on South Africa. The political conflict between the majority in the General Assembly and the Union started to grow sharper. At its eleventh session (1956) the General Assembly decided to look for new ways to ensure that South Africa fulfil the obligations incumbent on it under the Mandate, and after detailed consideration of this aspect, in 1959, it drew the attention of member States to the possibility of their bringing a contentious case against the Union, based on the submission to the jurisdiction contained in the Mandate. [17] The question was then discussed at the Second African States Conference held at Addis Ababa in June, 1960, at which Ethiopia and Liberia announced their intention of initiating contentious proceedings, as recommended. The Conference established a steering committee of four African States, including Ethiopia and Liberia, to determine the procedure and tactics incident to the conduct of the case.

In November, 1960, two contentious cases were accordingly instituted, by Ethiopia and Liberia respectively, against South Africa, jurisdiction being based upon the compromissory clause contained in the Mandate instrument. This action met with strong approval by the General Assembly, which also refused to see in the subsistence of the contentious proceedings at The Hague any reason to cause it to refrain from exercising its own responsibilities for the supervision of South-West Africa, as defined in the previous three advisory opinions of the Court.

The contentious cases were to give rise to one of the most complicated and, in the view of many, frustrating pieces of litigation ever decided by any international tribunal.

After the two memorials were filed (in substantially identical terms) the Court noted that the two applicant governments were "in the same interest" before the Court. It therefore joined the two proceedings. [18] The immediate consequences were that the two applicant governments were to act in concert to choose a single judge *ad hoc*, and that joint pleadings were filed in the subsequent phases.

In due course South Africa filed a series of preliminary objections. The first objection was to the effect that the Mandate itself had not survived the dissolution of the League of Nations and was no longer in force, and at any event its compromissory clause was no longer in force. The second, which was related, argued that since the compromissory clause conferred jurisdiction in respect to another member of the League of Nations, with the dissolution of the League the two applicant States lost that quality. The third objection consisted of the proposition that the dispute brought before the Court was not a dispute as envisaged in the compromissory clause since it did not affect any material interests of the applicant States or their nationals. The fourth was to the effect that if the dispute was one which came within the scope of the compromissory clause, it was not one which could not be settled by negotiation with the applicants, and that there had been no such negotiations with a view to its settlement. After heavy pleading the Court, in its judgment of 21 December 1962, by eight votes to seven found that it had jurisdiction to adjudicate upon the merits. [19]

The first two objections to a large extent raised issues which the Court had previously considered in its advisory cases, especially the principal one of 1950. The third and fourth, however, broke new ground. The third objection, in particular, raised fundamental issues of the kind of rights which can be protected by the international judicial process. As will be seen, it was on this issue that the contentious proceedings were ultimately to come to grief.

The case continued, therefore, in accordance with the normal procedure, and after extremely heavy pleading became ready for hearing on 23 December 1964. The hearings commenced in March 1965. At their commencement, South Africa made an application relating to the composition of the Court for the purposes of the case. A closed hearing took place, after which the Court decided not to accede to that application. [20] No details of this step have been officially published, and it is believed that the motion related to one or more of the judges who, previously to their election, had been responsible members of their countries' delegations at the General Assembly of the

United Nations when the South West Africa issue had been discussed.

Hearings lasted from March to November 1965, with a break for the summer vacation. In the course of these hearings, South Africa proposed that the Court should carry out an inspection *in loco* in South West Africa, and that it should also visit South Africa, Ethiopia, Liberia and one or two other countries of the Court's own choosing south of the Sahara. In an order of 29 November 1965 the Court, by eight votes to six, decided not to visit South West Africa and South Africa, and by nine votes to five it decided not to visit the applicant States and sub-Saharan African countries. [21]

Fourteen witnesses and experts were called by South Africa and subjected to examination, cross-examination and re-examination by the parties, and to questions put by members of the Court.

The complicated submissions by Ethiopia and Liberia covered all of the grievances of the African States against South Africa. They seem to have had two major ends in view—a pronouncement by the Court to the effect that the policy of *apartheid* is contrary to international law, and that the breaches of the Mandate perpetrated by South Africa must be remedied. For its part South Africa contended that the Mandate was no longer in force, and in the alternative that it was not in breach of any of its provisions.

On both sides, then, the submissions were directed to the merits of the dispute. The Court, however, found that there was one matter which appertained to the merits but which had an antecedent character, namely the question of the applicants' standing in the present phase of the proceedings, which it defined as their legal right or interest regarding the subject-matter of the claim as set out in their final submissions. On this the Court found that the applicants could not be considered to have established any legal right or interest appertaining to them in the subject-matter of the present claims, and accordingly, by the President's casting vote—the votes being equally divided—it decided to reject the claims. [22]

The explanation of this apparent reversal of the 1962 decision is that there the Court was solely concerned with the question of *jurisdiction*, while here the issue was the applicants' entitlement to bring the claim over which, in other respects, the Court would have jurisdiction.

Needless to say, this surprising result, reached after such prolonged proceedings, caused something of a shock, and the General Assembly, in its resolution 2145 (XXI) of 27 October 1966, decided that the Mandate for South West Africa was terminated and assumed direct responsibility for the Territory until its independence. It took various dispositions, designed to persuade South Africa to withdraw from the territory, but these were to no avail.

Early in 1968 the question of South West Africa was brought to the Security Council by the African States. On 25 January 1968 the Security Council adopted resolution 245 (1968) in which it backed the General

Assembly's 1966 decision. This was followed by resolution 246 (1968) of 14 March, censuring South Africa for its refusal to abide by the earlier resolutions. Further resolutions were adopted in 1969, and on 30 January 1970, in resolution 276 (1970), the Security Council established an *ad hoc* subcommittee to study ways and means for the effective implementation of the Council's resolutions. One of the recommendations of this subcommittee was for a further advisory opinion to be requested of the Court, and on 29 July 1970, in resolution 284 (1970), the Security Council decided to ask the Court what were the legal consequences for States of the continued presence of South Africa in Namibia notwithstanding Security Council resolution 276 (1970). The Court was asked to transmit its opinion to the Security Council at an early date. That resolution was adopted by twelve votes to none, Poland, the U.S.S.R. and the United Kingdom abstaining.

A large number of written statements were filed by the end of November, but before the public hearings could commence, a series of questions relating to the composition of the Court had to be solved. South Africa objected to the presence of three judges on the Court. In respect of two of these, the President Sir Muhammad Zafrulla Khan and Judge Padilla Nervo the Court was unanimous in rejecting the objection. In the third case, relating to Judge Morozov, the Court reached a similar decision by ten votes to four. These objections all related to previous activities by the members concerned in their national delegations in the General Assembly. In the third case, the member concerned had also been one of his country's representatives at the Security Council when the relevant resolutions had been adopted. In addition, the South African government applied for the appointment of a judge *ad hoc*. In a closed hearing (the record of which was subsequently made public) the application was heard, to be rejected by ten votes to five. [23]

Hearings lasted for six weeks in February and March, 1971. During the course of these South Africa requested that a plebiscite be held in the territory under the joint supervision of the Court and South Africa, and that South Africa should be permitted to adduce a considerable amount of evidence on factual issues. In May the Court announced its negative decision on these requests.

The advisory opinion was delivered on 21 June 1971. After explaining its reasons for its decisions on the composition of the Court it proceeded to reject a series of objections by South Africa to the giving of the opinion. It then turned to the substance of the matter, to a large extent covering ground previously traversed in the earlier opinions and judgments. By thirteen votes to two the Court found that the continued presence of South Africa in Namibia being illegal, South Africa is under obligation to withdraw its administration from Namibia immediately and thus put an end to its occupation of the territory. By eleven votes to four the Court indicated that States members of the United Nations are under obligation to recognize the illegality of South Africa's presence in Namibia and the invalidity of its acts on behalf of or concerning Namibia, and to refrain from any such acts and in particular any dealings with the Government of South Africa implying recognition of the legality of, or lending support or assistance to, such presence and administration. It is also incumbent upon States which are not members of the United Nations to give assistance in the action which has been taken by the United Nations with regard to Namibia. [24]

In resolution 301 (1971) of 20 October 1971 the Security Council, by twelve votes to none, with France and the United Kingdom abstaining, *inter alia* took note with appreciation of that opinion and expressed agreement with it. Both the Security Council and the General Assembly are continuing their efforts to find a satisfactory solution to the problem.

This history well illustrates the extraordinary complications which beset a dispute, in which there are important legal elements, between the majority of the United Nations, in the Security Council and in the General Assembly, and a member State. It also demonstrates the inherent limitations of the judicial process, especially the advisory competence, as an effective instrument for the resolution of these problems in the absence of the real consent of the parties concerned—the somewhat abstract and generalized consent to the functioning of the Court implicit in the bare fact of membership in the United Nations being insufficient as consent to the exercise of the judicial function in a concrete case. The purpose underlying the recourse to the contentious procedure in 1960 was to eradicate the ambiguity which is characteristic of the formally non-binding quality of the advisory opinions, and to obtain a binding decision on broadly similar grounds in the form of a judgment which could be brought before the Security Council for "execution".

The inability of the Court to meet this problem is due above all to institutional causes and the fragile basis on which modern international litigation rests. This, and the legalistic nature if not pure sophistry which many purport to see in some of the Court's pronouncements, have in their turn given rise to profound disappointment and misgivings. These reactions are not limited to the African States immediately concerned. With the 1966 judgment, the standing of the Court fell to its lowest point. It is significant that the profound changes in the composition of the Court, bringing it into line with the composition of the Security Council, were felt after that date, and that the Court itself, after the elections of 1966, took in hand a re-examination of its internal practices, leading firstly to the 1968 resolution on its internal judicial practice (see p. 103 above) and later to the 1972 revision of the Rules of Court (see p. 23 above). It is also since 1966 that the anxious political and professional review of the role of the Court has been initiated, in both political and academic circles.

RIGHTS OF U.S. NATIONALS IN (FRENCH) MOROCCO

On 28 October 1950 France instituted proceedings against the United States, on the basis of the compulsory jurisdiction, asking for a definition of the rights of United States nationals in Morocco. The dispute originated in measures of currency control and control of imports introduced in 1948, but it also raised complicated questions concerning the extent to which United States citizens enjoyed rights of exterritoriality under the system of capitulations, and the method of evaluating imports for customs purposes under the so-called Act of Algeciras of 1906, and a number of related topics. The United States made a formal reservation about the applicability of the compulsory jurisdiction in this case, but nevertheless agreed to the questions being decided by the Court. The United States also raised a technical objection designed to ascertain whether the judgment would be binding not only on France but also on Morocco, and when this point was cleared up, the objection was withdrawn. In a long and complicated judgment of 27 July 1952, the Court gave its decision on the various issues presented to it. [25]

RESERVATIONS TO INTERNATIONAL TREATIES

The Convention on the Prevention and Punishment of the Crime of Genocide which was signed on 9 December 1948 provided that it would come into force after twenty States had become parties to it. On the eve of the fifth session of the General Assembly in 1950 the Secretary-General was confronted with a novel problem: the number of States parties to the Convention was growing, but some of these had appended reservations to which other States had entered objections, and it seemed likely that he would run into difficulties in deciding whether in those circumstances the reserving States could be included in the twenty necessary to bring the Convention into force. On that basis he asked the General Assembly for directions. For practical purposes his difficulties were overcome on 14 October 1950 when five States ratified the Convention, bringing the total number up to twenty-four. Only two of these were affected by reservations, so there was no difficulty in determining the entry into force of the Convention. However the incident had disclosed great differences of opinion among the members about the applicable rules of law in circumstances such as these (which are fairly common), and it was decided to take the opinion of the Court on the basic question whether a reserving State could be regarded as being a party to the Convention if some of the other parties object to the reservation, but not others. Although the immediate problem of the Genocide Convention was therefore to some extent solved in fact, the questions were asked in relation to that Convention in order to enable the Court to consider the problems against a concrete background, and not entirely in the abstract. For the Court this became a normal question of treaty interpretation, of ascertaining the underlying intentions of the draftsmen, even though the issues involved were entirely novel. On 28 May 1951 the Court gave its opinion, which is mainly of technical interest to the professional international lawyer, and the General Assembly subsequently gave instructions to the Secretary-General based on the opinion. [26]

The underlying issues of this case, relating to highly technical matters of the law of international treaties, are important for the smooth conduct of international affairs. These issues had greatly troubled the responsible organs of the League of Nations as well as the General Assembly and the International Law Commission of the United Nations. This, indeed, had vacillated in its approach to the matter, between the attitude which was current in the League of Nations and the position adopted by the International Court in this case. Ultimately, that position prevailed, and is adopted, in a refined form, in Articles 19 to 23 of the Vienna Convention of 23 May 1969 on the Law of Treaties. [27]

A GREEK CITIZEN'S CLAIM FOR DAMAGES FOR BREACH OF CONTRACT

In 1919 a Greek shipowner, Nicholas Ambatielos, contracted with the British Government for the purchase of some steamships then abuilding, but the ships were not delivered as soon as anticipated and Mr. Ambatielos became indebted to the British Government for a considerable sum of money, part of which was secured by a mortgage on the ships. In the course of legal proceedings in London in 1920, certain interdepartmental minutes were not produced by the British Government—a fact which later gave rise to a claim by Ambatielos for "denial of justice". Ambatielos lost his case in the Court of Appeal in London, and made no attempt to take it to the House of Lords. Diplomatic correspondence then ensued, and at one time there was talk of referring the dispute to the Permanent Court, but the British Government took the position that there was no international dispute and did not consent to referring the matter to the Permanent Court. Proposals for arbitration were finally rejected by the British Government at the end of 1939. After the War the discussion was resumed, and on 9 April 1951 Greece instituted proceedings against the United Kingdom, basing the jurisdiction on a Treaty of Commerce and Navigation of 1926, which provided for the reference of certain disputes to the Permanent Court. The Court was asked to declare that by virtue of certain agreements between the parties, the United Kingdom was obliged to co-operate with Greece in establishing an Arbitration Commission to determine the merits of the dispute. It will thus be seen that the International Court itself was not asked to determine the merits of this complicated dispute: its task was limited to determining that a dispute existed between the parties for which the proper solution was to be found through a bilateral arbitration process.

The United Kingdom first challenged the jurisdiction of the International Court even for this limited purpose. In its judgment of 1 July 1952 the Court held that it was without jurisdiction to decide on the merits of the Ambatielos claim, but that it did have jurisdiction to decide whether the United Kingdom was under an obligation to submit the claim to arbitration. The issues that arose in this phase of the case were mostly technical issues of international treaty law. In a second judgment of 19 May 1953 the Court found that the United Kingdom was under the obligation to submit the dispute to arbitration. In the third phase of the proceedings before the arbitration commission (containing three "neutral" members), the final award was in favour of the United Kingdom. [28] It will be noted that the role of the International Court here was limited to deciding upon the "arbitrability" of the dispute, and its own jurisdiction to decide that issue. Since the parties had not agreed that it should decide the merits of the dispute, it was extremely careful in both its judgments not to encroach on the jurisdiction of the arbitral commission.

THE ANGLO-IRANIAN OIL CO.

Tension between Iran and the United Kingdom over the affairs of the Anglo-Iranian Oil Company has persisted throughout the present century. The original D'Arcy Concession was granted in 1901, and after the First World War the Iranian Government complained that the Company was not paying sufficient attention to Iran's national interests. In 1932 the dispute reached such a pitch that the United Kingdom Government contemplated referring it to the Permanent Court. In 1933 a new concession agreement was negotiated between Iran and the Company through the Council of the League, to which the United Kingdom had referred the dispute, and in 1949 a supplemental agreement, designed to increase Iran's benefits under the concession, was not ratified by the Iranian Parliament. Matters took a dramatic turn in March, 1951, when the Iranian Parliament enacted legislation, which received the Imperial assent on 1 May, for the nationalization of the oil industry throughout the country. The dispute became serious, and the British Government even started to make preparations for sending its armed forces into Iran in the event of danger to British nationals there. [29] Later, however, the British Government decided to refer the dispute to the Court, which it did by application instituting proceedings filed on 26 May. The application was based on the compulsory jurisdiction, which was said to be applicable by virtue of a somewhat complicated construction given in the document instituting the proceedings.

The filing of this application did not arrest the rapid deterioration in the situation, in the course of which there was a danger that the Company's installations would be damaged. Accordingly, on 22 June 1951 the British Government submitted to the Court an urgent request for an indication of interim measures of protection designed to protect the Company and its installations. The Iranian Government immediately denied that the Court had jurisdiction to deal with this request, and did not appear in the oral proceedings held on 30 June (nor was an Iranian judge *ad hoc* appointed at this stage). On 5 July the Court, being satisfied that it had jurisdiction for this purpose, made an order as requested. [30] This order was not implemented by Iran, and in September the United Kingdom referred to the Security Council the question of its enforcement, with the inconclusive results described earlier (p. 40 above).

In due course, the Iranian Government appointed its agent and also designated a judge *ad hoc*, but instead of pleading to the merits, filed preliminary objections. In a judgment of 22 July 1952 the Court found that it had no jurisdiction on a number of grounds, mostly of a technical character. However, in the course of explaining its reasons, it had to deal with one facet of the dispute which was complicating the legal relations between the parties. As stated, the concession agreement of 1933 had been negotiated between the Iranian Government and the Company through the good offices of the Rapporteur appointed by the Council of the League of Nations, and it was argued that in consequence the concession agreement itself could be regarded as an international convention. The Court decided that question in the negative. [31]

Almost simultaneously with the filing of the British Government's application in this case, the Anglo-Iranian Oil Company applied to the President, asking him to appoint an umpire for the arbitration tribunal between the Company and the Iranian Government, in accordance with a provision in the 1933 concession conferring that power on the President of the *Permanent* Court. The President deferred his decision until after the termination of the British Government's case, and then, in the absence of the necessary consent on the part of the Iranian Government, found that he was not authorized to make the appointment. [32]

WHOSE ARE THE CHANNEL ISLETS: MINQUIERS AND ECREHOS?

On 5 December 1951 the United Kingdom filed the text of a special agreement concluded a year earlier with France by which a dispute over the sovereignty of these two islets lying between Jersey and the French coast was submitted to the Court (see p. 87 above). Underlying this dispute were not only fishing interests of the two countries—for the area contains valuable oyster beds—but also other economic interests including certain French plans to exploit the tides for the purpose of generating electricity. Furthermore, the interested party on the British side was not the United Kingdom itself, but the Island of Jersey, whose parliamentary organization actually approved the submission of the case to the Court, as far back as 1948, after diplomatic negotiations had broken down. The United Kingdom delegation included the Attorney-General of Jersey. On 17 November 1953 the Court gave judgment in favour of the claim of the United Kingdom. [33]

By a separate agreement of 30 January 1951, made independently of the special agreement to submit the case to the Court, the British and French Governments reached accord on the question of the fishing rights without prejudice to the question of sovereignty over the groups. This was an instance of the two parties appearing before the Court "arm-in-arm", in the words of the Attorney-General of the United Kingdom.

A GERMAN NATIONAL CLAIMS RESTORATION OF HIS SEQUESTERED PROPERTY

Herr Friedrich Nottebohm was born at Hamburg in September, 1881, of German nationality. In 1905 he established himself in Guatemala, where he continued to have his fixed abode until 1943 when, Guatemala having declared war on Germany in 1941, he was arrested, deported to the United States, and interned, and his substantial property sequestered under the equivalent of the trading with the enemy legislation. In March, 1939, he paid a visit to Germany, and in October, shortly after the outbreak of the War, he visited Liechtenstein where he applied for, and was granted, Liechtenstein nationality after undertaking to make certain annual payments by way of "naturalization tax". He then applied for a Guatemalan visa on his new passport with which he returned to Guatemala there to resume his business activities. After the War Liechtenstein attempted to recover the sequestered property, and on the failure of the diplomatic negotiations filed an application in Court on 17 December 1951, on the basis of the compulsory jurisdiction. Further negotiations having been unsuccessful, the pleadings commenced. In due course Guatemala filed a preliminary objection to the effect that since Guatemala's acceptance of the compulsory jurisdiction had expired after the institution of the proceedings, the Court no longer had jurisdiction. By a judgment of 18 November 1953 the Court unanimously (there was no judge *ad hoc* for either party in this phase) dismissed the plea, which many lawyers believe to have been unarguable (a rare instance of this). In the next phase of the case, Guatemala contended that the claim was inadmissible on the ground that Liechtenstein was not entitled to rely against Guatemala on the nationality thus conferred for the purposes of exercising its right of diplomatic protection, so as to transform enemy (German) property into neutral property. The Court, in its judgment of 6 April 1955, upheld this contention. [34]

GOLD LOOTED FROM ROME IN 1943

In September, 1943, the Germans looted from a bank in Rome nearly 2,340 kilograms of monetary gold belonging to the National Bank of Albania and transferred it to Germany. The Paris Act on Reparation of 1946 provided that monetary gold found in Germany by the allied forces should be pooled for distribution as restitution proportionately among the countries which had lost gold through looting during the War. Both Italy and Albania were parties to the Paris Act, which established a Tripartite Commission, consisting of the United States, France and the United Kingdom, for the purpose of passing upon claims to a share out of the pool. Both Italy and Albania had claims, and since the Tripartite Commission was unable to solve them the Three Powers decided to submit the question to arbitration. On 20 February 1953 the arbitrator decided that the gold belonged to Albania.

At this point a complication appeared. The gold was in the hands of the Tripartite Commission, and the three Powers had agreed between themselves that if the arbitrator were to decide that the gold was Albanian, they would hand it over to the United Kingdom in partial satisfaction of the unpaid judgment debt in the *Corfu Channel* case, unless within a period of 90 days, either Albania or Italy instituted appropriate proceedings against them in the International Court, and for that purpose they agreed in advance to accept the Court's jurisdiction. Having lost before the arbitrator, the only way by which Italy could protect its claim to the gold was, therefore, by turning to the Hague Court, and on 19 May 1953 the proceedings were instituted against the three Governments. Albania, however, refused either to institute pro- ceedings of its own, or to intervene in the Italian suit, and before filing the memorial the Italian Government asked the Court to decide the preliminary question of whether, in such circumstances, it could exercise jurisdiction. In its judgment of 15 June 1954 the Court answered that question in the nega- tive, on the ground that in the absence of Albania, a directly interested party, it could not decide a case directly involving the international responsibility of Albania. The future of the gold was therefore returned to the diplomatic channel. [35]

The importance of this case is not so much in the pronouncement of the Court, interesting though that is from the legal point of view, as in the action of the three Powers in developing novel procedures for securing satisfaction of a judgment debt previously awarded to one of them by the International Court. This was an instance of the adoption of measures of economic self-help, in which provision was made for the application of judicial controls at the request of interested parties, including possible competitive claimants.

FRANCE'S DIFFICULTIES IN THE LEBANON

On two occasions, in 1953 and again in 1959, France has referred to the Court disputes with the Lebanon arising out of Lebanese attempts to modify concessions agreements with French companies. The first concerned the public services concession of the Electricité de Beyrouth Company, and the second the Compagnie du Port, des Quais et des Entrepôts de Beyrouth and the Société Radio-Orient. In the first case a settlement was reached after the memorial had been filed, and the case was accordingly discontinued. In the second, after the memorial had been filed, preliminary objections were raised and observations thereon filed and that case was ready for hearing. Negotiations for the settlement of the two disputes nevertheless continued outside the Court, and upon being notified the Court placed on record the settlement of the case. [36]

These are instances of the contentious jurisdiction being invoked to bolster up the diplomatic negotiations.

THE ADMINISTRATIVE TRIBUNALS

Three cases involving decisions of the United Nations and the I.L.O. Administrative Tribunals have come before the Court for advisory opinion. The first two had a similar background, namely, the rights of former staff members of the organization concerned, who had been discharged by the organization's administration because of their refusal to answer questions put to them by an investigating committee of the United States Senate relating to membership in the Communist Party or subversive activities in the United States. All the staff members concerned were United States nationals. After their discharge, they sought redress from the appropriate Administrative Tribunal which, in many instances, found that the circumstances of the discharge gave rise to a claim for compensation. The third case constitutes recourse by a staff member who felt that his case had been misjudged by the United Nations Administrative Tribunal.

In the first case, in accordance with normal practice, the Secretary-General had included appropriations in the 1953 budget to meet the compensation thus awarded. His action was challenged on the ground that the General Assembly was entitled to override the decisions of the Administrative Tribunal. The General Assembly thereupon decided to seek an advisory opinion on the legal issues. In its advisory opinion of 13 July 1954, the Court reached the conclusion that the General Assembly had no right on any grounds to refuse to give effect to an award of compensation made by the Administrative Tribunal in favour of a staff member whose contract of service had been terminated without his assent (this unusually broad language simply corresponds to the question as formulated by the General Assembly, and obviously need not be taken literally!). [37]

It was in the light of that advisory opinion that the General Assembly decided to introduce a system of review by the Court of the decisions of the Administrative Tribunals, as has been described earlier (see p. 83 above).

In the second case, the recourse to the Court was initiated in 1955 by the Executive Board of UNESCO which wanted to avail itself of the procedure for review existing under the current rules for the I.L.O. Administrative Tribunal, and challenge decisions of that Tribunal confirming its own jurisdiction. This was the first occasion on which this form of recourse had been employed, and it enabled the Court to indicate the kind of procedure which would be appropriate and how the Court would ensure that it had adequate information to enable it to give its opinion. In its advisory opinion of 23 October 1956, the Court, after first deciding that the exercise of the advisory function in this type of case was compatible with its judicial role, found that the Administrative Tribunal was competent, and that the validity of its decisions in the cases concerned was no longer open to question. [38]

In this case, the important feature is the special procedure which was devised to enable the interested persons, who had already obtained judgments in their favour in the Administrative Tribunal, to present their views to the Court. The Executive Board had decided, when it adopted the request for the advisory opinion, to enable these persons to submit their statements to UNESCO which would annex them to its own statement without comment, and this was done. The Court later decided not to hold oral proceedings, but instead to make provision for a second round of written pleadings, in which both UNESCO and the interested persons were able to comment briefly on the statements made in the first round of statements. The problem which the Court then faced was whether it could give the advisory opinion and remain faithful to the requirements of its judicial character as a Court in which only States can litigate their differences. Without prejudice to its future action, the Court found that in the circumstances it could, and that if there was any inequality between the "parties"—UNESCO on the one hand and the staff members on the other—it was purely nominal and did not affect the exercise by the Court of its judicial functions.

The important consequence of these two opinions has been to safeguard the judicial character of the two Administrative Tribunals, and this, in turn, is an important contribution towards the creation of an independent international civil service on which the effective functioning of the system of international organization depends.

In the third case, instituted in 1972, the appointment of a holder of a fixed-term appointment in the United Nations Secretariat was not renewed. In judgment No. 158 of 28 April 1972 the United Nations Administrative Tribunal made certain awards in his favour. However, the official concerned believed that his case had not fairly or fully examined and passed upon by the Tribunal, so he applied for review of that judgment. The Committee on Applications for Review of Administrative Tribunal Judgments decided to request an advisory opinion on the questions whether the Administrative Tribunal had failed to exercise jurisdiction vested in it and whether it had committed a fundamental error in procedure which had occasioned a failure of justice.

In its advisory opinion of 12 July 1973 the Court first decided to comply with the request for an opinion, and then proceeded to answer in the negative the two questions put to it. [39] The effect of this was to confirm the decision of the Administrative Tribunal.

THE IRON CURTAIN OVERFLOWN (I)—MILITARY AIRCRAFT

It has been seen (p. 70 above) that the procedure of the Court makes it possible for proceedings to be instituted even though there is at the time no basis for the jurisdiction of the Court, the application instituting proceedings containing an invitation to the respondent to confer jurisdiction on the Court to decide that concrete dispute. The first instances of this occurred on 3 March 1954, when the United States filed applications against the U.S.S.R., and Hungary relating to the treatment of aircraft and crew of the United States in Hungary. These applications referred to an incident which had occurred in 1951 when a United States military aircraft had been shot down over Hungary and its crew subjected to treatment which the United States regarded as contrary to international law. Attempts to reach a solution of these differences through the diplomatic channels had been unsuccessful. The respondent governments declined the invitation to adjudicate the dispute, and the Court was left with no alternative but to order the two cases to be removed from the list.

Further incidents of this kind continued, and in September, 1954, the United States asked the Security Council to deal with a situation which it thought could constitute a danger to the maintenance of international peace and security. The debate, in the Council's 679th and 680th meetings on 10 September, was inconclusive, and no resolution was proposed. Since then, the United States has instituted three similar cases against the Soviet Union and one against Czechoslovakia, between 1956 and 1959. In no case has the respondent government consented to confer jurisdiction on the Court, which could therefore take no action except to order the cases to be removed from the list. [40]

THE ANTARCTICA

Similar was the action of the United Kingdom in instituting proceedings against Argentina and Chile on 4 May 1955. In these applications the Court was asked to declare that the sovereignty over the disputed Falkland Islands Territories and other areas of the Antarctic belonged to the United Kingdom and that the claims of Argentina and Chile to those territories were, as against the United Kingdom, invalid. After the proceedings were instituted, the United Kingdom continued to make strenuous efforts to obtain the consent of the respondent governments to litigate the dispute, but finally conceded that the Court did not have jurisdiction, and the cases were accordingly removed from the list. [41]

As in the *Aerial Incident* cases, the effect of this action is to place the claim, and the main grounds on which it is based, on public record. The action of the United Kingdom may be regarded as a diplomatic phase in a dispute which has been in existence for some time.

SOME NORWEGIAN LOANS

The origins of this dispute lie in a flotation of loans by Norway at the turn of the century on various foreign markets, including that of Paris. The bonds contained a "gold clause". During the financial instability of the First World War, and again in the financial crisis of 1931, the convertibility of the notes was suspended, and has remained so. Diplomatic correspondence claiming fulfilment of the gold clause proceeded intermittently since 1925, in the course of which Norway rejected all proposals to submit the dispute to arbitration or adjudication on the ground that the matter came within its exclusive jurisdiction. On 6 July 1955 France instituted proceedings on the basis of the compulsory jurisdiction, and in due course Norway raised four objections to the jurisdiction and to the admissibility of the suit. However, by agreement between the parties, Norway agreed to postpone the decision on these objections until the merits.

The French declaration accepting the jurisdiction had contained a clause (since revoked) by which France excluded from the jurisdiction disputes relating to matters which are essentially within the national jurisdiction as understood by the French Government (see p. 72 above). One of the Norwegian objections was that the loan contracts were governed by domestic law and not by international law, but in the course of pleading that objection the Norwegian Government had sought to rely, in a subsidiary manner, on the subjective element of the French declaration (which Norway was entitled to invoke on the basis of reciprocity), and thus exclude the jurisdiction. In its judgment of 6 July 1957, the Court upheld that contention and found that it was without jurisdiction. [42]

RIGHT OF PASSAGE

This case, which was instituted by application filed by Portugal on 22 December 1955, is discussed in Chapter V.

WHO SHALL APPOINT A GUARDIAN OVER AN INFANT?

This dispute, which did not reflect any political tension between the two countries, had its origins in a family squabble between two branches of a mixed Dutch-Swedish family about the right to appoint a guardian over an infant born in May 1945. The child, who was the issue of a marriage between a Dutchman and a Swedish woman and was of Dutch nationality, had lived all its life in Sweden. After the death of the mother in 1953, the father became guardian by Dutch law, but later a female guardian was appointed by a Dutch civil Court dealing with children. However, about the same time a Swedish Court instituted measures of protective upbringing based on a Swedish Law of 1924 for the protection of children. The Swedish authorities refused to allow the child to be transferred to the Netherlands. The dispute was then taken up through the diplomatic channels, and on 9 July 1957 the Netherlands instituted proceedings against Sweden on the basis of the compulsory jurisdiction. The legal questions at issue related to the Hague Convention of 1902 on the Guardianship of Infants. In its judgment of 28 November 1958 the Court rejected the claim of the Netherlands, and decided to leave the existing arrangements untouched. [43]

The view is occasionally expressed that a case of this nature is somewhat trivial for the International Court. Such opinions must be examined with care. There is no doubt that the dispute raised difficult issues of interpretation of the Guardianship Convention of 1902, and there is no reason why the Court should not be asked to decide them. Although the dispute had no political implications, it should also be remembered that it involved conflicting decisions of the competent judicial authorities of two friendly States, and it seems clear that international legal proceedings are especially appropriate for overcoming that kind of difficulty.

THE INTERHANDEL COMPANY'S ASSETS

In 1942 the United States Government, acting under the Trading with the Enemy Act, vested in itself nearly all the shares of the General Aniline and Film Company, incorporated in the United States, on the ground that in reality they belonged to or were controlled by the I.G. Farbenindustrie of Frankfurt. Until 1940 I.G. Farben certainly controlled General Aniline and Film through a company incorporated in Switzerland, later known as Interhandel, but the Swiss Government alleged that in 1940 Interhandel severed its links with the German Company, so that the General Aniline assets became Swiss, and neutral, and were not enemy property when they were seised. Towards the end of the War property of Germans in Switzerland was blocked as a result of an agreement between Switzerland and the Western Allies, but the Swiss Compensation Office accepted the view that Interhandel was Swiss, and its assets there were not blocked. An agreement of 1946 provided for the unblocking of Swiss assets in the United States, and further discussions ensued regarding the character of Interhandel. No agreement was reached, and in 1948 proceedings were instituted in the United States Courts by Interhandel. One of the obstacles to those proceedings was the refusal of Interhandel to produce certain documents on the ground that their production would be a violation of Swiss law. In the course of the diplomatic correspondence between the two governments, the United States informed Switzerland (prematurely, as it later transpired) that in fact Interhandel had failed in its suit. Accordingly, on 2 October 1957 Switzerland instituted proceedings in reliance on the compulsory jurisdiction, asking for the restoration of Interhandel's assets. The next day Switzerland requested interim measures of protection asking the United States Government to take no steps to part with the property and in particular not to sell the shares which were being claimed as Swiss property. The United States immediately made a determination that the matters referred to came within the domestic jurisdiction of the United States, in accordance with the condition appearing in its acceptance of the compulsory jurisdiction (see p. 72 above).

Oral proceedings on the question of the measures of protection were held on 12 and 14 October 1957, and on 16 November the Court was informed that the Supreme Court had, on the 14th, but many hours after the International Court had terminated its meeting, issued an order readmitting Interhandel into its suit, and the United States informed the Court that it would not be proceeding to the sale of the shares. In those circumstances, and holding that there was no urgency the Court, by an order of 24 October 1957, found that although it had jurisdiction there was no need for it to indicate interim measures of protection.[44]

In due course the United States filed four preliminary objections, three arguing that the Court lacked jurisdiction, and one contending that the suit was inadmissible on the ground that Interhandel had not exhausted the local remedies provided by the law of the United States before Switzerland instituted the proceedings at The Hague. The three objections to the jurisdiction were each dismissed, but the Court, influenced by the fact that the legal proceedings in the United States were continuing, accepted the objection to the admissibility, and the suit was dismissed.[45]

The protracted domestic litigation came to an end in 1965 after proceedings in the United States Court of Appeals and the Supreme Court. Agreement in principle was reached between the principal parties for the settlement of the litigation, the intervention of the courts, however, being still required on certain matters of detail.[46]

THE IRON CURTAIN OVERFLOWN (II)–CIVIL AIRCRAFT

On 27 July 1955 an Israel civil aircraft on a scheduled commercial flight was shot down by the Bulgarian aerial defence service, having inadvertently penetrated into the Bulgarian airspace. All its fifty-eight occupants were killed. The victims were nationals of Israel, Austria, Belgium, Canada, France, Germany, South Africa, Sweden, the United Kingdom and the United States. A few days later the Bulgarian Government announced that its armed forces had shot the aircraft down, those armed forces having acted in haste and without taking all the necessary measures. The Bulgarian Government undertook to identify and punish the culpable persons, and to pay the compensation due. Negotiations and diplomatic correspondence followed in attempts by the various claimant governments to reach a friendly solution, but to no avail. On 16 October 1957, Israel instituted proceedings against Bulgaria with regard to the destruction of this aircraft. On 28 October and on 21 November, the United States and the United Kingdom also instituted proceedings in respect to the damage suffered by their nationals arising out of the destruction of the aircraft. Israel had invoked the compulsory jurisdiction, relying on a Bulgarian declaration of 1921 and the provisions contained in the present Statute for maintaining continuity in the domain of international jurisdiction (see p. 74 above). These were three separate proceedings: although they all arose out of the same incident, the three governments each represented different interests. Israel, in addition to claiming on behalf of its injured nationals, which included both the airline and the Israeli passengers and crew, was also interested in protecting its flag; whereas the other governments were interested in protecting the rights of their injured nationals. As a consequence, the three cases each took a separate course, and never remained in the same procedural stage.

When the time came for Bulgaria to reply to the Israel memorial, that governments filed five preliminary objections, two relating to the jurisdiction and three contesting the admissibility of the claim. One of the objections was that since Bulgaria had become a member of the United Nations and a party to the Statute of the Court ten years after the Charter had come into force (Bulgaria was admitted to the United Nations on 14 December 1955) the clause in the Statute providing for the maintenance in force of declarations accepting the jurisdiction of the Permanent Court did not apply to it. In its judgment of 26 May 1959, the Court upheld that objection to its jurisdiction.[47]

Following that judgment, the United Kingdom, without prejudice to its international claim, decided to discontinue its suit against Bulgaria.[48] The United States, however, on the basis of the rule that the judgment in the Israel case was only binding as between Israel and Bulgaria (see p. 114 above), continued with its case, and in due course Bulgaria filed four preliminary objections, one based on the very ground which the Court had upheld in the Israel case. Another of these objections pleaded, on the basis of reciprocity and following the Court's decision in the *Norwegian Loans* case, that Bulgaria was entitled as against the United States to determine that the matter came within the domestic jurisdiction of Bulgaria, and that the Court had no jurisdiction. The United States was originally prepared to contest this plea, but shortly before the case became ready for hearing had second thoughts, and entered notice of discontinuance.[49]

After further diplomatic negotiations Bulgaria made small payments in respect of the victims of the disaster.

BAERLE-DUC AND BAARLE-NASSAU–BELGIAN OR DUTCH?

On 26 November 1957 a special agreement between the Netherlands and Belgium was filed, asking the Court to decide whether sovereignty over certain parcels of land on the frontier, about 14 hectares (33 acres) in area, belonged to the Dutch Commune of Baarle-Nassau or the Belgian Commune of Baerle-Duc. In a judgment of 20 June 1959, the Court found in favour of Belgium.[50]

Underlying this seemingly insignificant dispute was an important conflict of economic interests which the two governments were unable to resolve themselves. The invocation of the Court procedures opened the way to the settlement.

One of the interesting features of this case was that neither side appointed a judge *ad hoc*, a rare occurrence.

THE FRONTIER BETWEEN HONDURAS AND NICARAGUA

The roots of this dispute go back go back to the distant past—to the period of Spanish rule in South America. In 1906 the King of Spain was asked to arbitrate the differences between the two countries, and in his award he fixed the frontier, for the greater part to the advantage of Honduras. [51] The frontier thus fixed was not delimited, however, and from about 1912 onwards Nicaragua began to challenge the regularity of the arbitration proceedings before the King of Spain and the validity of the arbitral award he had rendered. Various attempts to reach a settlement of this dispute failed, and in 1957 hostilities broke out between the two countries over the disputed territory. This incident was brought before the competent organs of the Organization of American States through the good offices of which the parties, in July 1957, agreed to submit their dispute to the International Court. It was further agreed that Honduras would submit its claim that the arbitral award should be carried out, and that Nicaragua would answer the claim in the normal course. On 1 July 1958 Honduras accordingly instituted the proceedings by application based on the Washington Agreement of 1957. The pleadings in this case were heavy, but proceeded without complication, and judgment was given on 18 November 1960. The Court was virtually unanimous in deciding that the award of the King of Spain was valid and binding, and that Nicaragua was under an obligation to give effect to it.

Both sides appointed a judge *ad hoc*, but neither of them was a national of the country by which he was chosen. One of the judges *ad hoc* was not even a national of any of the Latin American States.

After this judgment, negotiations proceeded between the parties. These related to the demarcation of the new frontier and the transfer of the population of the ceded territories. It was found that parts of the original award were obscure, and Nicaragua, the judgment debtor, referred the matter to the Inter-American Peace Committee. A Mixed Commission was set up, and its neutral chairman was granted certain powers of decision. He gave a reasoned decision on 5 August 1961 on the outstanding matters, after which the dispute was settled. [53]

The interesting feature of this case is the interplay of a regional international organization—the Organization of American States and its various bodies—and the International Court of Justice in the settlement of a grave dispute which had led to acts of hostility. The organization deployed its efforts first to bring the acts of hostility to an end, then to persuade the parties to submit their differences to the International Court, and then to assist them in executing the decisions binding upon them with the force of *res judicata.*

THE AFFAIRS OF THE BARCELONA TRACTION,
LIGHT AND POWER COMPANY

The above company was established in Toronto in 1911, but for the last twenty-five years most of its shares have been in Belgian hands. The Belgian Government alleged that it had been subjected to a variety of vexatious measures at the hands of the Spanish authorities, and was subsequently, in 1948, adjudicated bankrupt in Spain, and that in the measures of liquidation it was despoiled of its assets which were transferred to a Spanish group. On 23 September 1958 Belgium instituted proceedings against Spain, founding jurisdiction on the Treaty of Conciliation, Judicial Settlement and Arbitration between the two countries of 19 July 1927. In that application, Belgium asked for the restoration of the despoiled assets or alternatively for compensation for damage allegedly caused to the Company on account of acts said to be contrary to international law committed by organs of the Spanish State. After the memorial was filed Spain raised three preliminary objections. However, negotiations between the private interests concerned continued, and as part of those negotiations, and at the request of the private interests, the Belgian Government served notice of discontinuance of those proceedings, to which Spain agreed. [54] The negotiations led to no result, and in 1962 Belgium filed a new application instituting proceedings against Spain claiming reparation for the damage allegedly sustained by Belgian nationals, shareholders in the Company, on account of acts said to be contrary to international law committed in respect of the company by organs of the Spanish State. The amount of compensation claimed was of the order of $ 78,000,000 plus costs and interest, being the equivalent of 88% of the assets of the despoiled company. The impugned acts of the Spanish State come within the general rubric of "denial of justice" as a ground for a diplomatic claim put forward by a State in exercise of its right of diplomatic protection of its nationals abroad.

Against this new application Spain filed four preliminary objections, of which the first was new, and the remainder adaptations of those raised in the first case. The first objection to the jurisdiction was to the effect that the discontinuance of the first proceedings precluded the renewal of the case later. The second was to the effect that the compromissory clause on which the jurisdiction was based, namely the 1927 Treaty, had lapsed on the dissolution of the Permanent Court, Article 37 of the Statute notwithstanding. The third was an objection to the admissibility and really embraced the nub of the case. It was to the effect that Belgium was not entitled to exercise its right of diplomatic protection in favour of Belgian nationals who held shares in a Canadian registered commercial corporation. The fourth, also an objection to the admissibility, and also raising issues central to the whole dispute on the diplomatic level, was to the effect that the application to the Court was premature having regard to the well-known rule of international law requiring exhaustion of the local remedies before an international claim for denial of justice can be brought. The issues involved in the third objection had been thoroughly discussed in the diplomatic phase prior to the institution of the first proceedings, and Belgium had even intimated willingness for the Court to decide the point. No agreement had been reached, however, on submitting the dispute to the Court and, as stated, it was submitted unilaterally and without any agreement by Spain.

In its judgment of 24 July 1964 the Court dismissed the first two objections, but with a somewhat narrower majority decided to join the third and fourth to the merits; on the ground that they could not be decided at that stage until all the facts on the merits had been placed before the Court. Strenuous written and oral pleading followed (no less than 64 public hearings were held in this phase between April and July 1969, and the Court required the best part of six months to frame its judgment), and in its judgment of 5 February 1970 (delivered on the eve of the expiry of the term of office of the judges not re-elected in the election of 1969) the Court found that the Belgian Government had no *locus standi* in this case, and therefore rejected the claim.[55]

This case, coming relatively soon after the 1966 South West Africa judgment (where too the Court had decided the case on "antecedent" grounds related to the *locus standi* of the applicants), gave rise to similar misgivings, in both political and professional circles. It was widely felt that the particular issue was a question of law which could and should have been decided in the first phase. Criticism was also levelled at the prolixity of the pleadings, both written and oral: it was widely felt that the Court should have exercised more control over them. Another ground of reserve was that by joining the question of the *locus standi* of Belgium to the merits after it had been fully pleaded as a question of law in 1964, the parties had been put to much unnecessary expense. Not all this criticism is justified, and the fact that Spain had raised no less than four preliminary objections, and had fought them with tenacity, was a signal for caution. Nevertheless, there is no doubt that some of the revisions of the Rules of Court of 1972 designed to reduce the cost of international litigation and to reduce its delays were inspired by the experience of this case.

THE MARITIME SAFETY COMMITTEE

The Constitution of the Intergovernmental Maritime Consultative Organization establishes as one of the main organs of the Organization the Maritime Safety Committee. Among the members of the Organization to be represented on it are the eight largest ship-owning nations. At the first meeting of the

IMCO Assembly in 1959 the question of the meaning of that phrase arose—whether it meant the nations possessing the largest amount of registered tonnage or those beneficially owning the largest amount of tonnage. Beneath this formal dispute lay the vexed question of "flags of convenience", i.e. the registration of ships in a foreign country, usually for purposes of tax relief or for other reasons. If the first interpretation were adopted, Liberia and Panama, under whose flags over ten million and over four millions of tons of merchant shipping respectively are registered, would be entitled to be members of the Maritime Safety Committee. In the elections held in January, 1959, neither of those countries had been elected to the Committee, but at the same time the Assembly, recognizing that differences of opinion had arisen regarding the correct interpretation of the Constitution, decided to request an advisory opinion. In its opinion of 8 June 1960 the Court held that the Committee had not been properly constituted, and that as the proper criterion was registered tonnage, Liberia and Panama were entitled to be elected. [56] During the proceedings Liberia had agreed that if the Court should make such a finding, it would nevertheless raise no question as to the validity of the work of the Committee during the period prior to the date on which Liberia should become a member. Following the advisory opinion the IMCO Assembly decided to dissolve the Committee as previously elected, and to constitute a new one in accordance with the Court's interpretation of the constitution.

The significance of this case is that it is the first instance in which the International Court has held to be unconstitutional action taken by an international organization. On the other hand, the advisory opinion makes no attempt to solve the legal problems arising from the existence of the flags of convenience: the Court's opinion was for the most part based on a textual analysis of the relevant clause of the IMCO Constitution.

THE TEMPLE OF PREAH VIHEAR

On 6 October 1959 Cambodia, invoking the compulsory jurisdiction, instituted proceedings against Thailand alleging violation on the part of Thailand of Cambodia's territorial sovereignty over the region of the Temple of Preah Vihear and its precincts. The Court first dismissed challenges to its jurisdiction by judgment of 26 May 1961 and then went on to dispose over the merits. In a judgment of 15 June 1962, the Court found that the Temple was situated in territory under the sovereignty of Cambodia, and made various consequential findings. This decision caused great disappointment to Thailand. However, on 3 July 1962 the Government of Thailand announced that despite its profound sorrow at the result of the case it considered that "as a member of the United Nations, Thailand is bound to honour its obligations under the United Nations Charter. It will do so under protest and with reservation of her intrinsic rights." [57]

This case grew out of the dissolution of the French empire in Indo-China, and the local tension has to be viewed against the wider background of the crisis in South-East Asia. The case itself turned on the interpretation of boundary settlements made in the period 1904-8 between France, which at that time conducted the foreign relations of Cambodia, and Thailand.

Neither side chose a judge *ad hoc* in this case.

Witnesses and experts were called by both parties, and at one point the Court assembled in private, in the presence of the representatives of the parties, to attend a film of the place in dispute.

The judgment is of importance for its discussion of two legal issues, namely the effect of subsequent conduct on a State's legal position (some-times loosely known as "estoppel" or "preclusion" in international law) and the effect of error in a treaty. The Court's jurisprudence on these points was later consolidated in the codification of the law of treaties, as Articles 45 and 48 respectively of the Vienna Convention on the Law of Treaties of 1969.

THE NORTHERN CAMEROONS

On 30 May 1961 Cameroon filed an application instituting proceedings against the United Kingdom, alleging failure to respect certain obligations directly or indirectly flowing from the Trusteeship Agreement of 1946 (replacing the former Mandate) for the Territory of the Cameroons under British administration. Although the question of the disposition of the Northern Cameroons is long-standing, the present case grew out of dissatis-faction felt by the Republic of Cameroon, i.e. the successor of the Territory formerly under French administration, at the manner in which that Trustee-ship had been terminated. This had led to the Northern Cameroons being joined to Nigeria. Nigeria was not impleaded in these proceedings, and the Court was simply asked to make a series of general declarations, without redressing any alleged injustice or detaching any territory from Nigeria. The United Kingdom filed a series of preliminary objections. In its judgment of 2 December 1963 the Court, by ten votes to five, found that the circum-stances of this case and what it was being asked to do raised antecedent issues of whether the limits of the judicial function permitted it to entertain the claims submitted. That question it answered in the negative, primarily because any judgment which it might pronounce would be without object, and for that reason it found that it could not adjudicate upon the merits of the claim. [58]

It is believed that despite this curious result, this is an instance in which the judicial pronouncement, removed from the substance of the issues though it might be, nonetheless performed a useful function in facilitating the acceptance of a decision of the General Assembly of the United Nations (regarding the termination of the Trusteeship Agreement) which was political- ly unpalatable. From the point of view of the development of the Court's jurisprudence and its own concepts of its functions, the judgment is important for its discussion of the limits of judicial propriety when the Court is asked to render a declaratory judgment.

THE U.N. BUDGET

After the crisis in the Middle East at the end of 1956, the General Assembly established the United Nations Emergency Force (UNEF). The financing of UNEF presented what the Court called "perplexing problems". In the middle of 1960, the United Nations commenced its activities in the Congo, for which purpose it established another Force known as ONUC. The expenses of these two Forces became very heavy and the question of how to meet them gave rise to very serious difficulties, both for political and for legal reasons. In the summer of 1961, a Working Group appointed by the General Assembly reached the conclusion that, having regard to the differences of opinion which had been expressed about the legal nature of the financial obligations arising out of the peace-keeping operations, the General Assembly should request an advisory opinion from the Court, the precise formulation of the question being for the General Assembly to decide. In a Resolution of 21 December 1961, adopted by 52 votes to 11 with 32 abstentions, the General Assembly asked the Court whether certain expenditures authorised in a number of given Resolutions relating to ONUC and relating to UNEF constituted "expenses of the Organization" within the meaning of Article 17 (2) of the Charter. The power of the Court to give the Opinion in the terms requested was challenged both in the General Assembly and before the Court, although it will be noted that these challenges did not, as had been the case in the years 1948-50, question the power of the Court to interpret the Charter itself. In its Advisory Opinion of 20 July 1962 the Court dismissed all the challenges to its competence and, by nine votes to five, answered the question put to it in the affirmative. The Court found that it was required to answer a concrete question and, contrary to the practice adopted in all previous Advisory Opinions on the interpretation of the Charter, proceeded to deal with almost all the major legal contentions which had been advanced in the previous discussions. This case provided the first occasion since the establish- ment of the Permanent Court of International Justice for participation by a representative of the Soviet Union in the oral proceedings.[59]

This advisory opinion did not lead to a speedy solution of the crisis, which was at the same time financial and constitutional. Indeed, in the view of many it only served to aggravate it, since it introduced intractable questions of prestige into the diplomatic scene. In resolution 1854 (XVII) of 19 December 1962 the General Assembly accepted the advisory opinion after a bitter debate. That resolution was adopted by a vote of 76 to 17, with 14 abstentions, two of the permanent members of the Security Council being among those who voted against. At the same time the General Assembly adopted other resolutions for dealing with the financial aspects. Expectations that the advisory opinion and this resolution would lead the States concerned to change their attitude were unrealized, and in 1964 some of these States were two years in arrear in their payments found by the Court to be due to the United Nations. This brought into play Article 19 of the Charter, theoretically depriving them of their vote in the General Assembly. The nineteenth session of the General Assembly (1964) was held in the shadow and unreal atmosphere produced by that crisis. It conducted no substantive business, and the matters of routine with which it had to deal were solved without the necessity for a vote (i.e. by consensus). This ridiculous state of affairs was later rectified through diplomatic channels (although the financial aspect of the crisis was left unresolved), and in 1965 the General Assembly was able to resume its routine, albeit with reduced prestige. In the view of many, this exercise was an instance of abuse of the General Assembly and the advisory process by the Great Powers, and it did nothing to enhance the standing of the judicial process in the United Nations.

THE NORTH SEA CONTINENTAL SHELF

The discovery and exploitation of mineral resources in the bed of the North Sea during the sixties intensified competition amongst the littoral States—Norway, Denmark, the Federal Republic of Germany, the Netherlands, Belgium, France and the United Kingdom—over the delimitation of the sea-bed between them and the areas of the sea-bed over which each would exercise exclusive rights within the terms of the Geneva Convention on the Continental Shelf of 29 April 1958. As between most of these countries delimitation was effected as the result of negotiations. However, difficulties arose as between Denmark and the Federal Rupublic, and as between the Federal Republic and the Netherlands. In February 1967 two special agreements were concluded, in identical terms, between those two pairs of States. The Court was asked to decide what principles and rules of international law were applicable to the delimitation as between the parties of the areas of the continental shelf in the North Sea which appertain to each of them beyond boundaries previously determined. At the same time the parties agreed to delimit the continental shelf as between them by agreement in pursuance of the decision requested from the Court. Although the cases were somewhat different, the parties were agreed on their joinder, which the Court effected, and in its judgment of 20 February 1969 the Court answered the question put to it.

In accordance with the special agreement, negotiations between the parties continued, and in due course further agreement was reached on the ultimate delimitation of the continental shelf of the North Sea.[60]

Two interesting features of this case may be mentioned. Firstly, although the Court was not asked to decide any concrete dispute or to effect any delimitation of the areas in question, this exercise of the judicial function was directly related to the negotiations between the parties. This gave the judgment an object and a purpose. Secondly, much turned on the Court's interpretation of the 1958 Geneva Convention on the Continental Shelf, to which the Federal Republic was not a party, not having ratified it although it was subject to ratification. This Convention was one of four adopted at the first United Nations Conference on the Law of the Sea—the first United Nations codification conference working on the basis of a draft prepared by the International Law Commission. Discussion of this question led to an examination of whether that particular convention was "codificatory" or not. The significance of this was that if the answer was affirmative, the rules embodied in it, and especially the rules for the delimitation of adjacent and opposite areas of continental shelf, might be held to be applicable notwithstanding that the Federal Republic was not a party to the Convention. On this point, after close analysis of the history of the Convention, the Court gave a negative answer.

This was the first time that the Court had to consider, as a central issue in a case before it, the quality as "codification" or "development" of a multilateral treaty drawn up through the codifying machinery of the United Nations. With the increase in the number and scope of treaties coming out of these processes, this type of issue is coming more frequent. The criteria established by the Court are important for understanding the interaction of the two processes—of application of the law by the Court and its codification by States through the International Law Commission and international conferences. It may be added that the Court has since clarified that if it is satisfied that a rule embodied in such a treaty is codificatory, it will probably apply it as a rule of customary international law.

INDIA, PAKISTAN AND BANGLADESH

Following a serious incident of hijacking of an Indian civil aircraft to Pakistan and in the tension existing between those two countries throughout their long smouldering dispute, India in February 1971 suspended overflights by Pakistan civil aircraft of Indian territory. This, of course, impeded mutual access between what were then East and West Pakistan. Pakistan thereupon complained to the Council of the International Civil Aviation Organization, before which it laid its dispute with India on this question of overflying. This Council has a quasi-judicial competence, under the Chicago Air Agreement of 1944, in this type of case, subject to a right of appeal from its decision to the Court (exercising a transferred jurisdiction from the Permanent Court). In the Council proceedings, India raised some preliminary objections, which the Council decided to reject. India thereupon immediately appealed to the Court. The proceedings in the Court did not touch upon the merits of the dispute brought before the Council, but only on the Council's decision to reject India's preliminary objections. In those proceedings, Pakistan for its part also objected to the Court's jurisdiction, but did not raise these as preliminary objections. In its judgment of 18 August 1972 the Court first, by thirteen votes to three, rejected Pakistan's objections and then, by fourteen votes to two, dismissed India's appeal.[61]

The question of overlying Indian territory in 1971 was closely connected with what emerged later as a triangular relationship between India, Pakistan and Bangladesh. In that context, the tension provoked by the initial hijacking and by the subsequent litigation was marginal.

On 11 May 1973 Pakistan instituted proceedings against India relating to a number of Pakistani Prisoners of War taken by India in the 1971 fighting. From a joint statement by India and Bangladesh it appeared that 195 of these were to be handed to Bangladesh for trial for alleged acts of genocide and crimes against humanity, and Pakistan contested the legality of that. At the same time Pakistan applied for interim measures of protection to the effect that the repatriation of prisoners of war should not be interrupted by virtue of these charges, and that the persons should not be handed over to Bangladesh while the action was pending in the International Court. India contested the jurisdiction of the Court and was not represented at the first hearings in June 1973. In its order of 12 July 1973 the Court, after the request for interim measures had been withdrawn in the light of jurisdictional difficulties that arose, arranged for the case to proceed, with the issue of jurisdiction being tried first. [62]

ICELAND'S FISHERIES JURISDICTION

Since these cases are pending it will be sufficient to state that Iceland's aspiration to secure an exclusive fisheries zone extending fifty nautical miles from its base-lines has encountered strong opposition on the part of the United Kingdom and the Federal Republic of Germany. In April and in June 1972 these two countries respectively filed applications instituting proceedings against Iceland, asking the Court to declare that Iceland's claim to extend

Photo: United Nations

Balloting in the Security Council 1960

The Court deliberating in the Salle "Bol"

its exclusive fisheries jurisdiction to a zone of 50 nautical miles around Iceland is without foundation in international law and, in the second case, cannot be opposed to the Federal Republic and its fishing vessels. Iceland's reaction to the applications was that there was no basis for the Court to exercise jurisdiction, and that considering that the vital interests of Iceland were involved, the government was not willing to confer jurisdiction on the Court and would not appoint an agent.

As the date for the entry into force of the new regulations approached, the United Kingdom and the Federal Republic, in August 1972, respectively filed applications for the indication of interim measures of protection. Iceland repeated its position regarding the jurisdiction of the Court and objected to the indication of interim measures of protection. After hearings at which Iceland was not represented the Court, by two orders of 17 August adopted in each case by fourteen votes to one (no judge *ad hoc* has been chosen), indicated the interim measures substantially in the terms suggested by the applicant governments. By two further orders made the next day the Court, by nine votes to six, decided that the first pleadings should be addressed to the question of the jurisdiction of the Court to entertain the disputes, and fixed time-limits for the filing of the memorials and the counter-memorials. By judgments of 2 February 1973 the Court by fourteen votes to one found that it had jurisdiction to deal with the merits of the disputes. Iceland did not take part in the proceedings, and no judges *ad hoc* were appointed. [63] The pendency of this litigation unfortunately did not prevent the 1972 "cod war" from causing tension between the parties, but negotiations for the settlement of the dispute are still continuing.

NUCLEAR TESTS IN THE PACIFIC OCEAN

On 9 May 1973 Australia and New Zealand both instituted independent proceedings against France contesting the legality of atmospheric nuclear weapon tests by France in the South Pacific Ocean. On 16 and 18 May respectively Fiji made application to intervene in each of these cases, on the basis of Article 62 of the Statute and its particular concern in the proceedings. France, for its part, informed the Court of its view that the Court lacked jurisdiction, and it asked for the cases to be removed from the list. Both Australia and New Zealand also asked for interim measures calling upon France to desist from any further tests pending the judgment of the Court. After hearings at which France was not represented the Court, on 22 June 1973, issued two orders, by eight votes to six, calling upon the Governments concerned to ensure that no action was taken which might aggravate or extend the disputes submitted to it or prejudice the rights of the other party in respect of the carrying out of whatever decision might finally be rendered

by the Court. More particularly the Court called upon France to avoid nuclear tests causing the deposit of radioactive fall-out on Australian territory or
on the territory of New Zealand, the Cook Islands, Niue or the Tokelau
Islands. At that stage the Court could not accede to the French request to
remove the case from the list, but it ordered that the questions of its jurisdiction to entertain the disputes and the admissibility of the applications
should be pleaded first. [64]

EVALUATION

During the first twenty-five years of the existence of the present Court, from
1946 to the end of July, 1973, 60 cases were referred to the Court. Of these,
14 were requests for advisory opinion and the remaining 46 were contentious
cases (eight of them cases in which the Court would only have jurisdiction if
the respondent accepted the invitation to litigate, contained in the application instituting proceedings). These figures, especially when compared with
those of the Permanent Court (see Appendix 4), have led many observers to
the view that the contribution which the present Court has been enabled to
make to the maintenance of international peace has been less than was the
case for the Permanent Court. However, in the long run, the bare figures may
be misleading as the point for departure for an evaluation of the role of the
Court in the contemporary international scene.

The figures themselves are not without interest. On the one hand they
show virtual consistency in the number of *contentious* cases sought to be
referred by States to the decision of each Court. On the other hand, the real
and substantial decline is in the number of matters referred collectively to the
present Court for *advisory* opinion. It might fairly be concluded from this that,
contrary to a widespread impression, there is no real falling-off in the
readiness of States to refer appropriate bilateral disputes to the decision of
the Court. Against this, it is quite clear that in the modern political organs,
above all the General Assembly and the Security Council, the political difficulties in securing a majority to support properly drafted legal questions for
advisory opinion as an incident in the settlement of political disputes or
situations referred to them, are virtually insuperable in the absence of agreement of the parties to the dispute in question. Bearing in mind that the
effectiveness of the judicial method of settling international disputes depends
exclusively on the agreement of the parties to invoke judicial procedures, it is
not a cause for dismay that, in the absence of such agreement, the General
Assembly and the Security Council have shown themselves averse to employ-
ing even the indirect system of access to the Court provided by the advisory
competence. In the League's practice there was found a tendency, which was
not beyond criticism, for the political and judicial processes to coalesce

through the advisory procedure. But United Nations practices (especially the manner in which debates are conducted and decisions reached) demonstrate the opposite tendency—to differentiate between the two types of pacific solution for international disputes. Today States which refer disputes or situations to the political organs do so because they want a political and not a judicial settlement, and the way these organs work affords them plenty of opportunities to concentrate their diplomatic endeavours in an exclusively political direction.

The advisory procedure is dominated by two characteristic ambiguities. The first is the absence of "parties" in the strict sense of the term from the proceedings themselves. This produces two main consequences. The first is the apparent unwillingness of the Court to avail itself of the discretion accorded it by the Statute to assimilate advisory proceedings to contentious proceedings. This frame of mind is most marked in the refusal of the Court to appoint a South African judge *ad hoc* in *Namibia.* [65] It has also led to lack of clarity in regard to the treatment of "preliminary objections" and other similar matters in advisory cases, despite the persistence of this phenomenon throughout the period under review. The second consequence of the absence of "parties" is that the judicial pronouncement does not partake of the quality of *res judicata* implying the obligation of compliance, whatever else it might be. (This does not prevent an agreement outside the Court proceedings from conferring that quality upon the advisory opinion, but strictly speaking that is not a matter for the Court in the exercise of its general discretion whether to give an advisory opinion at all.)

The second characteristic ambiguity in the advisory procedure is that in the hierarchy of international legal norms, a resolution of a competent international organ adopting (in whatever language) an advisory opinion possesses no inherent status to distinguish it from any other resolution of that organ. If in principle—and *grosso modo* this is the position as regards resolutions of the General Assembly and even of the Security Council—the resolutions have the character of non-binding recommendations, the fact that such a resolution "adopts" an advisory opinion does not suffice to make it "binding".

That these features have influenced the attitude of States towards the advisory competence is undoubted. A recent report by the Sixth Committee of the General Assembly alluded to this in guarded terms when it recalled the position of a number of representatives, that the right to request advisory opinions should depend on the consent of all the States concerned if it was not to result in circumvention of the principle that a State could not be subject to any type of third party settlement of a dispute without its consent. It was also pointed out that a proposal to limit advisory opinions to questions that could not be presented as an actual case did not come to grips with the problem, since it would frequently be difficult to foresee the future development of a question on which an advisory opinion had been requested.

Besides, such an extension of the advisory role of the Court could be pre-judicial to its contentious jurisdiction proper which, under the Statute, was its primary responsibility. [66]

The differentiation between the contentious and advisory spheres has been further accentuated by the repeated emphasis placed by the political organs on the primacy and exclusiveness of their role in the United Nations.

On the substance, there are some striking differences between the kind of dispute brought before the present Court and the kind of dispute brought before its predecessor. As seen, the Permanent Court had much to do with marginal disputes closely connected with the major sources of international tension in the inter-War period. It had little to do with the central issues in other conflicts. The present Court, after a hesitant start which was not particularly successful, has not been asked by the States concerned to deal with disputes related even marginally to the major international tensions since the end of the Second World War. The attempts to involve it in the Cold War during the fifties were quite unproductive. This naturally has reduced the amount of business brought before the Court, but this is not necessarily dis-advantageous, for it has freed the Court from what might be misguided efforts to find legal solutions for conflicts which are not in reality legal problems at all. A similar evaluation can be made regarding the non-involvement of the Court in othe major international issues of global scope.

On the other hand (and leaving aside what might be termed routine legal disputes between States, of which the Court has possibly had more than its predecessor), the present Court has been asked to decide the central issues of several other major international disputes. Some of these, being in reality conflicts of interest and of national aspirations, even contained a sufficient number of elements to give rise to concern that they might constitute a threat to international peace, if not on a universal scale then at least on a regional scale. In situations of great tension and conflict, diplomacy has two ways of proceeding. It can by deliberate choice leave the dispute unsettled, while trying not to let it get out of hand. Alternatively, it can try to reach a definit-ive settlement. The timing and the method of the change from one approach to the other is usually a matter of the greatest delicacy, and depends upon considerations of domestic politics no less than on international factors. The International Court has shown that when States are agreed that the time has come for a final settlement of a given dispute, it is capable of assisting them, if they so desire, to reach their objective. This is the lesson of major conflicts settled by the Court, such as the *Fisheries* and *Honduras-Nicaragua Frontier* cases. On the other hand, if there is no underlying political agreement, as in the *Anglo-Iranian* and *Right of Passage* cases, the Court has shown that its procedures can be invoked not so much to reach a definitive settlement as to deflect into peaceful channels a phase of a complex diplomatic situation, and prevent that from getting out of hand and endangering world peace. Two contentious cases, *Anglo-Iranian* and the *Honduras-Nicaragua Frontier* cases, came before the Court either in close connection with fear that force would be used (the first of them) or after hostilities had actually broken out (the second of them). The *Right of Passage* sometimes conveys the impression that Portugal had recourse to the Court as a deliberate alternative to the Security Council, presumably out of a belief that its diplomacy would be the more likely to achieve its aims in a (for it) deteriorating situation at The Hague than at New York. In the long run, it failed.

The Permanent Court never had contentious cases of this character referred to it.

Another striking thing about the work of the present Court is its variety.

The substantive work of the Court is far from being confined to mere questions of treaty interpretation, which many people consider to have been the most prominent feature of the work of the Permanent Court. A great number of completely novel problems have come before it, covering vast areas of international legal and social relations previously untouched by the international judge.

Geographically, too, the substance of the Court's work is covering a wider area than its predecessor. All the cases before the Permanent Court (except one) were litigated exclusively between European States although some of them related to interests outside Europe. It is true that the majority of cases before the present Court relate to European affairs, but there have been a significant number of cases in which one of the parties has not been a European power. A complete innovation is the fact that two cases have concerned exclusively Latin-American powers, and three cases have concerned exclusively Asian powers. Since 1960 a further development is noticeable in that African powers have started seeing in the Court an instrument which their diplomacy can employ in their disputes with European powers. This applies not only to the cases concerning South-West Africa and the Northern Cameroons, but also to the case on the constitution of the Maritime Safety Committee of IMCO, in which the main protagonists were Liberia and the United Kingdom. In 1973 Australia and New Zealand were for the first time applicants in cases against a European power, and another Polynesian State requested to intervene. The Court is now truly universal.

On the negative side of the Court's work to date, noticeable is the fact that, albeit on technical grounds of lack of jurisdiction or inadmissibility, the Court has not found it possible to decide on the substance of any dispute relating to events occurring during the Second World War, whether or not that dispute ended up also by being a Cold War dispute (the *Monetary Gold from Rome, Nottebohm* and *Interhandel* cases). But this negative conclusion too requires further examination, for it is possibly not accidental. As a matter of fact, Article 107 of the Charter of the United Nations (of which the Statute of the Court is an integral part) can be interpreted as excluding from the normal competence of the United Nations and its different organs actions taken during the Second World War against enemy States. Although the Court has never directly referred to this Article, its action in declining to decide the merits of this type of case cannot necessarily be regarded as being contrary to the spirit of the Charter.

It is usual today to say that the expectations generated by the decision of the San Francisco Conference to make the Court a principal organ of the United Nations, and which led to the assumption that the new Court would be able to play a major role in the pacific settlement of international disputes, have not been fully realized. The reason for this state of affairs are many and complex, and are only partly due to the general attitude of reserve towards the Court manifested by some of the major contemporary world Powers. There is prevalent in the world today a widespread questioning of the contemporary international law. This feeling is based on the view that for the greater part international law is the product of European imperialism and colonialism and does not take sufficient account of the completely changed pattern of international relations which now exists. This feeling has been very marked in the prolonged discussions in the United Nations over questions of the codification of different aspects of international law. Its existence is not conducive to recourse to the Court. Whereas before the Second World War it was on the whole the small Powers who were inclined to look to international law and its organs as a means to protect themselves against the rapacity of the Great Powers, paradoxically enough the situation today is changing rapidly, and it is the Great Powers who are inclined to take refuge behind a formal position based on traditional international law when faced with claims by small and new States who object to the traditional position. This is particularly evident in the sphere of international economic relations.

What is perhaps not sufficiently known is that in this type of case the International Court has shown itself sympathetic towards the psychological attitudes of the new and of the small States. Careful scrutiny of the record of the Court may lead to the conclusion that it has displayed quite a remarkable sense of appreciation of the changing currents of internationalist thought. In this respect it has performed a major service to the international community as a whole, because the need to bring international law into line with present-day requirements and conditions is real and urgent. Here we recall our basic assumption that in most instances of international litigation the legal cases of the two parties are evenly balanced and that the decision is reached by a process of choice which enables the majority of the Court to reach a result which it considers just and tenable in the circumstances. Many observers feel that several of the great cases decided since 1946 which raised this type of issue would have been decided differently had they been brought before the Permanent Court. The International Court does not support the charge of rigid conservatism said to be characteristic of lawyers. If anything, it is the

International Court, together with the International Law Commission, which has infused new dynamism into the international law of today. As we have seen, but for the decisions of the Court it is extremely doubtful if the Conferences on the Law of the Sea would have succeeded in reaching agreement on a vast number of problems satisfactory to the extremely diversified international community of today. Another branch of law on which the Court has pronounced itself on many occasions is the Law of Treaties, the codification of which by the Commission is one of the most successful examples of ·codification by the United Nations.

Above all, in considering the work of the Court and the role which it has been called upon to play, it has to be remembered that, unlike the situation after the First World War, when, after a few years, the illusion of general pacification and relaxation of tension became commonplace, the period since the Second World War has been marked by unceasing international tension and unrelieved anxiety in the part of all statesmen and on the part of the public at large over what the future might bring. The international situation has lacked any element of relaxation and tranquility. The development of this situation has been marked by continuous weakening of the authority of all the international institutions established to deal with the intercourse of States in time of peace. This general atmosphere is not propitious for any extended use of international judicial techniques. In the light of the general international situation, the wonder perhaps is not so much what the Court has been able to do, as that in fact States continue to show willingness to refer a number of major disputes to its decision, and great interest in all that pertains to the Court. This is the encouraging feature of the experience of the International Court, for it shows that even if its jurisdiction is not compulsory, its permanency as an international organ enables it to play its own constructive role in the pacific settlement of international disputes despite the constantly disintegrating international situation.

THE CHARTER OF THE UNITED NATIONS AND THE STATUTE OF THE COURT

EXTRACTS FROM THE CHARTER

CHAPTER III

Organs

Article 7

1. There are established as the principal organs of the United Nations: a General Assembly, a Security Council, an Economic and Social Council, a Trusteeship Council, an International Court of Justice, and a Secretariat.

CHAPTER VI

Pacific Settlement of Disputes

Article 33

1. The parties to any dispute, the continuance of which is likely to endanger the maintenance of international peace and security, shall, first of all, seek a solution by negotiation, enquiry, mediation, conciliation, arbitration, judicial settlement, resort to regional agencies or arrangements, or other peaceful means of their own choice.
    2. The Security Council shall, when it deems necessary, call upon the parties to settle their dispute by such means.

Article 36

1. The Security Council may, at any stage of a dispute of the nature referred to in Article 33 or of a situation of like nature, recommend appropriate procedures or methods of adjustment.
    2. The Security Council should take into consideration any procedures for the settlement of the dispute which have already been adopted by the parties.
    3. In making recommendations under this Article, the Security Council should also take into consideration that legal disputes should as a general rule be referred by the parties to the International Court of Justice, in accordance with the provisions of the Statute of the Court.

CHAPTER XIV

The International Court of Justice

Article 92

The International Court of Justice shall be the principal judicial organ of the United Nations. It shall function in accordance with the annexed Statute, which is based upon the Statute of the Permanent Court of International Justice and forms an integral part of the present Charter.

Article 93

1. All members of the United Nations are *ipso facto* parties to the Statute of the International Court of Justice.

2. A state which is not a Member of the United Nations may become a party to the Statute of the International Court of Justice on conditions to be determined in each case by the General Assembly upon the recommendation of the Security Council.

Article 94

1. Each member of the United Nations undertakes to comply with the decision of the International Court of Justice in any case to which it is a party.

2. If any party to a case fails to perform the obligations incumbent upon it under a judgment rendered by the Court, the other party may have recourse to the Security Council, which may, if it deems necessary, make recommendations or decide upon measures to be taken to give effect to the judgment.

Article 95

Nothing in the present Charter shall prevent Members of the United Nations from entrusting the solution of their differences to other tribunals by virtue of agreements already in existence or which may be concluded in the future.

Article 96

1. The General Assembly or the Security Council may request the International Court of Justice to give an advisory opinion on any legal question.

2. Other organs of the United Nations and specialized agencies, which may at any time be so authorized by the General Assembly, may also request advisory opinions of the Court on legal questions arising within the scope of their activities.

STATUTE OF THE INTERNATIONAL COURT
OF JUSTICE

Article 1

THE INTERNATIONAL COURT OF JUSTICE established by the Charter of the United Nations as the principal judicial organ of the United Nations shall be constituted and shall function in accordance with the provisions of the present Statute.

CHAPTER I

Organization of the Court

Article 2

The Court shall be composed of a body of independent judges, elected regardless of their nationality from among persons of high moral character, who possess the qualifications required in their respective countries for appointment to the highest judicial offices, or are jurisconsults of recognized competence in international law.

Article 3

1. The Court shall consist of fifteen members, no two of whom may be nationals of the same state.

2. A person who for the purposes of membership in the Court could be regarded as a national of more than one state shall be deemed to be a national of the one in which he ordinarily exercises civil and political rights.

Article 4

1. The members of the Court shall be elected by the General Assembly and by the Security Council from a list of persons nominated by the national groups in the Permanent Court of Arbitration, in accordance with the following provisions.

2. In the case of Members of the United Nations not represented in the Permanent Court of Arbitration, candidates shall be nominated by national groups appointed for this purpose by their governments under the same conditions as those prescribed for members of the Permanent Court of Arbitration by Article 44 of the Convention of The Hague of 1907 for the pacific settlement of international disputes.

3. The conditions under which a state which is a party to the present Statute but is not a member of the United Nations may participate in electing the members of the Court shall, in the absence of a special agreement, be laid down by the General Assembly upon recommendation of the Security Council.

Article 5

1. At least three months before the date of the election, the Secretary-General of the United Nations shall address a written request to the members of the Permanent Court of Arbitration belonging to the states which are parties to the present Statute, and to

the members of the national groups appointed under Article 4, paragraph 2, inviting them to undertake, within a given time, by national groups, the nomination of persons in a position to accept the duties of a member of the Court.

2. No group may nominate more than four persons, not more than two of whom shall be of their own nationality. In no case may the number of candidates nominated by a group be more than double the number of seats to be filled.

Article 6

Before making these nominations, each national group is recommended to consult its highest court of justice, its legal faculties and schools of law, and its national academies and national sections of international academies devoted to the study of law.

Article 7

1. The Secretary-General shall prepare a list in alphabetical order of all the persons thus nominated. Save as provided in Article 12, paragraph 2, these shall be the only persons eligible.

2. The Secretary-General shall submit this list to the General Assembly and to the Security Council.

Article 8

The General Assembly and the Security Council shall proceed independently of one another to elect the members of the Court.

Article 9

At every election, the electors shall bear in mind not only that the persons to be elected should individually possess the qualifications required, but also that in the body as a whole the representation of the main forms of civilization and of the principal systems of the world should be assured.

Article 10

1. Those candidates who obtain an absolute majority of votes in the General Assembly and in the Security Council shall be considered as elected.

2. Any vote of the Security Council, whether for the election of judges or for the appointment of members of the conference envisaged in Article 12, shall be taken without any distinction between permanent and non-permanent members of the Security Council.

3. In the event of more than one national of the same state obtaining an absolute majority of the votes both of the General Assembly and of the Security Council, the eldest of these only shall be considered as elected.

Article 11

If, after the first meeting held for the purpose of the election, one or more seats remain to be filled, a second and, if necessary, a third meeting shall take place.

Article 12

1. If, after the third meeting, one or more seats still remain unfilled, a joint conference consisting of six members, three appointed by the General Assembly and three by the Security Council, may be formed at any time at the request of either the General

Assembly or the Security Council, for the purpose of choosing by the vote of an absolute majority one name for each seat still vacant, to submit to the General Assembly and the Security Council for their respective acceptance.

2. If the joint conference is unanimously agreed upon any person who fulfils the required conditions, he may be included in its list, even though he was not included in the list of nominations referred to in Article 7.

3. If the joint conference is satisfied that it will not be successful in procuring an election, those members of the Court who have already been elected shall, within a period to be fixed by the Security Council, proceed to fill the vacant seats by selection from among those candidates who have obtained votes either in the General Assembly or in the Security Council.

4. In the event of an equality of votes among the judges, the eldest judge shall have a casting vote.

Article 13

1. The members of the Court shall be elected for nine years and may be re-elected; provided, however, that of the judges elected at the first election, the terms of five judges shall expire at the end of three years and the terms of five more judges shall expire at the end of six years.

2. The judges whose terms are to expire at the end of the above-mentioned initial periods of three and six years shall be chosen by lot to be drawn by the Secretary-General immediately after the first election has been completed.

3. The members of the Court shall continue to discharge their duties until their places have been filled. Though replaced, they shall finish any cases which they may have begun.

4. In the case of resignation of a member of the Court, the resignation shall be addressed to the President of the Court for transmission to the Secretary-General. This last notification makes the place vacant.

Article 14

Vancancies shall be filled by the same method as that laid down for the first election, subject to the following provision: the Secretary-General shall, within one month of the occurrence of the vacancy, proceed to issue the invitations provided for in Article 5, and the date of the election shall be fixed by the Security Council.

Article 15

A member of the Court elected to replace a member whose term of office has not expired shall hold office for the remainder of his predecessor's term.

Article 16

1. No member of the Court may exercise any political or administrative function, or engage in any other occupation of a professional nature.

2. Any doubt on this point shall be settled by the decision of the Court.

Article 17

1. No member of the Court may act as an agent, counsel, or advocate in any case.

2. No member may participate in the decision of any case in which he has previously taken part as agent, counsel, or advocate for one of the parties, or as a member of a national or international court, or of a commission of enquiry, or in any other capacity.

3. Any doubt on this point shall be settled by the decision of the Court.

Article 18

1. No member of the Court can be dismissed unless, in the unanimous opinion of the other members, he has ceased to fulfil the required conditions.

2. Formal notification thereof shall be made to the Secretary-General by the Registrar.

3. This notification makes the place vacant.

Article 19

The members of the Court, when engaged on the business of the Court, shall enjoy diplomatic privileges and immunites.

Article 20

Every member of the Court shall, before taking up his duties, make a solemn declaration in open Court that he will exercise his powers impartially and conscientiously.

Article 21

The Court shall elect its President and Vice-President for three years; they may be re-elected.

2. The Court shall appoint its Registrar and may provide for the appointment of such other officers as may be necessary.

Article 22

1. The seat of the Court shall be established at The Hague. This, however, shall not prevent the Court from sitting and exercising its functions elsewhere whenever the Court considers it desirable.

2. The President and the Registrar shall reside at the seat of the Court.

Article 23

1. The Court shall remain permanently in session, except during the judicial vacations, the dates and duration of which shall be fixed by the Court.

2. Members of the Court are entitled to periodic leave, the dates and duration of which shall be fixed by the Court, having in mind the distance between The Hague and the home of each judge.

3. Members of the Court shall be bound, unless they are on leave or prevented from attending by illness or other serious reasons duly explained to the President, to hold themselves permanently at the disposal of the Court.

Article 24

1. If, for some special reason, a member of the Court considers that he should not take part in the decision of a particular case, he shall so inform the President.

2. If the President considers that for some special reason one of the members of the Court should not sit in a particular case, he shall give him notice accordingly.

3. If in any such case the member of the Court and the President disagree, the matter shall be settled by the decision of the Court.

Article 25

1. The full Court shall sit except when it is expressly provided otherwise in the present Satute.

2. Subject to the condition that the number of judges available to constitute the Court is not thereby reduced below eleven, the Rules of the Court may provide for allowing one or more judges, according to circumstances and in rotation, to be dispensed from sitting.

3. A quorum of nine judges shall suffice to constitute the Court.

Article 26

1. The Court may from time to time form one or more chambers, composed of three or more judges as the Court may determine, for dealing with particular categories of cases; for example, labour cases and cases relating to transit and communications.

2. The Court may at any time form a chamber for dealing with a particular case. The number of judges to constitute such a chamber shall be determined by the Court with the approval of the parties.

3. Cases shall be heard and determined by the chambers provided for in this Article if the parties so request.

Article 27

A judgment given by any of the chambers provided for in Articles 26 and 29 shall be considered as rendered by the Court.

Article 28

The chambers provided for in Articles 26 and 29 may, with the consent of the parties, sit and exercise their functions elsewhere than at The Hague.

Article 29

With a view to the speedy despatch of business, the Court shall form annually a chamber composed of five judges which, at the request of the parties, may hear and determine cases by summary procedure. In addition, two judges shall be selected for the purpose of replacing judges who find it impossible to sit.

Article 30

1. The Court shall frame rules for carrying out its functions. In particular, it shall lay down rules of procedure.

2. The Rules of the Court may provide for assessors to sit with the Court or with any of its chambers, without the right to vote.

Article 31

1. Judges of the nationality of each of the parties shall retain their right to sit in the case before the Court.

2. If the Court includes upon the Bench a judge of the nationality of one of the parties, any other party may choose a person to sit as judge. Such person shall be chosen preferably from among those persons who have been nominated as candidates as provided in Articles 4 and 5.

3. If the Court includes upon the Bench no judge of the nationality of the parties, each of these parties may proceed to choose a judge as provided in paragraph 2 of this Article.

4. The provisions of this Article shall apply to the case of Articles 26 and 29. In such cases, the President shall request one or, if necessary, two of the members of the

Court forming the Chamber to give place to the members of the Court of the nationality of the parties concerned, and, failing such, or if they are unable to be present, to the judges specially chosen by the parties.

5. Should there by several parties in the same interest, they shall, for the purpose of the preceding provisions, be reckoned as one party only. Any doubt upon this point shall be settled by the decision of the Court.

6. Judges chosen as laid down in paragraphs 2, 3, and 4 of this Article shall fulfil the conditions required by Articles 2, 17 (paragraph 2), 20, and 24 of the present Statute. They shall take part in the decision on terms of complete equality with their colleagues.

Article 32

1. Each member of the Court shall receive an annual salary.

2. The President shall receive a special annual allowance.

3. The Vice-President shall receive a special allowance for every day on which he acts as President.

4. The judges chosen under Article 31, other than members of the Court, shall receive compensation for each day on which they exercise their functions.

5. These salaries, allowances, and compensation shall be fixed by the General Assembly. They may not be decreased during the term of office.

6. The salary of the Registrar shall be fixed by the General Assembly on the proposal of the Court.

7. Regulations made by the General Assembly shall fix the conditions under which retirement pensions may be given to members of the Court and to the Registrar, and the conditions under which members of the Court and the Registrar shall have their travelling expenses refunded.

8. The above salaries, allowances, and compensation shall be free of all taxation.

Article 33

The expenses of the Court shall be borne by the United Nations in such a manner as shall be decided by the General Assembly.

CHAPTER II

Competence of the Court

Article 34

1. Only States may be parties in cases before the Court.

2. The Court, subject to and in conformity with its Rules, may request of public international organizations information relevant to cases before it, and shall receive such information presented by such organizations on their own initiative.

3. Whenever the construction of the constituent instrument of a public international organization or of an international convention adopted thereunder is in question in a case before the Court, the Registrar shall so notify the public international organization concerned and shall communicate to it copies of all the written proceedings.

Article 35

1. The Court shall be open to the states parties to the present Statute.

2. The conditions under which the Court shall be open to other states shall, subject to the special provisions contained in treaties in force, be laid down by the Security Council, but in no case shall such conditions place the parties in a position of inequality before the Court.

3. When a state which is not a Member of the United Nations is a party to a case, the Court shall fix the amount which that party is to contribute towards the expenses of the Court. This provision shall not apply if such state is bearing a share of the expenses of the Court.

Article 36

1. The jurisdiction of the Court comprises all cases which the parties refer to it and all matters specially provided for in the Charter of the United Nations or in treaties and conventions in force.

2. The states parties to the present Statute may at any time declare that they recognize as compulsory *ipso facto* and without special agreement, in relation to any other state accepting the same obligation, the jurisdiction of the Court in all legal disputes concerning:

  a. the interpretation of a treaty;
  b. any question of international law;
  c. the existence of any fact which, if established, would constitute a breach of an international obligation;
  d. the nature or extent of the reparation to be made for the breach of an international obligation.

3. The declarations referred to above may be made unconditionally or on condition of reciprocity on the part of several or certain states, or for a certain time.

4. Such declarations shall be deposited with the Secretary-General of the United Nations, who shall transmit copies thereof to the parties to the Statute and to the Registrar of the Court.

5. Declarations made under Article 36 of the Statute of the Permanent Court of International Justice and which are still in force shall be deemed, as between the parties to the present Statute, to be acceptances of the compulsory jurisdiction of the International Court of Justice for the period which they still have to run and in accordance with their terms.

6. In the event of a dispute as to whether the Court has jurisdiction, the matter shall be settled by the decision of the Court.

Article 37

Whenever a treaty or convention in force provides for reference of a matter to a tribunal to have been instituted by the League of Nations, or to the Permanent Court of International Justice, the matter shall, as between the parties to the present Statute, be referred to the International Court of Justice.

Article 38

1. The Court, whose function is to decide in accordance with international law such disputes as are submitted to it, shall apply:

  a. international conventions, whether general or particular, establishing rules expressly recognized by the contesting states;

b. international custom, as evidence of a general practice accepted as law;

c. the general principles of law recognized by civilized nations;

d. subject to the provisions of Article 59, judicial decisions and the teachings of the most highly qualified publicists of the various nations, as subsidiary means for the determination of rules of law.

2. This provision shall not prejudice the power of the Court to decide a case *ex aequo et bono*, if the parties agree thereto.

CHAPTER III

Procedure

Article 39

1. The official languages of the Court shall be French and English. If the parties agree that the case shall be conducted in French, the judgment shall be delivered in French. If the parties agree that the case shall be conducted in English, the judgment shall be delivered in English.

2. In the absence of an agreement as to which language shall be employed, each party may, in the pleadings, use the language which it prefers; the decision of the Court shall be given in French and English. In this case the Court shall at the same time determine which of the two texts shall be considered as authoritative.

3. The Court shall, at the request of any party, authorize a language other than French or English to be used by that party.

Article 40

1. Cases are brought before the Court, as the case may be, either by the notification of the special agreement or by a written application addressed to the Registrar. In either case the subject of the dispute and the parties shall be indicated.

2. The Registrar shall forthwith communicate the application to all concerned.

3. He shall also notify the Members of the United Nations through the Secretary-General, and also any other states entitled to appear before the Court.

Article 41

1. The Court shall have the power to indicate, if it considers that circumstances so require, any provisional measures which ought to be taken to preserve the respective rights of either party.

2. Pending the final decision, notice of the measures suggested shall forthwith be given to the parties and to the Security Council.

Article 42

1. The parties shall be represented by agents.

2. They may have the assistance of counsel or advocates before the Court.

3. The agents, counsel, and advocates of parties before the Court shall enjoy the privileges and immunities necessary to the independent exercise of their duties.

Article 43

1. The procedure shall consist of two parts: written and oral.

2. The written proceedings shall consist of the communication to the Court and to

the parties of memorials, counter-memorials and, if necessary, replies; also all papers and documents in support.

3. These communications shall be made through the Registrar, in the order and within the time fixed by the Court.

4. A certified copy of every document produced by one party shall be communicated to the other party.

5. The oral proceedings shall consist of the hearing by the Court of witnesses, experts, agents, counsel, and advocates.

Article 44

1. For the service of all notices upon persons other than the agents, counsel, and advocates, the Court shall apply direct to the government of the state upon whose territory the notice has to be served.

2. The same provision shall apply whenever steps are to be taken to procure evidence on the spot.

Article 45

The hearing shall be under the control of the President or, if he is unable to preside, of the Vice-President; if neither is able to preside, the senior judge present shall preside.

Article 46

The hearing in Court shall be public, unless the Court shall decide otherwise, or unless the parties demand that the public be not admitted.

Article 47

1. Minutes shall be made at each hearing and signed by the Registrar and the President.

2. These minutes alone shall be authentic.

Article 48

The Court shall make orders for the conduct of the case, shall decide the form and time in which each party must conclude its arguments, and make all arrangements connected with the taking of evidence.

Article 49

The Court may, even before the hearing begins, call upon the agents to produce any document or to supply any explanations. Formal note shall be taken of any refusal.

Article 50

The Court may, at any time, entrust any individual, body, bureau, commission or other organization that it may select, with the task of carrying out an enquiry or giving an expert opinion.

Article 51

During the hearing any relevant questions are to be put to the witnesses and experts under the conditions laid down by the Court in the rules of procedure referred to in Article 30.

Article 52

After the Court has received the proofs and evidence within the time specified for the purpose, it may refuse to accept any further oral or written evidence that one party may desire to present unless the other side consents.

Article 53

1. Whenever one of the parties does not appear before the Court, or fails to defend its case, the other party may call upon the Court to decide in favor of its claim.

2. The Court must, before doing so, satisfy itself, not only that it has jurisdiction in accordance with Articles 36 and 37, but also that the claim is well founded in fact and law.

Article 54

1. When, subject to the control of the Court, the agents, counsel, and advocates have completed their presentation of the case, the President shall declare the hearing closed.

2. The Court shall withdraw to consider the judgment.

3. The delibarations of the Court shall take place in private and remain secret.

Article 55

1. All questions shall be decided by a majority of the judges present.

2. In the event of an equality of votes, the President or the judge who acts in his place shall have a casting vote.

Article 56

1. The judgment shall state the reasons on which it is based.

2. It shall contain the names of the judges who have taken part in the decision.

Article 57

If the judgment does not represent in whole or in part the unanimous opinion of the judges, any judge shall be entitled to deliver a separate opinion.

Article 58

The judgment shall be signed by the President and by the Registrar. It shall be read in open Court, due notice having been given to the agents.

Article 59

The decision of the Court has no binding force except between the parties and in respect of that particular case.

Article 60

The judgment is final and without appeal. In the event of dispute as to the meaning or scope of the judgment, the Court shall construe it upon the request of any party.

Article 61

1. An application for revision of a judgment may be made only when it is based upon the discovery of some fact of such a nature as to be a decisive factor, which fact was,

when the judgment was given, unknown to the Court and also to the party claiming revision, always provided that such ignorance was not due to negligence.

2. The proceedings for revision shall be opened by a judgment of the Court express-ly recording the existence of the new fact, recognizing that it has such a character as to lay the case open to revision, and declaring the application admissible on this ground.

3. The Court may require previous compliance with the terms of the judgment before it admits proceedings in revision.

4. The application for revision must be made at latest within six months of the discovery of the new fact.

5. No application for revision may be made after the lapse of ten years from the date of the judgment.

Article 62

1. Should a state consider that it has an interest of a legal nature which may be affected by the decision in the case, it may submit a request to the Court to be permitted to intervene.

2. It shall be for the Court to decide upon this request.

Article 63

1. Whenever the construction of a convention to which states other than those con-cerned in the case are parties is in question, the Registrar shall notify all such states forthwith.

2. Every state so notified has the right to intervene in the proceedings; but if it uses this right, the construction given by the judgment will be equally binding upon it.

Article 64

Unless otherwise decided by the Court, each party shall bear its own costs.

CHAPTER IV

Advisory opinions

Article 65

1. The Court may give an advisory opinion on any legal question at the request of whatever body may be authorized by or in accordance with the Charter of the United Nations to make such a request.

2. Questions upon which the advisory opinion of the Court is asked shall be laid before the Court by means of a written request containing an exact statement of the question upon which an opinion is required, and accompanied by all documents likely to throw light upon the question.

Article 66

1. The Registrar shall forthwith give notice of the request for an advisory opinion to all states entitled to appear before the Court.

2. The Registrar shall also, by means of a special and direct communication, notify any state entitled to appear before the Court or international organization considered by the Court, or, should it not be sitting, by the President, as likely to be able to furnish information on the question, that the Court will be prepared to receive, within a time

limit to be fixed by the President, written statements, or to hear, at a public sitting to be held for the purpose, oral statements relating to the question.

3. Should any such state entitled to appear before the Court have failed to receive the special communication referred to in paragraph 2 of this Article, such state may express a desire to submit a written statement or to be heard; and the Court will decide.

4. States and organizations having presented written or oral statements or both shall be permitted to comment on the statements made by other states or organizations in the form, to the extent, and within the time-limits which the Court, or, should it not be sitting, the President, shall decide in each particular case. Accordingly, the Registrar shall in due time communicate any such written statements to states and organizations having submitted similar statements.

Article 67

The Court shall deliver its advisory opinions in open Court, notice having been given to the Secretary-General and to the representatives of Members of the United Nations, of other states and of international organizations immediately concerned.

Article 68

In the exercise of its advisory functions the Court shall further be guided by the provisions of the present Statute which apply in contentious cases to the extent to which it recognizes them to be applicable.

CHAPTER V

Amendment

Article 69

Amendments to the present Statute shall be effected by the same procedure as is provided by the Charter of the United Nations for amendments to that Charter, subject however to any provisions which the General Assembly upon recommendation of the Security Council may adopt concerning the participation of states which are parties to the present Statute but are not members of the United Nations.

Article 70

The Court shall have power to propose such amendments to the present Statute as it may deem necessary, through written communications to the Secretary-General, for consideration in conformity with the provisions of Article 69.

[Here follow the signatures]

PARTIES TO THE STATUTE

Members of the United Nations
(as at 30 September 1973)

Afghanistan	19 November 1946
Albania	14 December 1955
Algeria	8 October 1962
*Argentina	24 October 1945
*Australia	1 November 1945
Austria	14 December 1955
Bahamas	18 September 1973
Bahrain	21 September 1971
Barbados	9 December 1966
*Belgium	27 December 1945
Bhutan	21 September 1971
*Bolivia	14 November 1945
Botswana	17 October 1966
*Brazil	24 October 1945
Bulgaria	14 December 1955
Burma	19 April 1948
Burundi	18 September 1962
*Byelorussian SSR	24 October 1945
Cameroon	20 September 1960
*Canada	9 November 1945
Central African Republic	20 September 1960
Chad	20 September 1960
*Chile	24 October 1945
*China [1]	24 October 1945
*Colombia	5 November 1945
Congo [2]	20 September 1960
*Costa Rica	2 November 1945
*Cuba	24 October 1945
Cyprus	20 September 1960
*Czechoslovakia	24 October 1945
Dahomey	20 September 1960
*Denmark	24 October 1945
*Dominican Republic	24 October 1945
*Ecuador	21 December 1945
*Egypt [3]	24 October 1945

1. By resolution 2758 (XXVI) of 25 October 1971, the General Assembly decided "to restore all its rights to the People's Republic of China and to recognize the representatives of its Government as the only legitimate representatives of China to the United Nations, and to expel forthwith the representatives of Chiang Kai-shek from the place which they unlawfully occupy at the United Nations and in all the organizations related to it"
2. Formerly listed as People's Republic of the Congo.
3. Egypt and Syria were original Members of the United Nations from 24 October 1945. Following a plebiscite on 21 February 1958, the United Arab Republic was established

---

*Original Member

*El Salvador	24 October 1945
Equatorial Guinea	12 November 1968
*Ethiopia	13 November 1945
Fiji	13 October 1970
Finland	14 December 1955
*France	24 October 1945
Gabon	20 September 1960
Gambia	21 September 1965
German Democratic Republic	18 September 1973
Germany, Federal Republic	18 September 1973
Ghana	8 March 1957
*Greece	25 October 1945
*Guatemala	21 November 1945
Guinea	12 December 1958
Guyana	20 September 1966
*Haiti	24 October 1945
*Honduras	17 December 1945
Hungary	14 December 1955
Iceland	19 November 1946
*India	30 October 1945
Indonesia [4]	28 September 1950
*Iran	24 October 1945
*Iraq	21 December 1945
Ireland	14 December 1955
Israel	11 May 1949
Italy	14 December 1955
Ivory Coast	20 September 1960
Jamaica	18 September 1962
Japan	18 December 1956
Jordan	14 December 1955
Kenya	16 December 1963
Khmer Republic	14 December 1955
Kuwait	14 May 1963
Laos	14 December 1955
*Lebanon	24 October 1945
Lesotho	17 October 1966
*Liberia	2 November 1945
Libyan Arab Republic	14 December 1955
*Luxembourg	24 October 1945
Madagascar	20 September 1960
Malawi	1 December 1964

by a union of Egypt and Syria and continued as a single Member. On 13 October 1961, Syria, having resumed its status as an independent State, resumed its membership in the United Nations. On 2 September 1971, the United Arab Republic changed its name to Arab Republic of Egypt.

4. By letter of 20 January 1965, Indonesia announced its decision to withdraw from the United Nations "at this stage and under the present circumstances". By telegram of 19 September 1966, it announced its decision "to resume full co-operation with the United Nations and to resume participation in its activities". On 28 September 1966, the General Assembly took note of this decision and the President invited representatives of Indonesia to take seats in the Assembly.

Malaysia [5]	17 September 1957
Maldive Islands	21 September 1965
Mali	28 September 1960
Malta	1 December 1964
Mauritania	27 October 1961
Mauritius	24 April 1968
*Mexico	7 November 1945
Mongolia	27 October 1961
Morocco	12 November 1956
Nepal	14 December 1955
*Netherlands	10 December 1945
*New Zealand	24 October 1945
*Nicaragua	24 October 1945
Niger	20 September 1960
Nigeria	7 October 1960
*Norway	27 November 1945
Oman	7 October 1971
Pakistan	30 September 1947
*Panama	13 November 1945
*Paraguay	24 October 1945
People's Democratic Republic of Yemen	14 December 1967
*Peru	31 October 1945
*Philippines	24 October 1945
*Poland	24 October 1945
Portugal	14 December 1955
Qatar	21 September 1971
Romania	14 December 1955
Rwanda	18 September 1962
*Saudi Arabia	24 October 1945
Senegal	28 September 1960
Sierra Leone	27 September 1961
Singapore	21 September 1965
Somalia	20 September 1960
*South Africa	7 November 1945
Spain	14 December 1955
Sri Lenka	14 December 1955
Sudan (Democratic Republic of)	12 November 1956
Swaziland	24 September 1968
Sweden	19 November 1946
*Syria [3]	24 October 1945
Thailand	16 December 1946
Togo	20 September 1960
Trinidad and Tobago	18 September 1962
Tunisia	12 November 1956
*Turkey	24 October 1945
Uganda	25 October 1962

5. The Federation of Malaya joined the United Nations on 17 September 1957. On 16 September 1963, its name changed to Malaysia, following the admission to the new federation of Singapore, Sabah (North Borneo) and Sarawak. Singapore became an independent State on 9 August 1965 and a Member of the United Nations on 21 September 1965.

*Ukrainian SSR	24 October 1945
*USSR	24 October 1945
United Arab Emirates	9 December 1971
*United Kindom of Great Britain and	
Northern Ireland	24 October 1945
United Republic of Tanzania [6]	14 December 1961
*United States of America	24 October 1945
Upper Volta	20 September 1960
*Uruguay	18 December 1945
*Venezuela	15 November 1945
Yemen Arab Republic	30 September 1947
*Yugoslavia	24 October 1945
Zaire [7]	20 September 1960
Zambia	1 December 1964

(c) *Other States parties to the Statute*

Liechtenstein as from 29 March 1950.
San Marino as from 18 February 1954.
Switzerland as from 28 July 1948.
Japan as from 2 April 1954 until admission to U.N.

6. Tanganyika was a Member of the United Nations from 14 December 1961 and Zanzibar was a Member from 16 December 1963. Following the ratification, on 26 April 1964, of Articles of Union between Tanganyika and Zanzibar, the United Republic of Tanganyika and Zanzibar continued as a single Member, later changing its name to United Republic of Tanzania on 1 November 1964.
7. Formerly Democratic Republic of the Congo.

RULES OF COURT
Adopted on 6 May 1946, as amended on 10 May 1972

Preamble

The Court,

Having regard to Chapter XIV of the Charter of the United Nations;

Having regard to the Statute of the Court annexed thereto;

Acting in pursuance of Article 30 of the Statute;

Adopts the amendments to the Rules of Court approved on 10 May 1972 and authorizes the Registry to issue a new set of Rules embodying these amendments. The amended Rules will come into force on 1 September 1972 and will as from that date replace the Rules adopted by the Court on 6 May 1946, save in respect of any case submitted to the Court before 1 September 1972, or any phase of such a case, which shall continue to be governed by the Rules in force before that date.

Heading I

CONSTITUTION AND WORKING OF THE COURT

Section 1. Constitution of the Court

Judges and Assessors

Article 1

The term of office of Members of the Court elected in February 1946, begins to run on the date of their election. In the case of Members of the Court elected later, the term of office shall begin to run on the date of the expiry of the term of their predecessors. Nevertheless, in the case of a Member elected to fill an occasional vacancy, the term of office shall begin to run on the date of the election.

Article 2

1. Members of the Court elected during the same session of the General Assembly of the United Nations shall take precedence according to seniority of age. Members elected during an earlier session shall take precedence over Members elected at a subsequent session. A Member of the Court who is re-elected without interval, shall retain his former precedence. Judges chosen under Article 31 of the Statute from outside the Court shall take precedence after the other judges in order of seniority of age.

2. The Vice-President shall take his seat on the right of the President. The other judges shall take their seats on the left and right of the President in the order laid down above.

Article 3

1. Any State which considers that it possesses and which intends to exercise the right to choose a judge under Article 31 of the Statute shall so notify the Registry within the time-limit fixed for the filing of the Memorial or Counter-Memorial, as the case may be, or, when it is a case of summary procedure, the filing of the corresponding pleading. The name of the person chosen to sit as judge shall be stated either at the time of giving the notification above mentioned or within a time-limit to be fixed by the President. These notifications shall be communicated to the other parties and they may submit their views to the Court within a time-limit to be fixed by the President. If any doubt or objection should arise, the decision shall rest with the Court, if necessary after hearing the parties.

2. If, on receipt of one or more notifications under the terms of the preceding paragraph, the Court finds that there are several parties in the same interest and that none of them has a judge of its nationality upon the Bench, it shall fix a time-limit within which these parties, acting in concert, may choose a judge under Article 31 of the Statute. If, at the expiration of this time-limit, they have not notified their choice, the Court shall nevertheless proceed to examine and adjudicate upon the case.

Article 4

Where one or more of the parties are entitled to choose a judge under Article 31 of the Statute, the Court may sit with a number of judges exceeding the number of Members of the Court fixed by the Statute.

Article 5

1. The declaration to be made by every judge in accordance with Article 20 of the Statute shall be as follows:

"I solemnly declare that I will perform my duties and exercise my powers as judge honourably, faithfully, impartially and conscientiously."

2. This declaration shall be made at the first public sitting of the Court at which the judge is present after his election or after being chosen under Article 31 of the Statute.

Article 6

For the purpose of applying Article 18 of the Statute the President, or if necessary the Vice-President, shall convene the Members of the Court. The Member affected shall be allowed to furnish explanations. When he has done so the question shall be discussed and a vote shall be taken, the Member affected not being present. If the Members present are unanimous, the Registrar shall issue the notification prescribed in the above-mentioned Article.

Article 7

1. The Court may, either upon its own initiative or upon a request made not later than the end of the written proceedings, decide, for the purpose of a contentious case or request for advisory opinion, to appoint assessors to sit with it but without the power to vote.

2. When the Court so decides, the President shall take steps to obtain all the information relevant to the choice of the assessors.

3. The assessors shall be appointed, by secret ballot and by a majority of the votes of the Members of the Court composing it at the time, at a private meeting of the Court.

4.   The same functions shall belong to the Chambers provided for by Articles 26 and 29 of the Statute and to the Presidents thereof, and may be exercised in the same manner.

Article 8

Before entering upon their duties, assessors shall make the following declaration at a public sitting:

"I solemnly declare that I will perform my duties as an assessor honourably, faithfully, impartially and conscientiously, and that I will scrupulously observe all the provisions of the Statute and of the Rules of the Court."

The Presidency

Article 9

1.   The Court shall proceed to elect the President and the Vice-President in the course of the month following the date on which the judges elected at the periodic election of Members of the Court enter upon their duties. The President and Vice-President thus elected shall take up their duties forthwith. If, at the periodic election, the President is not re-elected a Member of the Court, the duties of President shall in the meantime be discharged in accordance with Article 11 and Article 12, paragraph 2, of these Rules.

2.   If the President or the Vice-President should cease to be a Member of the Court or should resign the office of President or Vice-President before the expiry of his normal term, an election shall be held for the purpose of appointing a successor for the unexpired portion of the term.

3.   The elections referred to in the present Article shall take place by secret ballot. The Member of the Court obtaining an absolute majority of votes shall be declared elected.

Article 10

The President shall direct the work and administration of the Court; he shall preside at the meetings of the Court.

Article 11

The Vice-President shall take the place of the President if the latter is unable to fulfil his duties or if the office of President is vacant.

Article 12

1.   Provision shall be made to ensure at the seat of the Court the continuous discharge of the duties of the office of President either by the President or the Vice-President.

2.   If at the same time both the President and the Vice-President are unable to fulfil their duties, or if both offices are vacant at the same time, the duties of President shall be discharged by the oldest among the Members of the Court who have been longest on the Bench.

Article 13

1.   If the President is a national of one of the parties to a case brought before the Court, he will abstain from exercising his functions as President in respect of that case. The same rule applies to the Vice-President or to any Member of the Court who may be called on to act as President.

2. If a case is begun before a periodic election of Members of the Court and continues after such election, the duties of President shall be discharged by the Member of the Court who presided when the case was last under examination. If he is unable to sit, the duties of President shall be performed by the newly elected President or, failing him, the newly elected Vice-President, provided that the President or the Vice-President, as the case may be, is qualified to sit in the case. If neither is able to sit, the duties of President shall be performed by the oldest among the Members of the Court who have been longest on the Bench.

The Registry

Article 14

1. The Court shall select its Registrar from amongst candidates proposed by Members of the Court. The Members of the Court shall receive adequate notice of the date on which the list of candidates will be closed so as to enable nominations and information concerning the nationals of distant countries to be received in sufficient time.

2. Nominations must give the necessary particulars regarding the candidates' age, nationality, university qualifications and linguistic attainments, their present occupation, their practical legal experience and their experience in diplomacy and in the work of international organizations.

3. The election shall be by secret ballot and by an absolute majority of votes.

4. The Registrar shall be elected for a term of seven years. He may be re-elected.

5. If the Registrar should cease to hold his office before the expiration of the term above mentioned, an election shall be held for the purpose of appointing a successor. Such election shall be for a term of seven years.

6. The Court shall appoint a Deputy-Registrar to assist the Registrar, to act as Registrar in his absence and, in the event of his ceasing to hold the office, to perform the duties until a new Registrar shall have been appointed. The Deputy-Registrar shall be appointed under the same conditions and in the same way as the Registrar.

Article 15

1. Before taking up his duties, the Registrar shall make the following declaration at a meeting of the Court:

"I solemnly declare that I will perform the duties incumbent upon me as Registrar of the International Court of Justice in all loyalty, dicretion and good conscience."

2. The Deputy-Registrar shall make a similar declaration in the same circumstances.

Article 16

The Registrar is entitled to two months' holiday in each year.

Article 17

1. The officials of the Registry, other than the Deputy-Registrar, shall be appointed by the Court on proposals submitted by the Registrar.

2. Before taking up his duties, each official shall make the following declaration before the President, the Registrar being present:

"I solemnly declare that I will perform the duties incumbent upon me as an official of the International Court of justice in all loyalty, discretion and good conscience."

Article 18

1. The Court shall prescribe and, when necessary, modify the plan of the organization of the Registry and for this purpose shall request the Registrar to make proposals.

2. The Regulations for the staff of the Registry shall be drawn up having regard to the plan of the organization prescribed by the Court and to the provisions of the Regulations for the Staff of the Secretariat of the United Nations to which they shall, as far as possible, conform. Their adoption by the President on the proposal of the Registrar is subject to subsequent approval by the Court.

Article 19

If neither the Registrar not the Deputy-Registrar can be present or if both these offices are vacant at the same time, the President shall appoint an official of the Registry to act as a substitute for the Registrar for such time as may be necessary.

Article 20

1. The General List of cases submitted to the Court for decision or for advisory opinion shall be prepared and kept up to date by the Registrar on the instructions and subject to the authority of the President. Cases shall be entered in the list and numbered successively according to the date of the receipt of the document bringing the case before the Court.

2. The General List shall contain the following headings:

I.	Number in list.
II.	Short title.
III.	Date of registration.
IV.	Registration number.
V.	File number in the archives.
VI.	Class of case (contentious procedure or advisory opinion).
VII.	Parties.
VIII.	Interventions.
IX.	Method of submission.
X.	Date of document instituting proceedings.
XI.	Time-limits for filing pleadings.
XII.	Prolongation, if any, of time-limits.
XIII.	Date of closure of the written proceedings.
XIV.	Postponements.
XV.	Date of the beginning of the hearing (date of the first public sitting).
XVI.	Observations.
XVII.	References to earlier or subsequent cases.
XVIII.	Result (nature and date).
XIX.	Removal from the list (cause and date).
XX.	References to publications of the Court relating to the case.

3. The General List shall also contain a space for notes, if any, and spaces for the inscription, above the initials of the President and of the Registrar, of the dates of the entry of the case, of its result, or of its removal from the list, as the case may be.

Article 21

1. The Registrar shall be the regular channel for communications to and from the Court.

2. The Registrar shall ensure that the date of despatch and receipt of all communications and notifications may be readily verified. Communications addressed to the agents of the parties shall be considered as having been addressed to the parties themselves. The date of receipt shall be noted on all documents received by the Registrar, and a receipt bearing this date and the number under which the document has been registered shall be given to the sender.

3. The Registrar shall, subject to the obligations of secrecy attaching to his official duties, reply to all enquiries concerning the work of the Court, including enquiries from the Press.

4. The Registrar shall publish in the Press all necessary information as the date and hour fixed for public sittings.

5. The Registrar shall communicate to the government of the country in which the Court, or a Chamber dealing with a case, is sitting, the names, first names and description of the agents, counsel and advocates appointed by each of the parties for the purposes of the case.

Article 22

A collection of the judgments and advisory opinions of the Court, and also of such orders as the Court may decide to include therein, shall be printed and published under the responsibility of the Registrar.

Article 23

1. The Registrar shall be responsible for the archives, the accounts and all administrative work. He shall have the custody of the seals and stamps of the Court. The Registrar or his substitute shall be present at all sittings of the Court and at sittings of the Chambers. The Registrar shall be responsible for drawing up the minutes of the meetings.

2. He shall undertake, in addition, all duties which may be laid upon him by these Rules.

3. Instructions for the Registry shall be drawn up by the Registrar and approved by the President.

The Chambers

Article 24

1. The Chamber of Summary Procedure to be formed annually under Article 29 of the Statute shall be composed of five Members of the Court, comprising the President and Vice-President of the Court, acting ex officio, and three other members elected in accordance with Article 27, paragraph 1, of these Rules. In addition, two Members of the Court shall also be elected annually to act as substitutes.

2. The election referred to in paragraph 1 of this Rule shall be held within three months after 6 February. The members of the Chamber shall enter upon their functions on election and continue to serve until the next election; they may be re-elected.

3. If a member of the Chamber is unable, for whatever reason, to sit in a given case, he shall be replaced for the purposes of that case by the senior in rank of the two substitutes.

4. If a member of a Chamber ceases to be a member of it otherwise than by replacement under paragraph 1, his place shall be taken by the senior in rank of the two substitutes, who shall thereupon become a full member of the Chamber and be replaced as substitute by the election of another one. Should vacancies exceed the number of

available substitutes, elections shall be held as soon as feasible in respect of the vacancies still existing after the substitutes have assumed full membership and in respect of the vacancies in the substitutes.

Article 25

1. When the Court decides to form one or more of the Chambers provided for in Article 26, paragraph 1, of the Statute, it shall determine the particular category of cases for which each Chamber is formed, the number of its members, the period for which they will serve, and the date at which they will enter upon their duties.

2. The members of the Chamber shall be elected in accordance with Article 27, paragraph 1, of these Rules, from among the Members of the Court having regard to any special knowledge, expertise or previous experience which any of the Members of the Court may have in relation to the category of case the Chamber is being formed to deal with.

3. The Court may decide upon the dissolution of a Chamber, but without prejudice to the duty of the Chamber concerned to finish any cases pending before it.

Article 26

1. When the Court, acting under Article 26, paragraph 2, of the Statute, decides, at the request of the parties, to form a Chamber to deal with a particular case, the President shall consult the agents of the parties regarding the composition of the Chamber, and shall report to the Court accordingly.

2. When the Court has determined, with the approval of the parties, the number of its Members who are to constitute the Chamber, it will proceed to their election, in accordance with the provisions of Article 27, paragraph 1, of these Rules. The same procedure shall be followed as regards the filling of any vacancy that may occur on the Chamber.

3. Any Member of a Chamber formed under this Rule who ceases to be a Member of the Court by reason of the expiry of his term of office, shall continue to sit in the case, whatever the stage reached when his term of office expires.

Article 27

1. Elections to all Chambers shall take place by secret ballot. The Members of the Court obtaining the largest number of votes constituting a majority of the Members of the Court composing it at the time shall be declared elected. If necessary to fill vacancies, more than one ballot shall take place, such ballot being limited to the number of vacancies that remain to be filled.

2. Subject to Article 13, paragraph 1, of these Rules, the President of the Court shall preside over any Chamber of which he is a member, and the same shall apply to the Vice-President of the Court in respect of any Chamber of which he, but not the President, is a member. Subject to the same provision, if neither the President nor the Vice-President is a member, the Chamber shall elect its own President by secret ballot and an absolute majority vote of its members.

3. The member of the Chamber who, not being its President, is senior in rank shall act as Vice-President. The provisions of Article 10 shall be applicable, *mutatis mutandis*, in respect of all the Chambers and their presidencies.

4. If in any particular case the President of the Chamber concerned is prevented from sitting, or from acting as President, the functions of the Presidency shall be assumed by the Vice-President of the Chamber or, failing him, by the next ranking member of the Chamber in a position to act.

5. Without prejudice to Article 26, paragraph 3, of these Rules the duty of a member of a Chamber who ceases to be a Member of the Court, to finish a case already begun by him, arises only if he ceases to be a Member of the Court after the date on which the Chamber convenes for the oral proceedings. When judgment has been pronounced, such a duty does not extend to sitting in future phases of the same case. If the member of the Chamber concerned is also its President, he shall continue to act as such.

Section 2. Working of the Court.

Article 28

1. In the absence of a special resolution by the Court, the dates and duration of the vacations of the Court are fixed as follows: *(a)* from 18 December to 7 January; *(b)* from the Sunday before Easter to the second Sunday after Easter; *(c)* from 15 July to 15 September. The duties of President shall nevertheless be continuously discharged at the seat of the Court. For this purpose, the President shall either himself maintain contact with the Registrar or shall request the Vice-President to take his place.

2. In case of urgency, the President may at any time convene the Members of the Court during the periods mentioned in the preceding paragraph.

3. The public holidays which are customary at the place where the Court is sitting will be observed by the Court.

Article 29

1. Any Member of the Court who desires to obtain leave in pursuance of Article 23, paragraph 2, of the Statute, shall send his request to the Registry. The Court shall consider the request, and the date and the duration of the leave which it grants to a judge shall be fixed having regard to what is required to ensure its proper working and to the distance between The Hague and his home.

2. The number of Members of the Court on leave at the same time must not exceed two. The President and the Vice-President must not both be absent on leave at the same time.

Article 30

Members of the Court who are prevented by illness or other serious reasons from attending a sitting of the Court to which they have been summoned by the President, shall notify the President who will inform the Court.

Article 31

1. The date and hour of sittings of the Court shall be fixed by the President.

2. The President of the Court shall fix the date for the convening of any Chamber referred to in Articles 26 and 29 of the Statute. The date and hour of the sittings of such Chamber shall be fixed by the President of the Chamber.

3. The Court, or if it is not sitting the President, may fix the place, other than The Hague, where one of the Chambers provided for by Articles 26 and 29 of the Statute shall sit and exercise its functions.

Article 32

If a sitting of the Court has been convened and it is found that there is no quorum, the President shall adjourn the sitting until a quorum has been obtained. Judges chosen under Article 31 of the Statute shall not be taken into account for the calculation of the quorum.

Article 33[1]

1. The Court shall sit in private to deliberate upon disputes which are submitted to it and upon advisory opinions which it is asked to give.

2. Only the judges, and the assessors, if any, shall take part in the deliberations. The Registrar or his substitute shall be present. No other person shall be admitted except in pursuance of a special decision taken by the Court.

3. Every judge who is present at the deliberations shall state his opinion together with the reasons on which it is based.

4. Any judge may request that a question which is to be voted upon shall be drawn in precise terms in both the official languages and distributed to the Court. Effect shall be given to any such request.

5. The decision of the Court shall be based upon the conclusions concurred in after final discussion by a majority of the judges. The judges shall vote in the order inverse to the order laid down by Article 2 of these Rules.

6. No detailed minutes shall be prepared of the private meetings of the Court for deliberation upon judgments or advisory opinions; the minutes of these meetings are to be considered as confidential and shall record only the subject of the debates, the votes taken, the names of those voting for and against a motion and statements expressly made for insertion in the minutes.

7. Unless otherwise decided by the Court, paragraphs 2, 4 and 5 of this Article shall apply to deliberations by the Court in private upon any administrative matter.

Heading II

CONTENTIOUS PROCEEDINGS

Article 34

The rules contained in Sections 1, 2 and 4 of this Heading shall not preclude the adoption by the Court of particular modifications or additions proposed jointly by the parties and considered by the Court to be appropriate to the case and in the circumstances.

---

1. On 6 May 1946, the Court took note of the Resolution of the Permanent Court of International Justice regarding that Court's judicial practice adopted on 20 February 1931, and revised on 17 March 1936, and decided to adopt provisionally the method of deliberation described in that Resolution. On 5 July 1968, the Court adopted a new Resolution Concerning the Internal Judicial Practice of the Court (see *I.C.J. Yearbook 1967-1968*, pp. 88-91).

Section 1. Procedure before the full Court

I. General Rules

Institution of Proceedings

Article 35

1. When a case is brought before the Court by means of a special agreement, Article 40, paragraph 1, of the Statute shall apply.

2. When a case is brought before the Court by means of an application, the application must, as laid down in Article 40, paragraph 1, of the Statute, indicate the party making it, the party against whom the claim is brought and the subject of the dispute. It must also, as far as possible, specify the provision on which the applicant founds the jurisdiction of the Court, state the precise nature of the claim and give a succinct statement of the facts and grounds on which the claim is based, these facts and grounds being developed in the Memorial, to which the evidence will be annexed.

3. The original of an application shall be signed either by the agent of the party submitting it or by the diplomatic representative of that party at the seat of the Court or by a duly authorized person. If the document bears the signature of a person other than the diplomatic representative of that party at the seat of the Court, the signature must be legalized by this diplomatic representative or by the competent authority of the government concerned.

Article 36

1. When a case is brought before the Court by means of an application, the Registrar shall forthwith transmit to the party against whom the claim is made a copy of the application certified as correct.

2. When a case is brought before the Court by means of a special agreement filed by one only of the parties, the Registrar shall forthwith notify the other party that it has been so filed.

Article 37

1. The Registrar shall forthwith transmit to all the Members of the Court copies of special agreements or applications submitting a case to the Court.

2. He shall also transmit copies: *(a)* to Members of the United Nations through the Secretary-General and *(b)*, by means of special arrangements made for this purpose between them and the Registrar, to any other States entitled to appear before the Court.

Article 38

1. When a case is brought before the Court by means of a special agreement, the appointment of the agent or agents of the party or parties filing the special agreement shall be notified at the same time as the special agreement is filed. If the special agreement is filed by one only of the parties, the other party shall, when acknowledging receipt of the notification of the filing of the special agreement or failing this, as soon as possible, inform the Court of the name of its agent.

2. When a case is brought before the Court by means of an application, the application, or the covering letter, shall state the name of the agent of the applicant government.

3. The party against whom the application is made and to whom it is notified shall,

when acknowledging receipt of the notification, or failing this, as soon as possible, inform the Court of the name of its agent.

4. Applications to intervene under Article 69 of these Rules, interventions under Article 71 and requests under Article 83 for the revision, or under Article 84 for the interpretation, of a judgment, shall similarly be accompanied by the appointment of an agent.

5. The appointment of an agent must be accompanied by a statement of an address for service at the seat of the Court to which all communications relating to the case should be sent.

Article 39

When a State which is not a party to the Statute is admitted by the Security Council, in pursuance of Article 35 of the Statute, to appear before the Court, it shall satisfy the Court that it has complied with any conditions that may have been prescribed for its admission: the document which evidences this compliance shall be filed in the Registry at the same time as the notification of the appointment of the agent.

Preliminary Consultation and Time-Limits

Article 40

1. In every case submitted to the Court, the President will ascertain the views of the parties with regard to questions of procedure; for this purpose he may summon the agents to meet him as soon as they have been appointed.

2. In the light of the information obtained by the President, the Court will make the necessary orders to determine, *inter alia*, the number and the order of filing of the pleadings and the time-limits within which they must be filed.

3. In making an order under paragraph 2 of this Article, any agreement between the parties which does not cause unjustified delay shall be taken into account.

4. The Court may, at the request of the party concerned, extend any time-limit, or decide that any step taken after the expiration of the time-limit fixed therefor shall be considered as valid, if it is satisfied that there is adequate justification for the request. In either case the other party shall be given an opportunity to state its views.

5. If the Court is not sitting, its powers under this Article shall be exercised by the President, but without prejudice to any subsequent decision of the Court. If the consultation referred to in paragraph 1 of this Article reveals persistent disagreement between the parties as to the application of Article 44, paragraph 2, or Article 45, paragraph 2, of these Rules the Court shall be convened to decide the matter.

Article 41

Time-limits may be assigned by the lapse of a specified period, but must always indicate definite dates. Such time-limits shall be as short as the character of the case permits.

Written Proceedings

Article 42

1. If the parties agree that the proceedings shall be conducted wholly in French, or wholly in English, the pleadings shall be submitted only in the language adopted by the parties.

2. In the absence of an agreement with regard to the language to be used, the pleadings shall be submitted either in French or in English.

3. If in pursuance of Article 39, paragraph 3, of the Statute a language other than French or English is used, a translation into French or English shall be attached to the original of each document submitted.

4. The Registrar is under no obligation to make translations of the pleadings or any documents annexed thereto.

Article 43[1]

1. The original of every pleading shall be signed by the agent and filed in the Registry. It shall be accompanied by the number of copies required by the Registry, but without prejudice to an increase in that number should the need arise later.

2. When communicating a copy of a pleading to a party in pursuance of Article 43 of the Statute, the Registrar shall certify that it is a correct copy of the original filed in the Registry.

3. All pleadings shall be dated. When a pleading has to be filed by a certain date, it is the date of the receipt of the pleading in the Registry which will be regarded by the Court as the material date.

4. If the Registrar at the request of the agent of a party arranges for the printing, at the cost of that party, of a pleading which it is intended to file with the Court, the text must be sent to the Registry in sufficient time to enable the printed pleading to be filed before the expiry of any time-limit which may apply to it. The printing is done under the responsibility of the party in question.

5. The correction of a slip or error in any document which has been filed can be made at any time with the consent of the other party, or by leave of the President.

Article 44

1. The written pleadings in a case begun by means of an application shall consist, in the following order, of:

a Memorial by the applicant;
a Counter-Memorial by the respondent.

2. The Court may authorize or direct that there shall be a Reply by the applicant and a Rejoinder by the respondent if the parties are so agreed, or if the Court decides, *proprio motu* or at the request of one of the parties, that these pleadings are necessary.

Article 45

1. In a case begun by the notification of a special agreement, the number and order of the written pleadings shall be governed by the provisions of the agreement, unless the Court, after ascertaining the views of the parties, decides otherwise.

2. If the special agreement contains no such provision, and if the parties have not subsequently agreed on the order of pleadings, they shall each deliver a Memorial and Counter-Memorial, within the same time-limits. The Court shall not authorize the presentation of Replies unless it finds them to be necessary.

Article 46

1. A Memorial shall contain a statement of the relevant facts, a statement of law, and the submissions.

---

1. The agents of the parties are requested to ascertain from the Registry the usual format of the pleadings.

2. A Counter-Memorial shall contain an admission or denial of the facts stated in the Memorial; any additional facts, if necessary; observations concerning the statement of law in the Memorial; a statement of law in answer thereto; and the submissions.

3. The Reply and Rejoinder, whenever authorized by the Court, shall not merely repeat the parties' contentions, but shall be directed to bringing out the issues that still divide them.

4. Every pleading shall contain the party's submissions at the relevant stage of the case, or a confirmation of the submissions previously made, without recapitulation of the arguments presented.

Article 47

1. There must be annexed to every Memorial and Counter-Memorial and other pleading, copies of all the relevant documents, a list of which shall be given after the submissions. If, on account of the length of a document, extracts only are attached, the document itself or a complete copy of it must, if possible, unless the document has been published and is available to the public, be communicated to the Registrar for the use of the Court and of the other party.

2. Every pleading and every document annexed which is in a language other than French or English, must be accompanied by a translation into one of the official languages of the Court. Nevertheless, in the case of lengthy documents, translations of extracts may be submitted, subject, however, to any subsequent decision by the Court, or, if it is not sitting, by the President.

Article 48

1. The Registrar shall transmit to the judges and to the parties copies of the pleadings and documents annexed in the case, as and when he receives them.

2. The Court, or the President if the Court is not sitting, may, after obtaining the views of the parties, decide that the Registrar shall in a particular case make the pleadings and annexed documents available to the government of any Member of the United Nations or of any State which is entitled to appear before the Court.

3. The Court, or the President if the Court is not sitting, may, with the consent of the parties, authorize the pleadings and annexed documents in regard to a particular case to be made accessible to the public before the termination of the case.

Article 49

Upon the closure of the written proceedings, the case is ready for hearing.

Article 50

1. Subject to the priority provided for by Article 66 of these Rules, cases submitted to the Court will be taken in the order in which they become ready for hearing. When several cases are ready for hearing, the order in which they will be taken is determined by the position which they occupy in the General List.

2. Nevertheless, the Court may, in special circumstances, decide to take a case in priority to other cases which are ready for hearing and which precede it in the General List.

3. If the parties to a case which is ready for hearing are agreed in asking for the case to be put after other cases which are ready for hearing and which follow it in the General List, the President may grant such a postponement: if the parties are not in agreement, the President shall decide whether or not to submit the question to the Court.

Oral Proceedings

Article 51

1. When a case is ready for hearing, the date for the commencement of the oral proceedings shall be fixed by the Court, or by the President if the Court is not sitting.

2. If occasion should arise, the Court or the President, if the Court is not sitting, may decide that the commencement or continuance of the hearings shall be postponed.

Article 52

1. After the closure of the written proceedings, no further documents may be submitted to the Court by either party except with the consent of the other party or as provided in paragraph 2 of this Article. The party desiring to produce a new document shall file the original or a certified copy thereof, together with the number of copies required by the Registry, which will be responsible for communicating it to the other party and will inform the Court. The other party shall be held to have given its consent if it does not lodge an objection to the production of the document.

2. In the absence of consent, the Court, after hearing the parties, may, if it considers the document necessary, authorize its production.

3. If a new document is produced under paragraph 1 or paragraph 2 of this Article, the other party shall have an opportunity of commenting upon it and of submitting documents in support of its comments.

4. No reference may be made during the oral proceedings to the contents of any document which has not been produced in accordance with Article 43 of the Statute or the present Article, unless the document is part of a publication readily available.

5. The application of the provisions of this Article shall not in any case constitute a ground for delaying the opening or the course of the oral proceedings.

Article 53

Without prejudice to the provisions of the Rules concerning the production of documents, each party shall communicate to the Registry, in sufficient time before the commencement of the oral proceedings, information regarding the evidence which it intends to produce or which it intends to request the Court to obtain. This communication shall contain a list of the surnames, first names, descriptions and places of residence of the witnesses and experts whom the party intends to call, with indications in general terms of the point or points to which their evidence will be directed.

Article 54

The Court shall determine whether the parties should present their arguments before or after the production of the evidence; the parties shall, however, retain the right to comment on the evidence given.

Article 55

The order in which the parties will be heard, and the number of counsel and advocates who will address the Court, and the method of handling the evidence and of examining any witnesses and experts shall be determined by the Court after the views of the parties have been ascertained in accordance with Article 40, paragraph 1, of these Rules.

Article 56

1. The oral statements made on behalf of each party shall be as succinct as possible within the limits of what is requisite for the adequate presentation of that party's contentions at the hearing. Accordingly, they shall be directed to the essential issues that divide the parties and shall not go over the whole ground covered by the written pleadings, nor simply repeat the facts and arguments these contain.

2. At the conclusion of the last statement made by a party at the hearing, its agent shall read that party's final submissions, without recapitulation of the arguments. Written copies of these, signed by the agent, shall at the same time be communicated to the Court and to the other party.

Article 57

1. The Court may at any time prior to or during the hearing indicate any points or issues to which it would like the parties specially to address themselves, or on which there has been sufficient argument.

2. The Court may, during the hearing, put questions to the agents, counsel and advocates, and may ask them for explanations.

3. Each judge has a similar right to put questions, but before exercising it he should make his intention known to the President, who is made responsible by Article 45 of the Statute for the control of the hearing.

4. The agents, counsel and advocates may answer immediately, later in the sitting, or subsequently, but in any event prior to the close of the oral proceedings.

Article 58

1. Witnesses and experts shall be examined by the agents, counsel or advocates of the parties under the control of the President. Questions may be put to them by the President and by the judges.

2. Each witness shall make the following declaration before giving his evidence in Court:

   "I solemnly declare upon my honour and conscience that I will speak the truth, the whole truth and nothing but the truth."

3. Each expert shall make the following declaration before making his statement in Court:

   "I solemnly declare upon my honour and conscience that my statement will be in accordance with my sincere belief."

Article 59

The Court may request the parties to call witnesses or experts, or may call for the production of any other evidence on points of fact in regard to which the parties are not in agreement. If need be, the Court shall apply the provisions of Article 44 of the Statute.

Article 60

Witnesses or experts who appear at the instance of the Court shall be paid out of the funds of the Court.

Article 61

The Court, or the President if the Court is not sitting, shall, at the request of one of the parties or on its own initiative, take the necessary steps for the examination of witnesses or experts otherwise than before the Court itself.

Article 62

1. If the Court considers it necessary to arrange for an enquiry or an expert opinion, it shall, after duly hearing the parties, issue an order to this effect, defining the subject of the enquiry or expert opinion, and stating the number and mode of appointment of the persons to hold the enquiry or of the experts and the procedure to be followed.

2. Every report or record of an enquiry and every expert opinion shall be communicated to the parties.

Article 63

1. At any stage in the proceedings before the termination of the hearing, the Court may, either *proprio motu*, or at the request of one of the parties communicated as provided in Article 53 of these Rules, request a public international organization, pursuant to Article 34 of the Statute, to furnish information relevant to a case before it. The Court, after consulting the chief administrative officer of the organization concerned, shall decide whether such information shall be presented to it orally or in writing, and the time-limits for its presentation.

2. When a public international organization sees fit to furnish, on its own initiative, information relevant to a case before the Court, it shall do so in the form of a Memorial to be filed in the Registry before the closure of the written proceedings. The Court shall retain the right to require such information to be supplemented, either orally or in writing, in the form of answers to any questions which it may see fit to formulate, and also to authorize the parties to comment, either orally or in writing, on the information thus furnished.

3. In the circumstances contemplated by Article 34, paragraph 3, of the Statute, the Registrar, on the instructions of the Court, or of the President if the Court is not sitting, shall proceed as prescribed in that paragraph. The Court, or the President if the Court is not sitting, may, as from the date on which the Registrar has communicated copies of the written proceedings, and after consulting the chief administrative officer of the public international organization concerned, fix a time-limit within which the organization may submit to the Court its observations in writing. These observations shall be communicated to the parties and may be discussed by them and by the representative of the said organization during the oral proceedings.

Article 64

1. In the absence of any decision to the contrary by the Court, all speeches and statements made and evidence given at the hearing in one of the official languages of the Court shall be interpreted into the other official language. If they are made or given in any other language, they shall be interpreted into the two official languages of the Court.

2. Whenever, in accordance with Article 39, paragraph 3, of the Statute, a language other than French or English is used, the necessary arrangements for interpretation into one of the two official languages shall be made by the party concerned; however, the Registrar shall make arrangements for the verification of the interpretation provided by a party of evidence given on the party's behalf. In the case of witnesses or experts who appear at the instance of the Court, arrangements for interpretation shall be made by the Registry.

3. A party on whose behalf speeches or statements are to be made, or evidence given, in a language which is not one of the official languages of the Court, shall so notify the Registrar in sufficient time for him to make the necessary arrangements.

4. Before first interpreting in any case, an interpreter provided by a party shall make the following declaration in open Court:

"I solemnly declare upon my honour and conscience that my interpretation will be faithful and complete."

Article 65

1. A verbatim record shall be made by the Registrar of every hearing, in the official language of the Court which has been used. When the language used is not one of the two official languages of the Court, the verbatim record shall be prepared in one of the Court's official languages.

2. When speeches or statements are made in a language which is not one of the official languages of the Court, the party on whose behalf they are made shall supply to the Registry in advance a text thereof in one of the official languages, and this text shall constitute the relevant part of the verbatim record.

3. The transcript of the verbatim record shall be preceded by the names of the judges present, the agents, counsel and advocates of the parties, and the surnames and first names, nationality, description and residence of witnesses or experts.

4. Copies of the transcript shall be circulated to the judges sitting in the case, and to the parties. The latter may, under the supervision of the Court, correct the transcripts of the speeches and statements made on their behalf, but in no case may such corrections affect the sense and bearing of the statement. The judges may likewise make corrections in the transcript of anything they may have said.

5. Witnesses and experts shall be shown that part of the transcript which relates to the evidence given, or the statements made by them, and may correct it in like manner as the parties.

6. One certified true copy of the eventual corrected transcript, signed by the President and the Registrar, shall constitute the authentic minutes of the sitting for the purposes of Article 47 of the Statute. The minutes of public hearings shall be printed and published by the Court.

II. Occasional Rules

Interim Protection

Article 66

1. A request for the indication of interim measures of protection may be filed at any time during the proceedings in the case in connection with which it is made. The request shall specify the case to which it relates, the rights to be protected and the interim measures of which the indication is proposed.

2. A request for the indication of interim measures of protection shall have priority over all other cases. The decision thereon shall be treated as a matter of urgency.

3. If the Court is not sitting, the Members shall be convened by the President forthwith. Pending the meeting of the Court and a decision by it, the President shall, if need be, take such measures as may appear to him necessary in order to enable the Court to give an effective decision.

4. The Court may indicate interim measures of protection other than those proposed in the request.

5. The rejection of a request for the indication of interim measures of protection shall not prevent the party which has made it from making a fresh request in the same case based on new facts.

6. The Court may indicate interim measures of protection *proprio motu*. If the Court is not sitting, the President may convene the Members in order to submit to the Court the question whether it is expedient to indicate such measures.

7. The Court may at any time by reason of a change in the situation revoke or modify its decision indicating interim measures of protection.

8. The Court shall only indicate interim measures of protection after giving the parties an opportunity of presenting their observations on the subject. The same rule applies when the Court revokes or modifies a decision indicating such measures.

Preliminary Objections

Article 67

1. Any objection by the respondent to the jurisdiction of the Court or to the admissibility of the application, or other objection the decision upon which is requested before any further proceedings on the merits, shall be made in writing within the time-limit fixed for the delivery of the Counter-Memorial. Any such objection made by a party other than the repondent shall be filed within the time-limit fixed for the delivery of that party's first pleading.

2. The preliminary objection shall set out the facts and the law on which the objection is based, the submissions and a list of the documents in support; copies of these documents shall be attached; it shall mention any evidence which the party may desire to produce.

3. Upon receipt by the Registrar of a preliminary objection filed by a party, the proceedings on the merits shall be suspended and the Court, or the President if the Court is not sitting, shall fix the time-limit within which the other party may present a written statement of its observations and submissions; documents in support shall be attached and evidence which it is proposed to produce shall be mentioned.

4. Unless otherwise decided by the Court, the further proceedings shall be oral.

5. The statements of fact and law in the pleadings referred to in paragraphs 2 and 3 above, and the statements and evidence presented at the hearings contemplated by paragraph 4, shall be confined to those matters that are relevant to the objection.

6. In order to enable the Court to determine its jurisdiction at the preliminary stage of the proceedings, the Court, whenever necessary, may request the parties to argue all questions of law and fact, and to adduce all evidence, which bear on the issue.

7. After hearing the parties, the Court shall give its decision in the form of a judgment, by which it shall either uphold the objection, reject it, or declare that the objection does not possess, in the circumstances of the case, an exclusively preliminary character. If the Court rejects the objection or declares that it does not possess an exclusively preliminary character, it shall fix time-limits for the further proceedings.

8. Any agreement between the parties that an objection submitted under paragraph 1 be heard and determined within the framework of the merits shall be given effect by the Court.

Counter-Claims

Article 68

When proceedings have been instituted by means of an application, a counter-claim may be presented in the submissions of the Counter-Memorial, provided that such counter-claim is directly connected with the subject-matter of the application and that it comes within the jurisdiction of the Court. In the event of doubt as to the connection between the question presented by way of counter-claim and the subject-matter of the application the Court shall, after due examination, direct whether or not the question thus presented shall be joined to the original proceedings.

Intervention

Article 69

1.   An application for permission to intervene under the terms of Article 62 of the Statute shall be filed in the Registry at latest before the commencement of the oral proceedings.

2.   The application shall contain:

a description of the case;

a statement of law and of fact justifying intervention; and

a list of the documents in support of the application; these documents shall be attached.

3.   The application shall be communicated to the parties, who shall send to the Registry their observations in writing within a time-limit to be fixed by the Court, or by the President, if the Court is not sitting.

4.   The Registrar shall also transmit copies of the application for permission to intervene: *(a)* to Members of the United Nations through the Secretary-General and *(b)*, by means of special arrangements made for this purpose between them and the Registrar, to any other States entitled to appear before the Court.

5.   The application to intervene shall be placed on the agenda for a hearing, the date and hour of which shall be notified to all concerned. Nevertheless, if the parties have not, in their written observations, opposed the application to intervene, the Court may decide that there shall be no oral argument.

6.   The Court will give its decision on the application in the form of a judgment.

Article 70

1.   If the Court admits the intervention and if the party intervening expresses a desire to file a Memorial on the merits, the Court shall fix the time-limits within which the Memorial shall be filed and within which the other parties may reply by Counter-Memorials; the same course shall be followed in regard to the Reply and the Rejoinder. If the Court is not sitting, the time-limits shall be fixed by the President.

2.   If the Court has not yet given its decision upon the intervention and the application to intervene is not opposed, the President, if the Court is not sitting, may, without prejudice to the decision of the Court on the question whether the application should be granted, fix the time-limits within which the intervening party may file a Memorial on the merits and the other parties may reply by Counter-Memorials.

3.   In the cases referred to in the two preceding paragraphs, the time-limits shall, so far as possible, coincide with those already fixed in the case.

Article 71

1.   A State which desires to avail itself of the right conferred upon it by Article 63 of the Statute shall file in the Registry a declaration to that effect. This declaration may be filed by a State even though it has not received the notification referred to in that Article.

2.   Such declarations shall be communicated to the parties. If any objection or doubt

should arise as to whether the intervention is admissible under Article 63 of the Statute, the decision shall rest with the Court.

3. The Registrar shall also transmit copies of the declarations: *(a)* to Members of the United Nations through the Secretary-General and *(b)*, by means of special arrangements made for this purpose between them and the Registrar, to any other States entitled to appear before the Court.

4. The Registrar shall take the necessary steps to enable the intervening party to inspect the documents in the case in so far as they relate to the interpretation of the convention in question, and to submit its written observations thereon to the Court within a time-limit to be fixed by the Court or by the President if the Court is not sitting.

5. These observations shall be communicated to the other parties and may be discussed by them in the course of the oral proceedings; in these proceedings the intervening party shall take part.

Appeals to the Court

Article 72

1. When an appeal is made to the Court against a decision given by some other tribunal, the proceedings before the Court shall be governed by the provisions of the Statute and of these Rules.

2. If the document instituting the appeal must be filed within a certain limit of time, the date of the receipt of this document in the Registry will be taken by the Court as the material date.

3. The document instituting the appeal shall contain a precise statement of the grounds of the objections to the decision complained of, and these constitute the subject of the dispute referred to the Court.

4. A certified copy of the decision complained of shall be attached to the document instituting the appeal.

5. It is incumbent upon the parties to produce before the Court any useful and relevant material upon which the decision complained of was rendered.

Settlement and Discontinuance

Article 73

If at any time before judgment has been delivered, the parties conclude an agreement as to the settlement of the dispute and so inform the Court in writing, or by mutual agreement inform the Court in writing that they are not going on with the proceedings, the Court, or the President if the Court is not sitting, shall make an order officially recording the conclusion of the settlement or the discontinuance of the proceedings; in either case the order shall direct the removal of the case from the list.

Article 74

1. If in the course of proceedings instituted by means of an application, the applicant informs the Court in writing that it is not going on with the proceedings, and if, at the date on which this communication is received by the Registry, the respondent has not yet taken any step in the proceedings, the Court, or the President if the Court is not sitting, will make an order officially recording the discontinuance of the proceedings and directing the removal of the case from the list. A copy of this order shall be sent by the Registrar to the respondent.

2. If, at the time when the notice of discontinuance is received, the respondent has already taken some step in the proceedings, the Court, or the President if the Court is not sitting, shall fix a time-limit within which the respondent must state whether it opposes the discontinuance of the proceedings. If no objection is made to the discontinuance before the expiration of the time-limit, acquiescence will be presumed and the Court, or the President if the Court is not sitting, will make an order officially recording the discontinuance of the proceedings and directing the removal of the case from the list. If objection is made, the proceedings shall continue.

Section 2. Procedure before the Chambers

Article 75

Procedure before the Chambers mentioned in Articles 26 and 29 of the Statute shall, subject to the provisions of the Statute and of these Rules relating to the Chambers and to any special rules which the Court may make, be governed by the provisions relating to procedure before the Court.

Article 76

1. When it is desired that a case should be dealt with by one of the Chambers which has been formed in pursuance of Article 26, paragraph 1, or Article 29 of the Statute, a request to this effect should either be made in the document instituting the proceedings or accompany it. Effect will be given to the request if the parties are in agreement.

2. Upon receipt by the Registry of this request, the President of the Court shall communicate it to the members of the Chamber concerned. He shall take such steps as may be necessary to give effect to the provisions of Article 31, paragraph 4, of the Statute.

3. A request for the formation of a Chamber to deal with a particular case as provided for in Article 26, paragraph 2, of the Statute, can be filed at any moment until the closure of the written proceedings. Upon receipt of such a request by the Registry, the President shall ascertain whether the other party assents. When both parties have assented, the President shall ascertain the views of the parties as to the composition of the Chamber. The Court shall decide upon the request for the formation of a Chamber in accordance with Article 26, paragraphs 2 and 3, of the Statute, and Article 29 of these Rules.

4. The President of the Court shall convene the Chamber at the earliest date compatible with the requirements of the procedure.

5. As soon as the Chamber has met to begin the hearing of the case submitted to it, the powers of the President of the Court shall be exercised in respect of the case by the President of the Chamber.

Article 77

1. Written proceedings in a case before a Chamber shall consist of a single written pleading by each side. In proceedings begun by means of an application, the pleadings shall be delivered within successive time-limits. In proceedings begun by the notification of a special agreement, the pleadings shall be delivered within the same time-limits, unless the parties have agreed on successive delivery of their pleadings. The time-limits referred to in this paragraph shall be fixed by the Court, or by the President if the Court is not sitting, in consultation with the Chamber concerned if it is already constituted.

2. If necessary the Chamber may, at the instance of either party permit, or on its

own initiative direct, the submission of further written pleadings, within such time-limits as it fixes. Both parties shall be consulted before further pleadings are so permitted or directed.

3.   Oral proceedings shall take place unless the parties agree to dispense with them, and the Chamber consents. Even when no oral proceedings take place, the Chamber may call upon the parties to supply information or furnish explanations orally.

4.   The provisions of Articles 42 to 50 shall be applicable in respect of any pleading submitted in a case before a Chamber, and those of Articles 51 to 65 in respect of any oral proceedings in such a case.

Article 78

Judgments given by a Chamber will be read at a public sitting of that Chamber.

Section 3. Judgments

Article 79

1.   The judgment shall contain:
   a statement whether it has been delivered by the Court or by a Chamber;
   the date on which it is delivered;
   the names of the judges participating;
   the names of the parties;
   the names of the agents of the parties;
   a summary of the proceedings;
   the submissions of the parties;
   a statement of the facts;
   the reasons in point of law;
   the operative provisions of the judgment;
   the decision, if any, in regard to costs;
   the number of the judges constituting the majority.

2.   Any judge may, if he so desires, attach his individual opinion to the judgment, whether he dissents from the majority or not, or a bare statement of his dissent.

Article 80

1.   When the judgment has been read in public, one original copy, duly signed and sealed, shall be placed in the Archives of the Court and another shall be forwarded to each of the parties.

2.   A copy of the judgment shall be sent by the Registrar to Members of the United Nations and to States entitled to appear before the Court.

Article 81

The judgment shall become binding on the parties on the day on which it is read in open Court.

Article 82

The party in whose favour an order for the payment of the costs has been made shall present his bill of costs within ten days after the judgment has been delivered. The Court shall decide any dispute concerning the bill.

Section 4. Requests for the Revision or Interpretation
on a Judgment

Article 83

1.   A request for the revision of a judgment shall be made by an application.

The application shall state the judgment of which the revision is desired, and shall contain the particulars necessary to show that the conditions laid down by Article 61 of the Statute are fulfilled, and a list of the documents in support; these documents shall be attached to the application.

2.   The request for revision shall be communicated by the Registrar to the other parties. The latter may submit observations within a time-limit to be fixed by the Court, or by the President if the Court is not sitting.

3.   If the Court admits the application for a revision, it will determine the written procedure required for examining the merits of the application.

4.   If the Court makes the admission of the application conditional upon previous compliance with the judgment to be revised, this condition shall be communicated forthwith to the applicant by the Registrar and proceedings in revision shall be stayed pending receipt by the Court of proof of compliance with the judgment.

Article 84

1.   A request to the Court to interpret a judgment which it has given may be made either by the notification of a special agreement between the parties or by an application by one or more of the parties.

2.   The special agreement or application shall state the judgment of which an interpretation is requested and shall specify the precise point or points in dispute.

3.   If the request for interpretation is made by means of an application, the Registrar shall communicate the application to the other parties, and the latter may submit observations within a time-limit to be fixed by the Court, or by the President if the Court is not sitting.

4.   Whether the request be made by special agreement or by application, the Court may invite the parties to furnish further written or oral explanations.

Article 85

If the judgment to be revised or to be interpreted was given by the Court, the request for its revision or interpretation shall be dealt with by the Court. If the judgment was given by one of the Chambers mentioned in Articles 26 or 29 of the Statute, the request for its revision or interpretation shall be dealt with by the same Chamber.

Article 86

The decision of the Court on requests for revision or interpretation shall be given in the form of a judgment.

Heading III

ADVISORY OPINIONS

Article 87

1.   In proceedings in regard to advisory opinions, the Court shall, in addition to the provisions of Article 96 of the Charter and Chapter IV of the Statute, apply the provi-

sions of the Articles which follow. It shall also be guided by the provisions of these Rules which apply in contentious cases to the extent to which it recognizes them to be applicable; for this purpose it shall above all consider whether the request for the advisory opinion relates to a legal question actually pending between two or more States.

2. When the body authorized by or in accordance with the Charter of the United Nations to request an advisory opinion informs the Court that its request necessitates an urgent answer, or the Court finds that an early answer would be desirable, the Court shall take all necessary steps to accelerate the procedure. If the Court is not sitting when such a request is made, it shall be convened for the purpose of proceeding to a hearing and deliberation on the request.

Article 88

All requests for advisory opinions shall be addressed to the Court by the Secretary-General of the United Nations or the chief administrative officer of the organization authorized to make the request. The documents referred to in Article 65, paragraph 2, of the Statute shall be transmitted to the Court at the same time as the request or as soon as possible thereafter, in the number of copies required by the Registry.

Article 89

If the advisory opinion is requested upon a legal question actually pending between two or more States, Article 31 of the Statute shall apply, as also the provisions of these Rules concerning the application of that Article.

Article 90

1. Advisory opinions shall be given after deliberation by the Court. They shall mention the number of judges constituting the majority.

2. Any judge may, if he so desires, attach his individual opinion to the advisory opinion of the Court, whether he dissents from the majority or not, or a bare statement of his dissent.

Article 91

1. The Registrar will in due time inform the Secretary-General of the United Nations and the appropriate organ of the institution, if any, which requested the advisory opinion, as to the date and the hour fixed for the sitting to be held for the reading of the opinion.

2. One original copy of the advisory opinion, duly signed and sealed, shall be placed in the Archives of the Court and another shall be sent to the Secretariat of the United Nations. Certified copies shall be sent by the Registrar to Members of the United Nations and to the States, specialized agencies and public international organizations directly concerned.

(Signed) Zafrulla Khan,
President.
(Signed) S. Aquarone,
Registrar.

COMPOSITION OF THE COURT

(A) *Permanent Court of International Justice*

First period, 1922-30

R. Altamira y Crevea	Spain
D. Anzilotti (President, 1928-30)	Italy
R. Barbosa (d. 1 March 1923)	Brazil
A.S. de Bustamente y Sirven	Cuba
Viscount Finlay (d. 9 March 1929)	U.K.
H. Fromageot (from 19 September 1929)	France
H.M. Huber (President, 1925-7, Vice-President 1928-31)	Switzerland
C.E. Hughes (8 September 1928-15 February 1930)	U.S.A.
C.J.B. Hurst (from 19 September 1929)	U.K.
F.B. Kellog (from 25 September 1930)	U.S.A.
B.C.J. Loder (President, 1922-4)	Netherlands
J.B. Moore (resigned 11 April 1928)	U.S.A.
D.G.G. Nyholm	Denmark
Y. Oda	Japan
E.d.S. Pessôa (from 10 September 1923)	Brazil
C.A. Weiss (Vice-President 1922-8, d. 31 August 1928)	France

Deputy-Judges

F.V.N. Beichmann	Norway
D. Negulesco	Romania
Wang Ch'ung-hui	China
M. Yovanovitch	Yugoslavia

Second Period, 1931-45

M. Adatci (President 1931-3, d. 28 December 1934)	Japan
R. Altamira y Crevea	Spain
D. Anzilotti	Italy
A.S. de Bustamente y Sirven	Cuba
Cheng Tien-Hsi (from 8 October 1936)	China
R.W. Erich (from 26 September 1938)	Finland
W.J.M. van Eysinga	Netherlands
H. Fromageot	France
J.G. Guerrero (Vice-President, 1931-36, President, 1936-46)	El Salvador
Åke Hammarskjöld (from 8 October 1936, d. 7 July 1937)	Sweden
M.O. Hudson (from 8 October 1936)	U.S.A.
C.J.B. Hurst (President 1934-6, Vice-President 1936-46)	U.K.

F.B. Kellog (resigned 9 September 1935)	U.S.A.
H. Nagaoka (from 17 September 1935, resigned 15 January 1942)	Japan
D. Negulesco	Rumania
E. Rolin-Jaequemyns (d. 11 July 1936)	Belgium
M.C.J. Rostworowski (d. 24 March 1940)	Poland
W. Schücking (d. 25 August 1935)	Germany
F.J. Urrutia (resigned 9 January 1942)	Colombia
Ch. de Visscher (from 27 May 1937)	Belgium
Wang Ch'ung-hui (resigned 15 January 1936)	China

Deputy-Judges
(Post abolished on 1 February 1936)

R.W. Erich	Finland
J.C. de Matta	Portugal
M. Novacovitch	Yugoslavia
J. Redlich	Austria

(B) *International Court of Justice*

(Judges in order of Precedence)

First period, 1946-9 and Second Period, 1949-52

***J.G. Guerrero (President 1946-9, Vice-President 1949-52)	El Salvador
***J. Basdevant (Vice-President 1946-9, President 1949-52)	France
***A. Alvarez	Chile
**I. Fabela	Mexico
**G.H. Hackworth	U.S.A.
*B. Winiarski	Poland
*M. Zoričić	Yugoslavia
**Ch. de Visscher	Belgium
***Sir A. McNair	U.K.
**H. Klaestad	Norway
*A.H. Badawi	Egypt
**S.B. Krylov	U.S.S.R.
*J.E. Read	Canada
*Hsu Mo	China
***J. Azevedo (d. 7 May 1951)	Brazil
****L. Carneiro (from 6 December 1951)	Brazil

*Elected for three-year term expiring on 6 February 1949.
**Elected for six-year term expiring on 6 February 1952.
***Elected for nine-year term expiring on 6 February 1955.
****Elected for remainder of predecessor's term.

Third Period, 1952-5

Sir A. McNair (President)	U.K.
J.G. Guerrero (Vice-President)	El Salvador

A. Alvarez	Chile
J. Basdevant	France
G.H. Hackworth	U.S.A.
B. Winiarski	Poland
M. Zoričić	Yugoslavia
H. Klaestad	Norway
A.H. Badawi	Egypt
J.E. Read	Canada
Hsu Mo	China
L. Carneiro	Brazil
Sir B. Rau (d. 30 November 1953)	India
E.C. Armand-Ugon	Uruguay
S.A. Golunsky (resigned 25 July 1953)	U.S.S.R.
F.I. Kojevnikov (from 27 November 1953)	U.S.S.R.
Sir M. Zafrulla Khan (from 7 October 1954)	Pakistan

Fourth Period, 1955-8

G.H. Hackworth (President)	U.S.A.
A.H. Badawi (Vice-President)	Egypt
J.G. Guerrero	El Salvador
J. Basdevant	France
B. Winiarski	Poland
M. Zoričic	Yugoslavia
H. Klaestad	Norway
J.E. Read	Canada
Hsu Mo (d. 28 June 1956)	China
E.C. Armand-Ugon	Uruguay
F.I. Kojevnikov	U.S.S.R.
Sir M. Zafrulla Khan	Pakistan
Sir H. Lauterpacht	U.K.
L.M. Moreno Quintana	Argentina
R. Córdova	Mexico
V.K. Wellington Koo (from 11 January 1957)	China

Fifth Period, 1958-61

H. Klaestad (President)	Norway
Sir M. Zafrulla Khan (Vice-President)	Pakistan
J.G. Guerrero (d. 25 November 1958)	El Salvador
J. Basdevant	France
G.H. Hackworth	U.S.A.
B. Winiarski	Poland
A.H. Badawi	U.A.R.
E.G. Armand-Ugon	Uruguay
F.I. Kojevnikov	U.S.S.R.
Sir H. Lauterpacht (d. 8 May 1960)	U.K.
L.M. Moreno Quintana	Argentina
R. Córdova	Mexico
V.K. Wellington Koo	China
J. Spiropoulos	Greece

Sir Percy Spender   Australia
R.J. Alfaro (from 29 September 1959)   Panama
Sir Gerald Fitzmaurice (from 16 November 1960)   U.K.

Sixth Period, 1961-4

B. Winiarski (President)   Poland
R.J. Alfaro (Vice-President)   Panama
J. Basdevant   France
A.H. Badawi   U.A.R.
L.M. Moreno Quintana   Argentina
R. Córdova   Mexico
V.K. Wellington Koo   China
J. Spiropoulos   Greece
Sir Percy Spender   Australia
Sir Gerald Fitzmaurice   U.K.
V.M. Koretsky   U.S.S.R.
K. Tanaka   Japan
J.L. Bustamente y Rivero   Peru
P.C. Jessup   U.S.A.
G. Morelli   Italy

Seventh Period, 1964-7

Sir Percy Spender (President)   Australia
V.K. Wellington Koo (Vice-President)   China
B. Winiarski   Poland
A.H. Badawi (d. 4 August 1965)   U.A.R.
J. Spiropoulos   Greece
Sir Gerald Fitzmaurice   U.K.
V.M. Koretsky   U.S.S.R.
K. Tanaka   Japan
J.L. Bustamente y Rivero   Peru
P.C. Jessup   U.S.A.
G. Morelli   Italy
Sir M. Zafrulla Khan   Pakistan
L. Padilla Nervo   Mexico
I. Forster   Senegal
A. Gros   France
F. Ammoun (from 16 November 1965)   Lebanon

Eighth Period, 1967-70

J.L. Bustamente y Rivero (President)   Peru
V.M. Koretsky (Vice-President)   U.S.S.R.
Sir Gerald Fitzmaurice   U.K.
K. Tanaka   Japan
P.C. Jessup   U.S.A.
G. Morelli   Italy
Sir M. Zafrulla Khan   Pakistan
L. Padilla Nervo   Mexico

I. Forster	Senegal
A. Gros	France
F. Ammoun	Lebanon
C. Bengzon	Philippines
S. Petrén	Sweden
M. Lachs	Poland
C.D. Onyeama	Nigeria

Ninth Period, 1970-3

Sir M. Zafrulla Khan (President)	Pakistan
F. Ammoun (Vice-President)	Lebanon
Sir Gerald Fitzmaurice	U.K.
L. Padilla Nervo	Mexico
I. Forster	Senegal
A. Gros	France
C. Bengzon	Philippines
S. Petrén	Sweden
M. Lachs	Poland
C.D. Onyeama	Nigeria
H.C. Dillard	U.S.A.
L. Ignacio-Pinto	Dahomey
F. de Castro	Spain
P.D. Morozov	U.S.S.R.
E. Jiménez de Aréchaga	Uruguay

Tenth Period, 1973-6

M. Lachs (President)	Nigeria
F. Ammoun (Vice-President)	Lebanon
I. Forster	Senegal
A. Gros	France
C. Bengzon	Philippines
S. Petrén	Sweden
C.D. Onyeama	Poland
H.C. Dillard	U.S.A.
L. Ignacio-Pinto	Dahomey
F. de Castro	Spain
P.D. Morozov	U.S.S.R.
E. Jiménez de Aréchaga	Uruguay
Sir Humphrey Waldock	U.K.
Nagendra Singh	India
J.M. Ruda	Argentina

Appendix 4

JUDICIAL STATISTICS

(A) *Permanent Court of International Justice*

Year	New Cases filed	Advisory Opinions	Judgments	Orders (since 1926)	Cases Dis-continued	Removed from List by Court
1922	4	3				
1923	5	5	2			
1924	5	1	2			
1925	5	3	3		1	
1926	3	1	1	2		
1927	5	1	4	4		
1928	6	2	2	17		
1929			3	8	2	
1930	2	2		7		
1931	8	4		12		
1932	7	3	3	19		
1933	3		2	17	5	
1934	1		2	2		
1935	4	2		6		
1936	3		1	14	1	
1937	2		3	11		
1938	2		1	12	1	
1939	1		3	4		
1940				2		
1941						
1942						
1943						
1944						
1945					2	
Total	66	27	32	137	12	

(B) *The International Court of Justice*

Year	New Cases filed	Advisory Opinions	Judgments	Orders	Cases Dis-continued	Removed from List by Court
1946						
1947	2			3		
1948	1	1	1	3		
1949	6	1	2	9		
1950	4	4	2	7	1	
1951	4	1	2	11		
1952			3	8		
1953	3		3	5		
1954	3	1	1	10	1	2
1955	8	1	1	3		
1956		2		9		4
1957	6		2	9		
1958	3		1	19		1
1959	4		3	12	1	1
1960	2	1	2	6	2	
1961	3		1	9	1	
1962	1	1	2	5		
1963			1	4		
1964			1	3		
1965				3		
1966			1	2		
1967	2			4		
1968				4		
1969			1			
1970	1		1	2		
1971	1	1		6		
1972	3		1	7		
1973	3	1	2	12		
Total	60	15	34	178	6	8

Note: The figures for the Permanent Court are taken from M. Hudson, *The Permanent Court of International Justice, 1920-1942*, p. 779. (Corrected on the basis of the Sixteenth Report of the Permanent Court (E/16), pp. 92-197.) For the above figures, preliminary objections and requests for interim measures of protection are not included as "new cases". Requests for interpretation of judgments (two by the Permanent Court and one by the Present Court) are so listed. The General List of the Permanent Court contained 79 folios, and that of the present Court 60 folios to September 1973.

Appendix 5

THE AUTHORITY TO REQUEST ADVISORY OPINIONS

(a) *Organs authorized directly by the Charter*

By Article 96, paragraph 1, of the Charter, the following organs are authorized to request an advisory opinion on any legal question: the General Assembly, the Security Council.

(b) *Organs authorized by the General Assembly*

By Article 96, paragraph 2, of the Charter, organs of the United Nations and specialized agencies may be authorized by the General Assembly to request advisory opinions on legal questions arising within the scope of their activities.

The following organs of the United Nations have been so authorized:

Organ	Scope of Authority	General Assembly Resolution
Economic and Social Council	All legal questions arising within the scope of the activities of the Council (including legal questions concerning mutual relationships of the United Nations and the Specialized Agencies).	89 (I) of 11 December 1946
Trusteeship Council	Legal questions arising within the scope of its activities.	171 B (II) of 14 December 1947
Interim Committee	Legal questions arising within the scope of the Committee's activities.	196 (III) of 3 December 1948 and 295 (IV) of 21 November 1949
Committee on Applications for Review of Administrative Tribunal Judgments	For the purpose of Article 11 of the Statute of the United Nations Administrative Tribunal.	957 (X) of 8 November 1955

The following specialized agencies have been authorized to request advisory opinions on legal questions arising within the scope of their *activities*, other than questions concerning the mutual relationships of that specialized agency and the United Nations or other specialized agencies. In each case, when requesting an opinion the specialized agency has to inform ECOSOC. The terms of the authorization are contained in the relationship agreement (see p. 38 above), and the authorization of the General Assembly itself appears in the resolution by which the relationship agreement was approved.

Agency	Organs	Article of Relationship Agreement	Resolution of General Assembly
I.L.O.	Conference. Governing Body when authorized by Conference.	IX	50 (I) of 14 December 1946
F.A.O.	Conference. Executive Committee when acting in pursuance of an authorization by the Conference.	IX	50 (I)
UNESCO	General Conference. Executive Board acting in pursuance of an authorization by the Conference.	IX	50 (I)
I.C.A.O.	Assembly or Council.	X	50 (I)
I.B.R.D.	The Bank.	VIII	124 (II) of 15 November 1947
I.D.A.	The Association.	I	1594 (XV) of 27 March 1961
I.M.F.	The Fund.	VIII	124 (II)
I.M.C.O.	Assembly. Council acting in pursuance of an authorization by the Assembly.	IX	204 (III) of 18 November 1948
I.F.C.	The Corporation.	I	1116 (XI) of 20 February 1957

The following specialized agencies have similarly been authorized to request advisory opinions on legal questions arising within the scope of their *competence*, other than questions concerning the mutual relationships of the specialized agency and the United Nations or other specialized agencies. In each case the specialized agency shall inform ECOSOC of the request.

Agency	Organs	Article of Relationship Agreement	Resolution of General Assembly
W.H.O.	Health Assembly. Executive Board acting in pursuance of an authorization by the Health Assembly.	X	124 (II)
I.T.U.	Plenipotentiary Conference. Administrative Council acting in pursuance of an authorization by the Plenipotentiary Conference.	VII	124 (II)
W.M.O.	Congress.	VII	531 (VI) of 20 December 1951

The International Atomic Energy Agency has been authorized by Resolution 1146 (XII) of 14 November 1957 to request advisory opinions on legal questions arising within the scope of its activities other than questions concerning the relationship between the Agency and the United Nations or any specialized agency. By Article X of the relationship agreement, the United Nations will take the necessary action to enable the General Conference or the Board of Governors to seek such advisory opinions. This agreement was approved by Resolution 1145 (XII) of 14 December 1957.

Although the Organization of American States is not authorized to request advisory opinions, Article LI of the American Treaty on Pacific Settlement (the Pact of Bogotá) of 1948 enables the parties concerned in the solution of a controversy to petition the General Assembly or the Security Council to request an advisory opinion on any legal question. Such petition shall be submitted through the Council of the Organization.

THE COURT'S FINANCES

Year	Court's Annual Audited Expences	Court's Annual Income	U.N's Annual Audited Expenses
	$	$	$
1946	423,983		19,330,287
1947	525,554		27,290,241
1948	596,658		38,387,531
1949	588,512	1,950	42,575,368
1950	590,544	29,282	43,746,264
1951	596,540	34,217	48,628,383
1952	627,116	32,206	50,270,153
1953	585,537	27,022	49,292,552
1954	557,656	27,865	48,510,009
1955	594,463	24,638	50,089,808
1956	582,041	27,106	50,508,095
1957	642,948	36,145	53,172,964
1958	674,966	41,723	60,848,555
1959	732,584	42,146	61,460,607
1960	732,207	47,220	65,264,181
1961	761,990	49,551	71,096,378
1962	938,781	58,772	84,452,350
1963	889,936	58,600	92,195,880
1964	1,017,893	66,608	102,948,977
1965	1,111,053	67,687	107,111,392
1966	1,103,429	76,400	119,543,680
1967	1,054,087	81,060	131,486,813
1968	1,391,345	83,500	141,161,623
1969	1,533,536	87,100	156,780,541
1970	1,406,133	87,100	168,375,776
1971	1,495,998	125,053	194,124,544
Total	21,758,490	1,212,998	3,078,652,952

Sources: Columns one and three are taken from the Annual Financial Reports and Accounts and Reports of the Board of Auditors submitted to the General Assembly, and published in its Official Records. Column two is taken from the Court's Yearbooks.

Note. From 1950 the Court's income includes amounts attributed to it through operation of Staff Assessment under the Tax Equalization Scheme.

NOTES TO CHAPTER I

1. Isaiah ii. 4; Micah iv. 3.
2. *De jure belli ac pacis* (1625), II, ch. xxiii § 8. English translation from Hugo Grotius, *The Law of War and Peace*, trans. Louise R. Loomis (New York, 1949), 252.
3. For the position in Ancient India, see H. Chatterjee, *International Law and Inter-- State Relations in Ancient India* (Calcutta, 1958), 129. For the position in Ancient China, see Chan Nay Chow, *La Doctrine du Droit international chez Confucius* (Paris, 1941), 89.
4. A. Rechid, "L'Islam et le droit des Gens", R.A.D.I., 60 (1937) (ii), 371; M. Khadduri, *War and Peace in the Law of Islam* (Baltimore, 1955), 231.
5. See C. Phillipson, *The International Law and Custom of Ancient Greece and Rome* (London, 1911); A. Raeder, L'Arbitrage international chez les Hellènes (Kristiania, 1912); M. Tod, *International Arbitration amongst the Greeks* (Oxford, 1913); J. Ralston, *International Arbitration from Athens to Locarno* (California, 1929); M. Taube, "Les Origines de l'arbitrage international: antiquité et moyen âge", R.A.D.I., 42 (1932) (iv), 1; G. Ténékidès, "International Law and Federal Communities in the Greece of the Cities", R.A.D.I., 90 (1956) (ii), 469.
6. E. Usteri, *Bienne-Beppet* Arbitration, in J.B. Moore (editor), *International Adjudications*, Ancient Series, II (New York, 1936).
7. See A.B. Bozeman, *Politics and Culture in International History* (Princeton, 1960), 266-7. Also J. Eppstein, *The Catholic Tradition in the Law of Nations* (London, 1935), 113 and *passim*. Yet a warning has been issued against exaggerating the role of the Church, while emphasizing its function in creating an atmosphere in which arbitration could flourish. R. Bainton, *Christian Attitudes towards War and Peace* (New York, 1960), 116-8.
8. J.B. Moore, *International Adjudications*, Modern Series, vols. 1-4 (New York, 1929-31). Vol. 5 of this Series deals with certain U.S.-Spanish and U.S.-French claims (the latter being settled, as regards individual U.S. claimants, by domestic commissions), and vol. 6 contains the proceedings of another U.S.-Great Britain Mixed Commission set up to arbitrate the title to islands in the Passamaquoddy Bay and the Bay of Fundy, between Maine and New Brunswick.
9. For text see A.G. de Lapradelle and N. Politis, *Recueil des Arbitrages internationales*, II (Paris, 1923), 713; J.B. Moore, *History and Digest of the Arbitrations to which the United States have been a party*, I (Washington, 1898), 653; British and Foreign State Papers, 62 (1871-2), 233; *U.S. Foreign Relations*, 1872, Pt. II, Papers relating to the Treaty of Washington of 1871, IV, 49 (42nd Cong. 3rd Sess., Ex. Doc. 1).
10. See J.B. Scott, *The Reports to the Hague Conferences of 1899 and 1907* (Oxford, 1917). The Tsar's initiative was not entirely disinterested. In the growing armaments race which preceded the outbreak of the First World War, Russia was lagging behind, and he was in danger of losing his own throne, and the Conferences were convened to promote peace and disarmament and to relieve international tension. In that objective they failed, but they did succeed in codifying a great deal of international law, including the law of international arbitration. See H.A.L. Fisher, *A History of Europe*, II (London, 1949), 1084; and V. Potiemkine, *Histoire de la Diplomatie*, II (Paris, 1946), 161. On the Permanent Court of Arbitration, see J.P.A. François in R.A.D.I., 87 (1955) (i), 460.

11. For modern analyses of the problem of fact-finding, see Carl W.A. Schurmann, *A Center for International Fact-Finding: A Review and a Proposal* (New York, 1963); and Report of the Secretary-General on Methods of Fact-Finding, G.A. O.R. 20th session, annexes, agenda items 90 and 94, doc. A/5694. And see Resolution 2104 (XX), 20 December 1965. On international conciliation, see Jean-Pierre Cot, *International Conciliation* (London, 1972).

12. The codification of the rules of arbitral procedure which resulted from the Hague Conference has proved useful in practice, even for arbitration proceedings which were formally not conducted before a panel of the Permanent Court of Arbitration, and the rules are often incorporated in international arbitration treaties. A recent attempt by the International Law Commission of the United Nations to bring this branch of the law up to date was only partially successful. In 1958 the Commission submitted a set of Model Rules on Arbitral Procedure to the General Assembly, Yearbook of the International Law Commission, 1958, II, 83. By Resolution 1262 (XIII) of 14 November 1958, the General Assembly brought these Articles to the attention of Member States for their consideration and use, in such cases and to such extent as they consider appropriate, in drawing up treaties of arbitration. An alternative method, quite common today, is to incorporate into arbitration treaties relevant rules from the practice of the International Court.

13. M. Hudson, *International Tribunals, Past and Future* (Washington, 1944), 7.

14. See *Annual Digest and Reports of International Law Cases*, 16 vols. covering the period 1919-1949, and *International Law Reports*, continuous since 1950. A convenient collection of international arbitrations will be found in the U.N. series of *Reports of International Arbitral Awards*, vols. 9-11 covering the period 1902-1920, vols. 1-3 covering the period 1920-1940, and vols. 12 and 16 covering the period 1945-1965. The remaining volumes contain a miscellaneous collection of decisions of various mixed commissions (other than those established by the 1919 Peace Treaties). For the resolution of the Permanent Administrative Council of the Permanent Court of Arbitration of 3 March 1960, inviting new States to adhere to the First Hague Convention of 1907, see *American Journal of International Law*, 54 (1960), 933. See also *Succession of States to multilateral Treaties*: studies prepared by the [U.N.] Secretariat, II. Permanent Court of Arbitration and the Hague Conventions of 1899 and 1907, doc. A/CN.4/200, Yearbook of the International Law Commission, 1968, vol. II at 26. Generally see A.M. Stuyt, *Survey of International Arbitrations, 1794-1970* (Leyden and Dobbs Ferry, New York, 1972).

15. There is reason to believe that this type of constitution of an arbitration tribunal originated in Jewish private law. C.W. Jenks, *The Common Law of Mankind* (London, 1958), 99.

16. On international arbitration, see: A. Mérignhac, *Traité théorique et pratique de l'arbitrage international* (Paris, 1895); J.H. Ralston, *The Law and Procedure of International Tribunals* (Stanford, 1926); J.C. Wittenberg, *L'Organisation judiciaire, la procédure et la sentence internationales* (Paris, 1937); K.S. Carlston, *The Process of International Arbitration* (New York, 1946); M. Bos, *Les conditions du procès en droit international public* (Leyden, 1957); J.L. Simpson and H. Fox, *International Arbitration, Law and Practice* (London, 1959); U.N. Secretariat, *Memorandum on Arbitral Procedure*, doc. A/CN.4/35, Yearbook of the International Law Commission, 1950, II, 157; same, *Commentary on the draft Convention on Arbitral Procedure*, doc. A/CN.4/92 (New York, 1955). For general bibliography, see U.N. doc. A/CN.4/29, 20 June 1950.

Apart from the Permanent Court of Arbitration, mention must also be made, for the sake of completeness, of two other attempts to establish permanent international tribunals, both of which were unsuccessful, although their failure may have contributed to the later success of the Permanent Court of International Justice. The first was the attempt, also made at The Hague in 1907, to establish an International Prize Court to deal with claims by neutrals against belligerents arising out of the exercise of the right of prize at sea. Apart from difficulties inherent in the nature of the subject matter, the principal technical obstacle to the establishment of a permanent tribunal of this character lay in the inability to find a satisfactory procedure for electing the judges and guaranteeing their independence. The second was the Central American Court of Justice, established by the Treaty of Washington of 20 December 1907, between Costa Rica, Guatemala, Honduras, Nicaragua and El Salvador. This Court was in existence between 1908 and 1917, and dealt with a number of cases. It foundered, however, because of serious faults in its organization, including inadequate measures to assure the independence of its members, and in the definition of its jurisdiction, but above all it collapsed on the rock of political difficulties, including some which originated outside Central America.

17. These obligations were completed by Article 15 giving the Council competence over disputes which were not settled by arbitration or judicial settlement. After the adoption of the Statute of the Permanent Court of International Justice, the references to arbitration in the Covenant were changed to "arbitration or judicial settlement".

18. See *Documents presented to the Committee [of Jurists] relating to existing plans for the establishment of a Permanent Court of International Justice* (London, 1920); *Procès-Verbaux of the Proceedings of the Committee* (The Hague, 1920); *Documents concerning action taken by the Council of the League of Nations under Article 14 of the Covenant and the adoption by the Assembly of the Statute of the Permanent Court* (Geneva, 1921). See also N. Politis, *La Justice Internationale* (Paris, 1924). The leading treatise on the Permanent Court is M. Hudson, *The Permanent Court of International Justice, 1920-1942* (New York, 1943). This magisterial and definitive work —indispensable for an understanding of the Permanent Court—contains a full account of the drafting of the Covenant, the Statute and the Rules of Court, with complete references to all the documentation.

19. Acts and Documents concerning the Organization of the Court, No. 2, Rules of Court adopted on 6 May 1946, as amended on 10 May 1972. For text see Appendix 2. For details of these amendments, see I.C.J. Yearbook, 1971-1972 at 3. See also Eduardo Jiménez de Aréchaga, "The Amendments to the Rules of Procedure of the International Court of Justice", *American Journal of International Law*, 67 (1973), 1; and Sh. Rosenne, "The 1972 Revision of the Rules of the International Court of Justice", *Israel Law Review*, 8 (1973), 197.

20. See the following cases: *S.S. Wimbledon*, A 1 (1923); *German Settlers in Poland*, B 6 (1923); *Acquisition of Polish Nationality*, B 7 (1923); *Polish Postal Service in Danzig*, B 11 (1925); *German Interests in Polish Upper Silesia*, A 6 (1925), A 7 (1926); *Factory of Chorzów*, A 9 (1927), A 12 (1927), A 13 (1927), A 17 (1928); *Jurisdiction of the Danzig Courts*, B 15 (1928); *Minority Schools in Upper Silesia*, A 15 (1928); *River Oder Commission*, A 23 (1929); *Danzig and the International Labour Organization*, B 18 (1930); *German Minority Schools in Upper Silesia*, A/B 40 (1931); *Polish War Vessels in Danzig*, A/B 43 (1931); *Treatment of Polish Nationals in Danzig*, A/B 44 (1932); *Prince von Pless*, A/B 52 (1933), A/B 54 (1933), A/B 57 (1933), A/B 59 (1933); *Polish Agrarian Reform*, A/B 58 (1933), A/B 60 (1933); *Danzig Legislative Decrees*, A/B 65 (1935).

21. See the following cases *Railway Traffic between Poland and Lithuania*, A/B 42 (1931); *Memel Statute*, A/B 47 (1932), A/B 49 (1932).

22. See the following cases: *Polish-Czechoslovakian Frontier (Jaworzina)*, B 8 (1923); *Monastery of Saint Naoum (Albanian Frontier)*, B 9 (1924); *Treaty of Neuilly (Art. 4)*, A 3 (1924), A 4 (1925); *European Commission of the Danube*, B 14 (1927); *Inter-*

pretation of Greco-Turkish Protocol of 1926, B 16 (1928); *Greco-Bulgarian Communities*, B 17 (1930); *Interpretation of Greco-Bulgarian Agreement of 1927*, A/B 45 (1932); *Minority Schools in Albania*, A/B 64 (1935).

23. See the following cases: *Mavrommatis Palestine Concessions*, A 2 (1924), A 5 (1925), A 11 (1927); *Exchange of Greek and Turkish Populations*, B 10 (1925); *Frontier between Turkey and Iraq*, B 12 (1925); *Lighthouses*, A/B 62 (1934), A/B 71 (1937) (this dispute was finally settled only in 1956 by an arbitral award rendered through a Tribunal operating under the Hague Convention of 1907). See 12 Reports of International Arbitral Awards 155.

24. See the following cases: *Tunis and Morocco Nationality Decrees*, B 4 (1923); *Phosphates in Morocco*, A/B 74 (1938). For a case relating to commercial matters in the Congo, see *Oscar Chinn*, A/B 63 (1934).

25. The most significant instances of this are the *Lotus* and the *Borchgrave* cases. A 10 (1927) and A/B 72 and 73 (1937, 1938).

26. The *Eastern Carelia* case, B 5 (1923).

27. Loc. cit. in n. 13, 238.

28. The leading treatise on this aspect is Sir Hersch Lauterpacht, *The Development of International Law by the International Court* (London, 1958). For a systematic presentation of the law as applied by the Court, see E. Hambro, *The Case Law of the International Court*, A repertoire of the judgments, advisory opinions and orders of the Permanent Court of International Justice and the International Court of Justice, 6 vols. (Leyden, 1952-1972); V. Bruns (editor), *Fontes Juris Gentium*, Series A, Part I, vols 3-5, *Digest of the Decisions of the Permanent Court of International Justice* 1922-40 (Berlin, 1931-64); R. Bernhardt (editor), *Digest of the Decisions of the International Court of Justice*, 1947-58 (Cologne, 1961); K. Marek, *Répertoire des décisions et documents de la procédure écrite et orale de la Cour Permanente de Justice Internationale et de la Cour Internationale de Justice*, 2 vols. (Geneva, 1961-7); and volume 3 of same, ed., L. Caflisch (1973).

29. Herbert W. Briggs, *The International Law Commission* (Ithaca, New York, 1965). Also Sh. Rosenne, "The International Law Commission, 1949-59", *British Year Book of International Law*, 36 (1960), 104; same, "The Role of the International Law Commission". *Proceedings of the American Society of International Law*, vol. 64 (1970), 24; same, *League of Nations, Committee for the Progressive Codification of International Law*, 2 vols. (Dobbs Ferry, New York, 1972); R.B. Dhokalia, *The Codification of Public International Law* (Manchester and Dobbs Ferry, New York, 1970).

30. For instance, the Socialist writers are highly critical of the law as applied by the Court, and to a large degree this criticism stems from the fact that the Marxist-Leninist concept of the role and nature of the law is considerably different from that held by other political and social philosophies, and this of necessity leads to different scales of values for assessing the work of any Court—including the International Court. For a recent East European study on the Court, see C. Elian, *The International Court of Justice* (Leyden, 1971).

NOTES TO CHAPTER II

1. For the Report of the Informal Inter-Allied Committee, see British Parliamentary Paper, Cmd. 6531 (1944). It was also republished in *American Journal of International Law*, 39 (1945), Supplement section of documents, 1.

2. For the Dumbarton Oaks proposals (which take their name from the estate in Washington, D.C., in which the Conference was held at which they were finally drafted), see Documents of the United Nations Conference on International Organization (abbreviated U.N.C.I.O.), vol. 3.

3. For the records of the Washington Committee of Jurists, which was in session between 9-20 April 1945, see U.N.C.I.O., vol. 14. A selection of documents illustrating the work of this Committee is contained in *The International Court of Justice, Selected Documents relating to the Drafting of the Statute* (Washington, 1946), Department of State, Publication 2491, Conference Series 84.

4. For the records of Committee IV/1 see U.N.C.I.O., vol. 13. And see *The United Nations Conference on International Organization*, selected documents (Washington, 1946), Department of State, Publication 2490, Conference Series 83. For a comprehensive index to the proceedings of the San Francisco Conference, see U.N.C.I.O., vol. 21.

5. Judge Azevedo, Rep. 1950, at 82.

6. For judicial discussion of this inter-action between Article 7 and Article 92 of the Charter, see particularly in the *Interpretation of the Peace Treaties* case. Rep. 1950, 65 at 71-2. For application of this principle in contentious proceedings, see *Northern Cameroons* case, Rep. 1963 at 15, passim.

7. *Peace Treaties* case, Rep. 1950, 65 at 71-2, repeated in *Reservations, Expenses* and *Namibia* cases, 1951, 15 at 19; 1962, 151 at 155; and 1971, 16 at 27.

8. See discussion in the 76th meeting of the Security Council on 15 October 1946. Off. Rec. 1st yr. 2nd series, No. 19, 466 ff.

9. Doc. A/C.6/L.454, G.A. O.R. 14th session, annexes, agenda item 63 (1959).

10. Cf. *Namibia* case, Rep. 1971 at 24.

11. For a general survey, see *Survey of International Law*, Working Paper prepared by the Secretary-General in the light of the decision of the [International Law] Commission to review its programme of work, doc. A/CN.4/245, paras. 120-149. Yearbook of the International Law Commission, 1971, Vol. II part 2.

12. General Assembly Resolution 171 (II), 14 November 1947. See G.A. O.R., 2nd session, Plenary meetings, doc. A/459, p. 1559.

13. General Assembly Resolution 2625 (XXV), 24 October 1970. For the principal discussions on judicial settlement, see Report of the 1966 Special Committee on Principles of International Law concerning Friendly Relations and Co-operation among States, G.A. O.R., 21st session, annexes, agenda item 87, doc. A/6230, paras. 210-220; Report of the 1967 Special Committee, ib., 22nd session, annexes, agenda item 87, doc. A/6799, paras. 384-393.

14. G.A. O.R., 25th session, annexes, agenda item 96, doc. A/8238; ib., 26th session, annexes, agenda item 90, docs. A/8382 and Add. 1-4, A/8568; ib., 27th session, annexes, agenda item 90, docs. A/8747 and A/8967.

15. 338th meeting, 15 July 1948.

16. Instances are the *South-West Africa Voting Procedure*, Rep. 1955, 67; the *Grant of Hearings to Oral Petitioners on South-West Africa*, Rep. 1956, 23; and the *Constitution of the Maritime Safety Committee of I,M.C.O.* case, Rep. 1960, 150. Nevertheless, the conception of requiring the Court as a matter of course to adjudicate upon the constitutionality of action by the General Assembly or the Security Council is not widely held. It would probably not be suitable for the expeditious conduct of international affairs nor is it likely to assist in preserving the independence of the Court.

17. Review of the United Nations Charter. Staff Studies prepared for the use of the Subcommittee on the United Nations Charter of the Committee on Foreign Relations. 83rd Congress, 2nd Session, Senate Document no. 164 (Washington, 1955), 223 at 236.

18. See *Reports of International Arbitral Awards*, vol. 12, pp. 351 ff.

19. See *Judgments of the United Nations Administrative Tribunal*, vol. 1, Nos. 1-86, vol. 2, Nos. 87-113, continuing.

20. Of all the principal organs of the United Nations, the Court is the only one which did not submit an annual report to the General Assembly. In this respect, the Court followed the tradition of the Permanent Court in its relations with the League. In 1968 this was changed, and the Court then commenced the practice of submitting an annual report to the General Assembly, which in its turn has so far limited itself to taking note of the document. The Court explained this change on the ground that it felt that such a report would contribute to a better understanding of its functions and of its activities within the framework of the United Nations. G.A. O.R. 23rd session, annexes, agenda item 14, doc. A/7181. For trenchant criticism, see S. Engel, "Annual Reports of the International Court of Justice to the General Assembly?", *British Year Book of International Law*, vol. 44 (1970), 193.

21. For the texts of the Relationship Agreements see *Agreements between the United Nations and the Specialized Agencies and the International Atomic Energy Agency*, doc. ST/SG/14 (1961).

22. This undertaking does not appear in the agreements with the international financial organizations or with the Universal Postal Union.

23. *Judgments of the Administrative Tribunal of the I.L.O. upon complaints made against UNESCO* case, Rep. 1956, 77; *Constitution of the Maritime Safety Committee of I.M.C.O.* case, Rep. 1960, 150.

24. S.C. O.R. 6th yr., 559th-563rd and 565th meetings, 1-19 October 1951.

25. Statute, Article 33.

26. Statute, Article 32. And see General Assembly Resolution 2890 B (XXVI), 22 December 1971. The salaries have been raised several times since they were first fixed in 1946. The principal reason has been the continuing inflation.

27. General Assembly Resolution 2367 (XXII), 14 December 1967 as modified by Resolution 2890 A (XXVI), 22 December 1971.

28. G.A. O.R. 21st session, 5th Committee, pp. 23-5 (1966).

NOTES TO CHAPTER III

1. As regards the other principal collegiate organs of the United Nations, this is specifically written into Article 86 of the Charter dealing with the composition of the Trusteeship Council. On the other hand, no such formal stipulation appears in Article 61, dealing with the composition of the Economic and Social Council, but in fact it has always been applied there until the elections held in 1960.

2. See the cautious resolution adopted by the Institute of International Law on 26 April 1954 on the basis of the important report by Prof. Max Huber, former President of the Permanent Court of International Justice. *Annuaire de l'Institut de Droit International*, 45 (1954), t.1, 407, t.2, 60-107, 296. The question of the increase in the size of the Court has been placed on the agenda of the General Assembly in 1956, 1957 and 1958, but no decisions were adopted. For the procedure of amending the Statute, see Statute, Article 69, and Charter, Articles 108 and 109. And see Security Council Resolution 272 (1969) of 23 October 1969 and General Assembly Resolution 2520 (XXIV) of 4 December 1969. Further details in G.A. O.R. 24th session, annexes, agenda item 93.

3. See Statute, Articles 4-7. Very few details are in fact available of the manner in which the nominating process is carried out. In the nature of things this is done discreetly. An instance is reported in which the Supreme Court of the Argentine was consulted in 1946 concerning the qualification of a candidate whom the Argentinian National Group proposed nominating. R.R. Araya, *El Derecho Internacional interpretado por la Corte Suprema de la Nación (1836-1956)* (Rosario, 1958), 71. For the consultations of the United States National Group in 1960, with the Chief Justice of the United States, the Presidents of the American Society of International Law and of various Bar Associations, and the Deans of a number of Law Schools, see R.R. Baxter, "The Procedures employed in connection with the United States Nominations for the International Court in 1960", *American Journal of International Law*, 55 (1961), 445. For further information on the internal practice of the United States, cf. Marjorie M. Whiteman, *Digest of International Law*, vol. 12 (Washington, 1971), at 1202. For particulars of the composition of the national groups of the Permanent Court of Arbitration, see the annual reports of the Permanent Administrative Committee of the Permanent Court of Arbitration.

The question of the personal qualifications or the individual members arises for some other organs of the United Nations, notably the functional commissions of the Economic and Social Council. Here a different principle is followed, whereby, although States are elected to these Commissions, the actual representative is designated by the Government concerned after consultation with the Secretary-General, and is subject to confirmation by the Council. J.G. Hadwen and J. Kaufmann, *How United Nations Decisions are Made* (Leyden, 1960), 18. Such a system would not be appropriate for the International Court.

4. It is not too clear on what the assumption was based. Of the members of the Court serving in 1939, who continued in office until the dissolution of the Permanent Court in 1946, five had been first elected prior to the general election of 1930, and a further two had previously been deputy-judges (a post which was abolished in 1936). Three judges were continuously members of the Court from its establishment to its dissolution. They

served two full terms of nine years plus the further six War years. Of the fifteen judges elected to the present Court in 1946, only three remained on the Court after the election of 1960, and only one served until the election of 1967. It seems that the present system of triennial partial elections has in fact increased the rate of turn-over among the judges. This, in turn, is believed by many observers to have had an unsettling effect on the Court, and obstructed the creation of its "esprit de corps".

5. A majority of eight is therefore sufficient in the Security Council, the only instance of voting in that organ by which a decision can be reached by a simple majority. For all other decisions, whether or not the "veto" applies, the minimum number of positive votes required is nine out of the membership of fifteen. The relevant rules are now interpreted as requiring an absolute majoirty in the General Assembly, i.e. one half plus one of the total number of votes entitled to be cast. This is a change from the practice in the League Assembly where a simple majority, i.e. one half plus one of the votes actually cast, was required. The reasons for this change are not entirely clear. Cf. A.W. Rudzinski, "Election Procedure in the United Nations", *American Journal of International Law*, 53 (1959), 81. It was decisive for the election of Sir Zafrulla Khan in 1954. For the participation of non-members, parties to the Statute, in the General Assembly, see Resolution 264 (III) of 8 October 1948 on the basis of the recommendation made by the Security Council in its resolution 58 (1948) of 28 September 1948.

6. Statute, Articles 8-12. And see Rules 152 and 153 of the Rules of Procedure of the General Assembly (A/520/Rev. 11) and Rules 40 and 61 of the Provisional Rules of Procedure of the Security Council (S/96/Rev. 5). These Rules incorporate the current interpretation of the word "meeting", to the effect that it continues until as many candidates as are required for all the seats to be filled have obtained in one or more ballots an absolute majority of votes.

7. Statute, Articles 14, 15.

8. It is interesting to observe the full results of the voting in this election. In the General Assembly, the required majority was 52. In the first meeting, the results were as follows: first ballot (101 valid ballots); Messrs. Jessup (U.S.A.), 77; Koretsky (U.S.S.R.), 62; Tanaka (Japan), 51; Bustamente y Rivero (Peru), 42; Zafrulla Khan (Pakistan), 42; Morelli (Italy), 41; Klaestad (Norway), 37; Sapena Pastor (Paraguay), 37; Pal (India), 31; Armand-Ugon (Uruguay), 14; Nisot (Belgium), 11; Guggenheim (Switzerland), 10; Bartoš (Yugoslavia), 7; Kojevnikov (U.S.S.R.), 6; Petrén (Sweden), 5; Tunkin (U.S.S.R.), 3; Matine-Daftary (Iran), 3; Barros (Chile), 3; Hackworth (U.S.A.) 3; Castrén (Finland), 3; Flor (Ecuador), 1; Prodjodikoro (Indonesia), 1. Second Ballot (100 valid ballots): Tanaka, 56; Bustamente y Rivero, 48; Morelli, 43; Zafrulla Khan, 34; Klaestad, 33; Sapena Pastor, 31; Pal, 28; Bartoš 3; Guggenheim, 2; Armand-Ugon, 2; Matine-Daftary, 2; Nisot, 1; Petrén, 1; Prodjodikoro, 1. Third ballot (94 valid ballots): Bustamente y Rivero, 46; Morelli, 40; Klaestad, 28; Sapena Pastor, 28; Zafrulla Khan, 17; Pal, 13; Guggenheim, 5; Flor, 1; Armand-Ugon, 1; Matine-Daftary, 1; Nisot, 1; Prodjodikoro, 1; Petrén, 1; Sørensen (Denmark), 1. Fourth Ballot (98 valid ballots): Bustamente y Rivero, 53; Morelli, 45; Sapena Pastor, 29; Klaestad, 27; Zafrulla Khan, 16; Pal, 11; Guggenheim, 4; Nisot, 3; Sørensen 1; Flor, 1; Prodjodikoro, 1. Fifth ballot (97 valid ballots): Morelli, 56; Klaestad, 24; Pal, 8; Zafrulla Khan, 5; Sapena Pastor, 3; Matine-Daftary, 1. Second meeting, first ballot (89 valid ballots): Bustamente y Rivero, 66; Sapena Pastor, 13; Zafrulla Khan, 4; Pal, 3; Klaestad, 2; Guggenheim, 1. Four of the candidates who obtained votes in the General Assembly, Messrs. Hackworth, Kojevnikov, Tunkin and Prodjodikoro, had withdrawn their candidature before the voting commenced. In the Security Council, the required majority was 6. The result of the first ballot of the first meeting (11 valid ballots) was: Messrs. Jessup, 11; Koretsky, 9; Morelli, 7; Sapena Pastor, 6; Tanaka, 6; Bustamente y Rivero, 5; Klaestad, 4; Pal, 3; Armand-Ugon, 2; Zafrulla

Khan, 2. The result of the first ballot of the second meeting was: Bustamente y Rivero, 10; Sapena Pastor, 1. The point of order raised by India between the first and second ballots of the first meeting of the General Assembly was sustained on a roll-call vote by a majority of 47 to 27, with 25 abstentions.

9.   Statute, Article 20; Rules of Court, Article 5.

10. Statute, Article 16.

11. See correspondence between the Prime Minister of Australia (R. Menzies) and Judge Sir Percy Spender, the *Times* (London), 12 September 1958. Also in *Revue Général de Droit international public*, 63 (1959) at 94.

12. Statute, Article 17.

13. Statute, Article 18; Rules of Court, Article 6.

14. Statute, Article 23; Rules of Court, Articles 29, 30.

15. Statute, Article 24. The Statute does not contain anything corresponding to the continental system of *récusation*, i.e. a direct appeal by a party against the participation of a judge on ground of relationship or known personal bias towards one or other of the parties. The question was raised in both the *South West Africa* and *Namibia* cases. See Rep. 1965 at 3 and 1971 at 3, 6 and 9 for relevant orders, and ib., at 18 for discussion by the Court of some of the principles involved. It is also believed that the Statute permits discreet action to be taken in the same direction should one of the parties feel this to be necessary. Cf. Jeremy D. Morley, "Relative Incompatibility of Functions in the International Court", *The International and Comparative Law Quarterly*, 19 (1970) at 316.

16. Statute, Article 21; Rules of Court, Article 9.

17. Statute, Article 21; Rules of Court, Articles 9-12.

18. Statute, Article 32, paragraphs 2 and 3.

19. Rules of Court, Articles 2, 33.

20. Rules of Court, Articles 11-13.

21. Article 31.

22. For instances of this, see *South West Africa* and *Continental Shelf* cases. Rep. 1961 at 13, 1968 at 9.

23. *Nemo judex in causa sua*.

24. This was the view of the Informal Inter-Allied Committee of 1944, in support of its recommendation that the institution of judge *ad hoc* be retained.

25. Statute, Article 25; Rules of Court, Articles 29-32.

26. Statute, Article 29; Rules of Court, Articles 24 and 27.

27. Statute, Article 26, paragraph 1; Rules of Court, Articles 25 and 27.

28. Statute, Article 26, paragraph 2; Rules of Court, Articles 26 and 27.

29. Rules of Court, Articles 7 and 8. For the simplified procedure before the chambers, see Articles 75 to 78 of the Rules of Court.

30. See I.C.J. Yearbook, 1946-7, 55-87 for a description of the organization of the Registry, the Staff Regulations and the Instructions for the Registry.

31. See I.C.J. Yearbook, 1970-1 at 110.

NOTES TO CHAPTER IV

1. *Continental Shelf*, Rep. 1969, 3 at 47, citing with approval the Permanent Court in *Free Zones*, A 22 (1929), 13.

2. *Nottebohm* case (second phase), Rep. 1955, 19.

3. This is specifically laid down in Article 34 (1) of the Statute.

4. In the present Court see the following cases: *Ambatielos, Anglo-Iranian Oil Co., Nottebohm, Interhandel, Guardianship, Barcelona Traction*. This practice compares unfavourably with, for example, that of the European Court of Human Rights, as manifested in the *Lawless* case (1960-1). See Sh. Rosenne, "Reflections on the Position of the Individual in Inter-State Litigation in the International Court of Justice", *International Arbitration, Liber Amicorum* for Martin Domke (1967) at 240.

5. Statute, Article 34 (2). No instance of this has yet occurred.

6. *Reparation* case.

7. Statute, Article 35 (2).

8. *Corfu Channel* (in a later stage), *Minquiers and Ecrehos, Frontier Land, Continental Shelf* and *Fisheries Jurisdiction* (Federal Republic of Germany v. Iceland).

9. *Asylum* and *Honduras-Nicaragua Frontier* cases. The *Monetary Gold* case may be seen as a variation on this theme, in very special circumstances.

10. See U.N. Conference on the Law of the Sea (1958), O.R. II, 7, 33, for the discussion which brought out all the underlying political issues. For the text of the Optional Protocol of Signature concerning the Compulsory Settlement of disputes, see U.N.T.S., 450, at 169. A similar solution was adopted in the cases of the 1961 Vienna Convention on Diplomatic Relations, the 1963 Vienna Convention on Consular Relations and the 1969 New York Convention on Special Missions. For trenchant criticism, see Herbert W. Briggs, "The Optional Protocols of Geneva (1958) and Vienna (1961, 1963) concerning the Compulsory Settlement of Disputes", *Recueil d'Etudes de Droit international en hommage à Paul Guggenheim* (1968), at 628. For the different solution reached in the 1969 Vienna Convention on the Law of Treaties, see Sh. Rosenne, "The Settlement of Treaty Disputes under the Vienna Convention of 1969", 31 *Zeitschrift für ausländisches öffentliches Recht und Völkerrecht*, 1 (1971). For difficulties experienced in the League of Nations codification effort, see Sh. Rosenne, *Committee of Experts for the Progressive Codification of International Law* [1925-1928], I at lxii-lxiv (1972).

11. Cf. the following cases: *French Nationals in Egypt, South West Africa* (two cases), *Northern Cameroons, ICAO Council, Nuclear Tests* (two cases) and *Pakistani Prisoners of War*.

12. Cf. the following cases: *Haya de la Torre, Ambatielos, Barcelona Traction* (two cases), *Fisheries Jurisdiction* (two cases).

13. Cf. the following cases: *Electricité de Beyrouth, Compagnie du Port de Beyrouth*.

14. See the various *Aerial Incident* cases (except those concerning the incident of 27 July 1955) and the *Antarctica* cases.

15. M. Hudson, *The Permanent Court of International Justice, 1920-1942* (New York, 1943), 473.

16. See in general, Herbert W. Briggs, "Reservations to the Acceptance of the Compulsory Jurisdiction of the International Court of Justice", R.A.D.I., 93 (1958) (i), 223.

17. Covenant of the League of Nations, Article 15 (8).

18. Charter of the United Nations, Article 2 (7).

19. Such reservations have been made at one time or another by France, India, Liberia, Malawi, Mexico, Pakistan, South Africa, Sudan and, as stated, by the United States, and in a different form by the United Kingdom. Since 1957, those by France, India, Pakistan and the United Kingdom have been withdrawn. The Executive Branch of the United States Government has also attempted to obtain the advice and consent of the Senate to the withdrawal of this reservation from the United States acceptance, but without success. For some reason or other, the issue raises emotional reactions in the United States.

20. In the Court this view was advanced with great vigour by the late Sir Hersch Lauterpacht, as well as by other judges, especially in the *Norwegian Loans* and *Interhandel* cases. There is little doubt that some of the withdrawals of this type of reservation were prompted by that criticism. On the other hand its inclusion in some more recent declarations made by new States indicates that the factors which led to it in the first place are not entirely dormant.

21. On 31 December 1972 declarations by the following States accepting the compulsory jurisdiction were deposited with the Secretary-General of the United Nations: Australia, Austria, Belgium, Botswana, Cambodia, Canada, Costa Rica, Denmark, Egypt, Finland, France, Gambia, Honduras, India, Israel, Japan, Kenya, Liberia, Liechtenstein, Malawi, Malta, Mauritius, Mexico, Netherlands, Nigeria, Norway, Pakistan, Philippines, Portugal, Somalia, Sudan, Swaziland, Sweden, Switzerland, Uganda, United Kingdom and United States of America. In addition, declarations made by the following States in relation to the Permanent Court are still recorded as in force: Colombia, Dominican Republic, El Salvador, Haiti, Luxembourg, New Zealand, Nicaragua, Panama and Uruguay. The declaration of Egypt was made on 18 July 1957 regarding the operation of the Suez Canal, and is not a general acceptance of the jurisdiction, as are the others. For full particulars, see the current edition of *Multilateral Treaties in respect of which the Secretary-General performs Depositary Functions*, ch. I, sect. 4. Doc. ST/LEG/SER.D/—. This publication is issued annually.

22. In chronological order the cases are: *Fisheries, Anglo-Iranian Oil Co., U.S. Nationals in Morocco, Nottebohm, Norwegian Loans, Interhandel, Right of Passage, Guardianship Convention, Aerial Incident of 27 July 1955* (three cases) and *Temple*. The compulsory jurisdiction was also invoked as a second title of jurisdiction in the *Nuclear Tests* cases.

23. Statute, Articles 36 (5) and 37.

24. This seems to be the combined effect of the *Aerial Incident of 27 July 1955* and the *Temple* case.

25. *Barcelona Traction* (preliminary objections), Rep. 1964, 26-39. Reiterated in *ICAO Council*, Rep. 1972, at 53. Note that no objection on this point was raised in *South West Africa*, although the issue was raised indirectly. Cf. Rep. 1962, at 334-5.

26. Statute, Article 41, and see Article 66 (previously 61) of the Rules of Court.

27. See p. 40 above. For the order indicating the interim measures, see Rep. 1951, 89.

28. *Interhandel* case, Rep. 1957, 105.

29. Rep. 1972, 12, 30. These orders were originally made for one year, but they were later prolonged until final judgment. Rep. 1973, 302, 313.

30. Rep. 1973, 99 (Australia) and 135 (New Zealand).

31. Rep. 1973, 328.

32. Cf. *Right of Passage* case, Rep. 1957, 152. And see p. 101 above.

33. Statute, Articles 36 (6) and 53. Rules of Court, Article 67 (previously 62).

34. See *Monetary Gold* case.

35. Cf. *Interhandel* case, Rep. 1959 at 20.

36. This follows the principle of Roman law—*reus excipiendo actor est*—according to which, by opposing an exception to the plaintiff's claim, the defendant acts as plaintiff.

37. *ICAO Council*, Rep. 1972, at 56.

38. *Prince von Pless Administration*, Ser. A/B 52 (1933).

39. *ICAO Council*, Rep. 1972, at 52.

40. Rep. 1972 at 181 and 188 and 1973 at 3 and 49: Rep. 1973 at 105 and 142; Rep. 1973 at 328.

41. *ICAO Council*, Rep. 1972, at 60.

42. Cf. F. Frankfurter, "A Note on Advisory Opinions", *Harvard Law Review*, 37 (1924), 1002. Generally see K.J. Keith, *The Extent of the Advisory Jurisdiction of the International Court of Justice* (Leyden, 1971).

43. Charter, Article 96.

44. Statute, Articles 65-68. Rules of Court, Articles 87-91 (formerly 82-85).

45. *Frontier between Turkey and Iraq* case, B 12 (1925). And cf. the separate opinion of Sir Hersch Lauterpacht in the *South West Africa* (voting procedure) case. Rep. 1955, 67 at 98. See on this M. Pomerance, *The Advisory Function of the International Court in the League and U.N. Eras* (Baltimore and London, 1973).

46. *Eastern Carelia* case, B 5 (1923). In the opinion of many, this doctrine may have been considerably weakened, if not overruled entirely, by the jurisprudence of the present Court, notably in the *Peace Treaties* and *Namibia* cases. Rep. 1950 at 71 and 1971 at 23.

47. The following cases: *Competence of Assembly, Conditions of Admission to UN, Peace Treaties* (two opinions), *Reparation, South West Africa* (status), *Reservations to Genocide Convention, UN Administrative Tribunal, South-West Africa* (voting procedure), *South West Africa* (petitioners), *ILO Administrative Tribunal. Maritime Safety Committee, UN Expenses, Namibia, Appeal from Administrative Tribunal Judgment No. 158 (Fesla case).*

48. By virtue of Article 14 of the Statute of the UN Administrative Tribunal (AT/11/Rev.3), the competence of the Tribunal has been extended also to ICAO. In addition, the Tribunal has competence to deal with applications alleging non-observance of the UN Joint Staff Pension Fund as regards ILO, UNESCO, FAO, ICAO, and WHO. As for the ILO Administrative Tribunal, its competence has been extended to include the staff of WHO, UNESCO, ITU, WMO, FAO, IAEA, as well as a number of organizations not authorised to request advisory opinions, namely: UPU, Interim Commission for the ITO, European Organization for Nuclear Research, BIRPI, European Organization for the Safety of Air Navigation. In these cases, no recourse to the Court is possible through the special advisory procedure (but this does not exclude recourse through the normal advisory procedure, with the assistance of an authorised organ).

NOTES TO CHAPTER V

1. Statute, Article 43.
2. For an example, see the orders of 18 August 1972 in *Fisheries Jurisdiction*. Rep. 1972, 181, 188. These orders directed that the memorials and the counter-memorials should be addressed to the question of the jurisdiction of the Court to entertain the dispute.
3. Rules of Court, Article 35 (2) (formerly 32 (2)).
4. Statute, Article 39; Rules of Court, Articles 42 and 64 (formerly 39 and 58).
5. Rules of Court, Article 55 (amendment of 1972, formerly Article 51).
6. Agents were not appointed, and the respondent was not represented, in various phases in the following cases: *Corfu Channel, Anglo-Iranian Oil Co., Nottebohm, Compagnie du Port, Fisheries Jurisdiction, Nuclear Tests* and *Pakistani Prisoners of War.* Nevertheless, jurisprudence on this delicate aspect is fragmentary.
7. Statute, Article 40.
8. Rules of Court, Article 38 (5) (formerly 35 (5)).
9. Statute, Article 62; Rules of Court, Articles 69-70 (formerly 64-5). The Court deferred its decision pending the outcome of the jurisdictional phase. Rep. 1973, 320, 324.
10. Statute, Article 63; Rules of Court, Article 71 (formerly 66).
11. Rules of Court, Article 40 (5) (amendment of 1972, formerly Article 41).
12. Rules of Court, Article 46 (3) (amendment of 1972, formerly 42).
13. Rules of Court, Article 48 (formerly 44).
14. Rules of Court, Article 49 (formerly 45).
15. Rules of Court, Article 66 (2) (formerly 61 (2)).
16. Rules of Court, Article 52 (amended in 1972, formerly 48).
17. Statute, Article 46. In the *Namibia* case closed hearings were held on 27 January 1971 in connexion with one government's claim to be entitled to choose a judge *ad hoc*. I.C.J. Rep. 1971, 12. Later the Court decided to make the record of that hearing accessible to the public. Rep. 1971, at 19.
18. Rules of Court, Article 57 (amendment of 1972, formerly 52).
19. Rules of Court, Articles 54 and 55 (formerly 50 and 51).
20. Rep. 1965, 9.
21. A roneographed provisional record of the day's proceedings is distributed, together with an unofficial translation by the Registry, each evening. This is known as the C.R. (*compte rendu*). Subject to correction by the speakers under the control of the Court, this transcript becomes the formal minutes of the meetings and is published. Statute, Article 47; Rules of Court, Article 65 (amended in 1972, formerly 60).
22. Rules of Court, Article 57 (amended in 1972, formerly 52).
23. Statute, Article 48; Rules of Court, Article 56 (new article, added in 1972).
24. Statute, Article 56.
25. Statute, Article 55. Two cases, *Lotus* (in the Permanent Court) and *South West Africa* (in the present Court), have been decided by the casting vote of the President. In each case the decision was unacceptable politically, and led to political action to undo the effect of the judgment.
26. Statute, Article 57.
27. Rules of Court, Article 33 (formerly 30).

28. Rules of Court, Article 79 (formerly 74).

29. For text, see Sh. Rosenne, *The Law and Practice of the International Court*, 2 (1965) at 599. For descriptions of how deliberations were conducted under that resolution, cf. M. Hudson, *The Permanent Court of International Justice, 1920-1942*, (1943), 579; E. Hambro, "The reasons behind the decisions of the International Court of Justice", *Current Legal Problems*, 7 (1954), 212.

30. I.C.J. Yearbook, 22 (1967-8), 88 And see F.L. Grieves, "Reform of the Method of rendering decisions in the International Court of Justice", 64 *American Journal of International Law* (1970), 144; E. Hambro, "The Drafting Procedure of the International Court of Justice", *Festschrift Frangistas* (1968), 341; H. Mosler, "La procédure de la Cour internationale de Justice et de la Cour européenne des Droits de l'Homme", *René Cassin Amicorum Discipulorumque Liber, I (1969)*, 196.

31. Statute, Article 58.

32. Rules of Court, Article 80 (formerly 75). An analogous system of public reading and of circulation is prescribed for advisory opinions. Rules of Court, Article 91 (amended in 1972, formerly 85). Orders indicating interim measures of protection are sent to the Security Council. Where orders are not read in open court, copies are sent to the parties and are made available to the public. An appropriate press release is issued regarding all activities, including judicial activities, of the Court.

33. Rules of Court, Article 22. The Registrar is responsible for the Court's publications. For details, see p. 242 below. The Court's publications are obtainable through the local United Nations Sales Agents in each country.

34. The relevant date, 5 February 1930, was the date on which India's first declaration accepting the jurisdiction of the Permanent Court of International Justice took effect. For discussion of this technical, but significant, aspect of the work of the Court, see our work cited in note 29 above, vol. 1 at chapter IX passim.

35. *Maritime Safety Committee*. This is not the only example.

36. Sir Hersch Lauterpacht, *The Development of International Law by the International Court* (1958), 68-9. For a recent striking defence of the practice, see Judge de Castro in *ICAO Council* case, Rep. 1972, at 116.

37. This was subsequently exceeded, notably in *South West Africa* and in *Barcelona Traction*. Here, indeed, it has been claimed that the record came to exceed 18,000 pages!

38. Statute, Article 13; Rules of Court, Article 13.

39. Statute, Article 53.

40. Preliminary Objections, Annex B, Nos. 2 and 3. See *Right of Passage* case, Pleadings, vol. I, pp. 217 ff.

41. Rules of Court, Article 74 (previously 69). For an important analysis of the legal implications, see *Barcelona Traction*, Rep. 1964, 18 ff.

42. Rules of Court, Article 73 (previously 68).

43. Statute, Article 38 (1). This provision was amended in 1945 when the words "whose function is to decide in accordance with international law such disputes as are submitted to it" were added. The effect of this addition is controversial.

44. The technical name for this kind of finding is *non liquet*—literally "it is not clear"—a term borrowed from Roman law. It is now generally accepted that an international tribunal is in principle not entitled to bring a finding of *non liquet*.

45. See discussion at the 888th meeting of the Commission. I.L.C. Yearbook, 1966, vol. I part 2, 295-6.

46. Statute, Article 59, which is specifically recalled in Article 38.

47. Statute, Article 38 (2). The words mean "right and equitable", and their implication is that the application by the judge of a reasonable corrective to rules of law

which have become out-dated would be an acceptable decision. This concept, of which instances are extremely rare in international practice, must not be confused with the English concept of "equity", at least in its modern form.

48. At the same time it should be mentioned that other States have expressed disquiet over this development of the law and have taken steps to protect themselves against it. See Sh. Rosenne, *The Time Factor in the Jurisdiction of the International Court of Justice* (Leyden, 1960), especially at 21. Cf. also article 73 of the Vienna Convention on the Law of Treaties, partly designed to prevent excessive generalization of the law as expressed in this part of this case.

49. See discussions at the 987th and 988th meetings of the Security Council on 18 December 1961. The Court's judgment was hardly mentioned.

50. It is believed that this is the first instance in the experience of the Permanent Court and the present Court in which each one of a series of multiple objections has been rejected and in which the objecting State has nonetheless emerged as the substantive victor.

51. Statute, Article 64; Rules of Court, Article 82 (previously 77). There has been no instance in the International Court in which costs have been awarded.

52. Statute, Articles 59 and 60; Rules of Court, Article 81 (previously 76).

53. Statute, Article 60; Rules of Court, Articles 84-6 (previously 79-81).

54. Statute, Article 61; Rules of Court, Articles 83, 85-6 (previously 78, 80-1).

55. Yearbook of the International Court of Justice, 1948-9, 41.

NOTES TO CHAPTER VI

1. For the proceedings in the Security Council, see the *Official Records* of its 95th, 107th, 109th, 111th, 114th, 120th-122nd and 125th meetings, between 20 January and 3 April 1947. For the three judgments of the Court, see Rep. 1948, 15; 1949, 4, and 244; and for the orders regarding the appointment of the committees of experts, Rep. 1948, 124, and 1949, 237.

2. For the decisions of the General Assembly, see resolutions 113 B (II) of 17 November 1947 and 197 (III) of 8 December 1948. For the opinion of the Court, see Rep. 1948, 57. In these proceedings, written statements were submitted by China, El Salvador, Guatemala, Honduras, India, Canada, the United States of America, Greece, Yugoslavia, Belgium, Iraq, the Ukrainian S.S.R., U.S.S.R., and Australia. Oral statements were made on behalf of the Secretary-General of the United Nations, and France, Yugoslavia, Belgium, Czechoslovakia and Poland.

3. See General Assembly resolution 296 J (IV) of 22 November 1949. For the opinion of the Court, see Rep. 1950, 4. In these proceedings, written statements were submitted by the Secretary-General and by the Byelorussian S.S.R., Czechoslovakia, Egypt, the Ukrainian S.S.R., U.S.S.R., the United States, Argentina and Venezuela. An oral statement was made by France.

4. Resolution 258 (III) of 3 December 1948, adopted unanimously by fifty-three votes with no abstention. For the opinion of the Court, see Rep. 1949, 174. In these proceedings, written statements were submitted by India, China, the United States, the United Kingdom, France. Oral statements were made on behalf of the Secretary-General, and Belgium, France and the United Kingdom. For the action subsequently taken by the General Assembly, see resolution 365 (IV) of 1 December 1949.

5. Rep. 1951, 116.

6. See the Geneva Convention of 1958 on the Territorial Sea and Contiguous Zone. Both these issues were discussed in the Conference's First Committee. See *Official Records*, vol. III, *passim*. It may be noted that this Conference also dealt with another aspect of the law of the sea, emerging from the decision of the Permanent Court of International Justice in the *Lotus* case. There it had been held that a State could exercise criminal jurisdiction over a foreign ship on the high seas, if as a result of a collision on the high seas its nationals were injured. That decision was badly received in maritime circles, but the general rule of international law which the Court found to be applicable could only be changed by an international convention. The 1958 Convention on the High Seas (Article 11) now limits the jurisdiction, in such circumstances, to the flag State or the State of which the ship's officer concerned was a national.

7. Rep. 1950, 59.

8. Rep. 1950, 266.

9. Rep. 1950, 395.

10. Rep. 1951, 71.

11. See General Assembly resolution 294 (IV) of 22 October 1949. For the opinions of the Court, see Rep. 1950, 65, 221. In the first stage of these proceedings, written statements were submitted by the United States, the United Kingdom, Bulgaria, the Ukrainian S.S.R., U.S.S.R., the Byelorussian S.S.R., Romania, Czechoslovakia, Hungary and Australia. Oral statements were made on behalf of the Secretary-General, the United

States and the United Kingdom. In the second phase, a further written statement was submitted by the United States, and oral statements were made on behalf of the Secretary-General, the United States and the United Kingdom.

12. Resolution 385 (V) of 3 November 1950.

13. For the change of name from South West Africa to Namibia, see General Assembly resolution 2372 (XXII), 12 June 1968.

14. See General Assembly resolution 338 (IV) of 6 December 1949. The resolution was adopted by forty votes to seven, with four abstentions. For the Court's opinion, see Rep. 1950, 128. Written statements were submitted by Egypt, South Africa, the United States, Poland and India. Oral statements were made on behalf of the Secretary-General, the Philippines and South Africa.

15. See resolutions 844 (IX) of 11 October 1954 and 904 (IX) of 23 November 1954. That resolution was adopted by twenty-five votes to eleven, with twenty-one abstentions. For the Court's opinion, see Rep. 1955, 67. Written statements were submitted by the United States, Poland, India, Israel, China, Yugoslavia and the Secretary-General. No State requested to make an oral statement.

16. See resolution 942 (X) of 3 December 1955, adopted by thirty-two votes to five, with nineteen abstentions. For the Court's opinion, see Rep. 1956, 23. In addition to the Secretary-General's statement, written statements were submitted by the United States, China and India, and an oral statement was made on behalf of the United Kingdom.

17. Resolution 1361 (XIV), 17 November 1959.

18. Rep. 1961, 13.

19. Rep. 1962, 319.

20. Rep. 1965, 3.

21. Rep. 1965, 9.

22. Rep. 1966, 6.

23. Rep. 1971, 3, 6, 9 and 12.

24. Rep. 1971, 16. In these proceedings written statements were submitted by the United Nations and Czechoslovakia, Finland, France, Hungary, India, the Netherlands, Nigeria, Pakistan, Poland, South Africa, the United States and Yugoslavia. Oral statements were made on behalf of the Secretary-General of the United Nations, the Organization of African Unity, Finland, India, the Netherlands, Nigeria, Pakistan, South Africa, Viet-Nam and the United States of America. Apart from the preliminary questions of the composition of the Court, objections raised by South Africa to the giving of the opinion were based on a number of grounds. These included political pressure to which the Court might have been subjected, invalidity of the resolution of the Security Council by which the opinion was requested, that the opinion related to a dispute to which South Africa was a party and the consent of South Africa to the giving of the opinion should have been obtained, and procedural irregularities in the Security Council. All these objections were rejected by the Court.

25. Rep. 1951, 109; 1952, 176. Questions relating to the Act of Algeriras were also raised before the Permanent Court in the *Phosphates in Morocco* case (1938).

26. See resolution 478 (V) of 16 November 1950, adopted by a majority of forty-seven votes to five with five abstentions. For the Court's opinion, see Rep. 1951, 15. Written statements were submitted by the United Nations, the Organization of American States and the International Labour Organization, and by the United States, U.S.S.R., Jordan, United Kingdom, Israel, Poland, Czechoslovakia, the Netherlands, the Ukrainian S.S.R., Bulgaria, the Byelorussian S.S.R., and the Philippines. Oral statements were made on behalf of the Secretary-General, Israel, United Kingdom and France. In its opinion the Court dismissed challenges to its jurisdiction, which were similar to those put forward in

the *Peace Treaties* case. Pakistan later invoked this convention as a basis for jurisdiction in the *Pakistani Prisoners of War* case.

27. For the position in the League of Nations, see Rosenne, *The Progressive Codification of International Law* (Dobbs Ferry, N.Y., 1972), I, lxxii, lxxiv, II, 25. For the early position of the International Law Commission, see its Yearbook, 1950, II, at 381 and 1951, II, 125. For subsequent evolution, leading to the Vienna Convention, see the Yearbook, 1962, II, 175, 1965, II, 161 and 1966, II 202.

28. Rep. 1952, 28; 1953, 10. For the award of 6 March 1956, see 23 *International Law Reports* 306 and 24 ib. 291. Also in 12 *Reports of International Arbitral Awards* 91.

29. C.R. Attlee, *As it Happened* (New York,1954), 246. See also I.S. Macadam and H. Latimer, *The Annual Register*, 1951 (London, 1952), 50.

30. Rep. 1951, 89.

31. Rep. 1952, 93.

32. International Court of Justice, Yearbook, 1952-3, 45. In the new agreement of September 1954, by which the dispute was finally settled, a similar power was conferred on the President of the present Court. For text, see J.C. Hurewitz, *Diplomacy in the Near and Middle East*, II (New York, 1956), 348.

33. Rep. 1953, 47.

34. Rep. 1953, 111; 1954, 4.

35. Rep. 1954, 19. For the award of 20 February 1953, see 20 *International Law Reports* 441. Also in 12 *Reports of International Arbitral Awards* 19.

36. Rep. 1954, 107; 1960, 186.

37. Resolution 785 A (VIII) of 6 December 1953, adopted by forty-one to six, with thirteen abstentions. For the Court's opinion, see Rep. 1954, 47. Written statements were presented by the United Nations, the I.L.O., France, Sweden, the Netherlands, Greece, the United Kingdom, the United States, the Philippines, Mexico, Chile, Iraq, China, Guatemala, Turkey, Ecuador, Canada, U.S.S.R., Czechoslovakia and Egypt. Oral statements were made on behalf of the United Nations, France, the United States, Greece, the United Kingdom and the Netherlands.

38. Resolution of the Executive Board of UNESCO of 25 November 1955, adopted by twelve votes to five, with four abstentions. For the Court's opinion, see Rep. 1956, 77. Written statements were submitted by UNESCO, the United States, France, the United Kingdom and China. No oral proceedings were held.

39. For the judgment of the Administrative Tribunal (*Fesla* case), see doc. AT/DEC/158. For the proceedings in the Committee for Review, see doc. A/AC.86/14. The decision to request the advisory opinion was adopted on a roll-call vote by 15 votes to 3, with one abstention. For the advisory opinion, see Rep. 1973, 166. Written statements were submitted by the Secretary-General of the United Nations and by the applicant (through the Secretary-General). No oral proceedings were held.

40. For these cases, see Rep. 1954, 99, 103; 1956, 6, 9; 1958, 158; 1959, 276.

41. Rep. 1956, 12, 15.

42. Rep. 1957, 9.

43. Rep. 1958, 55.

44. Rep. 1957, 105.

45. Rep. 1959, 6.

46. See Annual Report, Office of Alien Property, Department of Justice (Washington D.C.), Fiscal Year ended June 30, 1958, at 63; id., Fiscal Year ended June 30, 1965, at 10.

47. Rep. 1959, 127. In the course of these proceedings, Bulgaria withdrew the other objection to the jurisdiction and agreed to defer consideration of two of the three objections to the admissibility until the proceedings on the merits.

48. Rep. 1959, 264.
49. Rep. 1960, 146.
50. Rep. 1959, 206.
51. Award of 23 December 1906, 11 *Reports of International Arbitral Awards* 107.
52. Rep. 1960, 192.
53. For the text of his decision see 30 *International Law Reports* 76.
54. Rep. 1961, 9.
55. Rep. 1964, 6; 1970, 3.
56. See resolution A.12 (I) adopted by the Assembly of IMCO on 19 January 1959. For the Court's opinion, see Rep. 1960, 150. Written statements were presented by Belgium, France, Liberia, the United States, China, Panama, Switzerland, Italy, Denmark, the United Kingdom, Norway, the Netherlands, and India. Oral statements were made on behalf of Liberia, the United States, Panama, Italy, the Netherlands, Norway, and the United Kingdom. The resolution of the IMCO Assembly was adopted unanimously, with one abstention. In April, 1961, the IMCO Assembly dissolved the Maritime Safety Committee and reconstituted it to conform to the terms of the advisory opinion.
57. For the Court's judgment see Rep. 1961, 17 and 1962, 6. For the statements of the Thailand government see *Foreign Affairs Bulletin* issued by the Thailand Ministry for Foreign Affairs, vol. 1 No. 6, June-July 1962, 129.
58. Rep. 1963, 15.
59. General Assembly resolution 1731 (XVI) of 20 December 1961, adopted by 52 votes to 11 with 32 abstentions. For the advisory opinion, see Rep. 1962, 151. Written statements were submitted by Australia, Bulgaria, Byelorussia, Canada, Czechoslovakia, Denmark, France, Ireland, Italy, Japan, Mexico, Netherlands, Philippines, Poland, Portugal, Romania, South Africa, Spain, Ukraine, U.S.S.R., United Kingdom, United States and Upper Volta, and the Secretary-General submitted a comprehensive introductory note to the documentation. In the oral proceedings, statements were made by Australia, Canada, Ireland, Italy, Netherlands, Norway, U.S.S.R., United Kingdom and United States.
60. For the joinder, see Rep. 1968, 9. For the judgment, see Rep. 1969, 3. For the subsequent agreements, see I.C.J. Yearbook, 1970-71, 117, and 1971-72, 142.
61. Rep. 1972, 46.
62. Rep. 1973, 328.
63. Rep. 1972, 12, 181 and 1973, 3, 93 (United Kingdom); 1972, 30, 188 and 1973, 49, 96 (Federal Republic).
64. Rep. 1973, pp. 99, 135.
65. For a defence of this, see Judge Jiménez de Aréchaga, "Judges *ad hoc* in Advisory Proceedings", 31 *Zeitschrift für ausländisches öffentliches Recht und Völkerrecht* 697 (1971).
66. Report of the Sixth Committee, *Official Records of the General Assembly*, twenty-sixth session (1971), annexes, agenda item 90, doc. A/8568, paras. 45-6.

NOTE ON BIBLIOGRAPHY

The publications of the Permanent Court of International Justice (P.C.I.J.) were organized in the following Series:

    A. Judgments and Orders. Nos. 1-24 (1922-30)

    B. Advisory opinions. Nos. 1-18 (1922-30).

These were amalgamated in 1931 to form

    A/B. Judgments, orders and advisory opinions. Nos. 40-80 (1931-40).

    C. Acts and Documents relating to judgments and advisory opinions (Pleadings). Nos. 1-19 (1922-30), 52-88 (1931-45).

    D. Acts and Documents concerning the organization of the Court. Nos. 1-6 (1922-40).

    E. Annual Reports. Nos. 1-16 (1925-45).

    F. General Indexes. Nos. 1-4 (1922-36).

The publications of the International Court of Justice (I.C.J.) are now organized as follows:

Reports of Judgments, Advisory Opinions and Orders (Rep.). Annual since 1948.

Pleadings, Oral Arguments, Documents (Pleadings). One or more volumes, containing the Court record, for each case.

Acts and Documents concerning the Organization of the Court (Acts). Two volumes to date (1946, 1972), containing the basic texts relating to the Court, including the Rules of Court.

Yearbook. Yearbook of the International Court of Justice, covering the period 16 July-15 July. Annual since 1946-7.

The Bibliography of the International Court of Justice. Nos. 1-18 formed Chapter IX of the *Yearbook* up to the 1963-64 edition. Beginning with No. 19 the *Bibliography* has been issued annually as a separate fascicle, arranged so as to facilitate the binding of several numbers together.

All the above are in bilingual editions except Series E and the Yearbook (*Annuaire*), which are published in separate English and French editions.

Since 1968 the annual *Report of the International Court of Justice*, covering the period 1 August-31 July, has been published as a Supplement to the *Official Records of the General Assembly*. It is available in the official languages of the General Assembly.

The abbreviation R.A.D.I. used in the Notes refers to the *Recueil des Cours* of the Academy of International Law, which is also situated in the Peace Palace at The Hague. The abbreviation O.R. refers to the *Official Records* of the various organs of the United Nations.

INDEX OF NAMES

INDEX OF CASES

GENERAL INDEX

Act of Algeciras (1906), 138, 239
Acting-President, 57, 102
   And see President of the Court
Admissibility of Claim –
   See Jurisdiction, disputes over
Advisory Opinions, 20, 21, 23, 27-8, 34, 38, 67, 80-4, 104, 106, 124-5, 126, 130-1, 132-3, 135-7, 138-9, 144-6, 154-5, 157-8, 162-3, 236, 242
Advocates, 89-90, 96-8
Afghanistan, 183
Agent, 88, 89, 91, 92, 93, 95, 96-8, 100, 109, 235
Albania, 40, 121-3, 143, 183
Algeria, 183
Amphictyonies, Delphic, 11
Appeals to the Court, 80, 159-60
Application instituting Proceedings, 87, 88, 89, 90, 99, 116, 119, 121, 126, 128, 129, 130, 133, 137, 139, 140, 142, 143, 144, 146, 147, 149, 150, 152, 153, 155, 156, 160, 161, 162
Arbitration, 11-20, 22, 28, 36, 68, 69, 70, 76
   – Award, see Judgment
   – Procedure, 18, 76, 92
   – Treaties of, 17
   – Tribunal, 14-5, 17
      And see Permanent Court of Arbitration
Arbitrators, 14-5, 16, 18
   And see Judges
Argentina, 48, 71, 147, 183, 229, 238
Australia, 48, 161-2, 164, 183, 231, 233, 236, 236, 241
Austria, 48, 183, 233

Bahamas, 183
Bahrain, 183
Bangladesh, 70, 160
Barbados, 183
Belgium, 47, 48, 151, 152-4, 183, 230, 236, 238, 241

Bhutan, 183
BIRPI, 234
Bolivia, 183
Botswana, 184, 233
Brazil, 13, 48, 183
Bulgaria, 130-1, 150-1, 183, 238, 239, 240, 241
Burma, 183
Burundi, 183
Byelorussian SSR, 183, 238, 239, 241
Byzantium, 12

Cambodia – see Khmer Republic
Cameroon, 156-7, 165, 183
Central African Republic, 183
Central American Court of Justice, 224
Ceylon – see Sri Lanka
Chad, 183
Chambers of the Court, 60-1
Chile, 48, 71, 147, 183, 230, 240
China, 29, 45, 148, 183, 223, 238, 239, 240, 241
Claims Commissions, 12-3, 17
Colombia, 48, 128-30, 183, 233
Commissions of Enquiry, 16
Committee for Review of Administrative Tribunal Judgments, 82, 83, 146, 218
Compliance with
   Advisory opinion, 80-1, 163
   Judgment, 13, 18, 39-40
Compromis, Compromissory Clause
   See Special Agreement
Concert of Europe, 15, 19
Conciliation, 12, 16, 17, 115
Congo, 183
Consultations on Procedure, 91
Costa Rica, 183, 223, 225
Costs, 90, 102, 119
Counsel, see Advocates
Counter-Memorial, see Written Pleadings
Court, 14, 27-42, 74
   – Composition, 14, 20, 35, 43-9, 56, 57-60, 101-2, 105, 111, 211-5